Strategic Multilateral Exchange

to my daughter Laurence

Strategic Multilateral Exchange

General Equilibrium with Imperfect Competition

Jean J. Gabszewicz
Université Catholique de Louvain

Edward Elgar

Cheltenham, UK · Northampton, MA, USA

Published by
Edward Elgar Publishing Limited
Glensanda House
Montpellier Parade
Cheltenham
Glos GL50 1UA
UK

Edward Elgar Publishing, Inc.
136 West Street
Suite 202
Northampton
Massachusetts 01060
USA

A catalogue record for this book is available from the British Library

Library of Congress Cataloging in Publication Data

Gabszewicz, Jean Jaskold.
    Strategic multilateral exchange : general equilibrium with imperfect
    competition / Jean J. Gabszewicz.
        p.cm.
    Includes bibliographical references and index.
        1. Foreign exchange. 2. Equilibrium (Economics) 3. Competition,
    Imperfect. 4. Oligopolies. I. Title.

HG3821.G22 2002
338.6'048–dc21

ISBN 1-85898-028-3

Printed and bound in Great Britain by MPG Books Ltd, Bodmin, Cornwall

Contents

Acknowledgements

The research contributions contained in this volume were developed over a long time span, starting from the 'Golden Sixties', a period during which general equilibrium theory was superbly flourishing, and finishing today, a much darker period for this field of microeconomic theory. Numerous scholars specialising in the field were visiting the Center for Operations Research and Econometrics (CORE) during this period, and created an exceptional research environment. This atmosphere was the origin of my own interest in the subject. I would like to thank all those who have contributed to developing this environment, in particular: Bob Aumann, Truman Bewley, Gérard Debreu, Jacques Drèze, Stefaan Gepts, Birgit Grodal, Werner Hildenbrand, Jean-François Mertens, Jean-Philippe Vial and Karl Vind. To this group of scholars, I must add Benjamin Shitovitz, with whom I share his enthusiasm for the mixed model of exchange economies, and Philippe Michel, with whom I developed the concept of oligopoly equilibrium. I am also deeply grateful to the doctoral students with whom I have renewed my interest in this domain of research during the last decade, namely Giulio Codognato, Tito Cordella and Lisa Grazzini.

Like the other scholars who have enjoyed the intellectual atmosphere at CORE, I am indebted to Jacques Drèze for giving me the opportunity of sharing all the benefits of this vicinity. I would like also to thank Sheila Weyers for her editorial assistance in handling several papers from which this book is derived, and Fabienne Henry for correcting numerous versions of the manuscript. Finally, I wish to express my gratitude to Nathalie Sonnac and Jacques Thisse, who encouraged the project of this book in a more personal way, by convincing me that it could bring about a fresh look at the analysis of market power.

Introduction

The new wine of monopolistic competition should not be poured into the old goatskins of partial equilibrium methodology

(Triffin 1940, 89)

This volume is devoted to the study of strategic multilateral exchange. We consider models in which economic agents *exchange* goods among themselves, as in the pure exchange model which was initially proposed to analyse competitive trade. But, contrary to the classical competitive paradigm in which agents are assumed to behave as price-takers, we allow traders to behave consciously as *strategic agents* who aim at influencing trade to their own advantage. This is usually done in oligopoly theory using a partial equilibrium approach. Here we want to go beyond this approach and consider a system of *interrelated markets* where the influence of what happens at some point is fully spread throughout the whole system.

The present approach relies on the building blocks proposed earlier by the pioneers of general equilibrium and imperfect competition theories. It is unnecessary to say that the main contributors to the theory of imperfect competition have never considered that perfect competition is an adequate model of the real world. On the contrary, they took as a postulate that market imperfections and the search for power by economic agents are the rules that govern the market mechanism. Perfect competition, when considered, was viewed mainly as an ideal version of the functioning of markets, or, at best, as a reference point with which market outcomes in an imperfect environment could be compared. This should be contrasted with the developments in general equilibrium theory in the second half of the twentieth century, which were mainly centered around the competitive paradigm. This is perfectly understandable, since the Walrasian model was built for analysing the interplay of competitive markets. Also, important questions, such as the existence of a competitive equilibrium and the welfare properties of the competitive equilibrium, had not yet been completely solved when entering into the second half of the twentieth century. What is perhaps more surprising, however, is that the first emergence of game theory into general equilibrium was also entirely oriented towards the competitive paradigm, the basic objective being to study the relationship between the cooperative concept of core and the set of competitive allocations in economies with many agents. This approach culminated in Aumann's equivalence theorem, showing that, in economies with an atomless continuum of traders, these two concepts coincide. This 'competitive mania' is surprising because game theory was especially tailored for analysing the outcome of situations with strategically interacting agents, while perfect competition excludes by definition such interactions. Nevertheless, the works of Debreu and Scarf (1963), Aumann (1964) and Hildenbrand (1974) about the cooperative concept of core opened the door of general equilibrium to game theory, and Aumann's version of the model spontaneously invited economic theorists to develop a variant of it, which had already been suggested earlier by Shapley (1961). This variant proposes a *mixed* version of the exchange model, including both a competitive sector, represented by an atomless continuum of traders, and a sector consisting of 'significant' traders, represented in the model by *atoms*. To quote from Aumann:

> Of course, to the extent that individual consumers or merchants are in fact not anonymous (think of General Motors), the continuous model is inappropriate, and our results do not apply to such a situation. But in that case, perfect competition does not obtain either. In many real markets the competition is indeed far from perfect; such markets are probably best represented by a mixed model, in which some of the traders are points in a continuum, and others are individually significant (Aumann, 1964, 41).

The first part of this monograph uses this mixed exchange model to study the relationship between the core and the set of price allocations in economies embodying significant traders. The profound work of Edgeworth (1881) on bilateral monopoly and the contract curve, which received little attention from the economics profession before it was rediscovered by game theorists, is at the basis of the concept of core. In contrast with Cournot, Edgeworth based his approach to imperfect competition on an assumption of cooperation between agents leading to Pareto-optimal outcomes. His definition of the contract curve coincides with the definition of the core in the case of two commodities, as discovered by Shubik (1959). He anticipated the convergence result obtained in 1963 by Debreu and Scarf, according to which the core shrinks to the set of competitive allocations when the number of traders increases without limit. Edgeworth also introduced the role of collusion, *via* the distinction he made between a *coalition* of economic agents – which can always dissolve before the outcome is settled – and a *combination* of traders, which is an institutional collusive agreement between agents, and which cannot dissolve before the outcome is reached (see Edgeworth 1881). This distinction forms the basis of the idea of a *syndicate*, viewed as a group of agents which do not enter into a broader coalition, except in unison. As we shall see, the 'significant' traders in the mixed exchange model, as represented by atoms, can also be interpreted as Edgeworth's combinations of traders.

Cournot (1838) is the other founder of the theory of imperfect competition. His contribution to economic theory goes far beyond the discovery of the notion of *non-cooperative equilibrium*. In fact, Cournot developed the theory of monopoly, the theory of oligopoly, and the theory of competition as the limiting case of oligopoly. He settled all the important questions relating to market structure and stressed the importance of demand – *la loi de débit*, as he called it – in the explanation of price formation. He would have constructed the complete foundations of micro theory had he also considered the need for a general equilibrium approach, a task assigned to Walras some fifty years later. At any rate, he was the first to suggest that the lack of cooperation among the agents operating in a market must guide the market outcome towards a non-cooperative equilibrium, a concept reinvented by Nash (1950) in the abstract framework of game theory. The work of Cournot has been cast using partial equilibrium analysis. In the second part of this book, we propose an extension of his non-cooperative approach to the case of multilateral exchange. This extension also allows for *all* traders to behave strategically, while Cournot was implicitly assuming that only the selling side of the market was behaving in that way, the demand side taking the price as given.

There are good reasons for economists not to be content with a partial equilibrium approach to imperfect competition. First of all, modern economies are characterised by the existence of large firms operating simultaneously in several markets. The interplay of their strategies can hardly be analysed without taking into account the full complexity of the economic system. Of course one should not expect the exchange model to portray the full complexity observed in the context of strategic multinational firms. It constitutes however the simplest 'maquette' through which strategic behaviour combined with market interdependence can be analysed. Second, the partial equilibrium approach allows us to capture in isolation some effects of economic agents' market power on the allocation of resources, thus permitting the analysis of the market distortions which it may create in a particular industry. However this method does not account for the overall impact of imperfectly competitive behaviour on the whole economy: the general equilibrium methodology is needed to capture all the corresponding implications. Again one should not expect the present approach to reflect even a small portion of the great richness of phenomena analysed in modern industrial economics. This is the price to be paid when the analysis of the overall impact is attempted, compared with an analysis relying on a detailed description of a particular industry. Finally, recent theoretical developments in industrial economics look like a highly coloured patchwork of often unrelated investigations, which mirror the incredible complexity of real market phenomena. A general equilibrium synthesis of these partial equilibrium theories may well be required with the aim of checking their robustness in a broader setting, as well as their mutual consistency. Even if the present contribution does not have the pretention to realise even the smallest part of these objectives, it proposes a methodological starting point from which this ambitious programme could be initiated.

Most of the work contained in this book relies on research contributions in which I have participated, and I have explicitly chosen to centre this approach on my own research efforts. This is the reason why it does not do justice to other scientists who have made crucial contributions in the same field. In the first part of this volume, the theory which is presented is entirely centered around the concept of core, while other authors have used the mixed exchange model to examine the behaviour of other cooperative concepts, like the von Neumann-Morgenstern solutions (Hart 1974), the bargaining set (Mas-Colell 1986, Shitovitz 1987), or the non-transferable Shapley value (Guesnerie 1977). But it is mainly in respect to the non-cooperative approach, considered in the second part of this book, that alternative research efforts provided by other authors concerning similar topics have not been sufficiently reported. In particular, we have in mind the theory of *strategic market games*, which has been introduced by Shapley and Shubik (1977). Admittedly, this theory shares several features with the research pursued in the second part of this book. As in Part 2, it presents a non-cooperative theory of exchange in which traders' strategies are quantity signals sent to the different markets in order to manipulate the price structure. It is accordingly a true general equilibrium approach of exchange. Nevertheless the main objective of this research is again related to the competitive paradigm: it aims at replacing the Walrasian auctioneer who quotes competitive prices with a strategic mechanism which would lead to the same competitive prices when agents are sufficiently numerous. Shapley and Shubik show that price manipulation vanishes when the number of traders grows indefinitely: the price constellation at the non-cooperative equilibrium approaches the competitive prices because they result from vanishing responsiveness to the traders' decisions. As stated by Shapley (1977), their approach must be viewed 'as an essay to throw some light into the shadowy transition between "many" and "few"'. By no means should it be viewed as an approach aiming at explaining the outcomes to be expected in an economy in which there is an inherent asymmetry in the market power of strategic agents, as in the case of Cournot. Of course asymptotic results of the kind referred to above have also been considered by Cournot and his successors, but in the framework of economies with 'significant' agents, who individually manipulate the price constellation, while some anonymous traders behave as price-takers. Another crucial difference between the strategic market games approach and the one considered in Part 2 is related to the institutional mechanism through which prices are obtained in the different markets. Since the main objective of the Shapley-Shubik games is to dispense with the existence of an auctioneer, it is clear that they do not consider the usual market clearing mechanism leading to prices balancing supply and demand in each market. In fact, they do not suggest a unique mechanism, but several different ones, which have been considered in this stream of literature (see Shapley and Shubik 1977, Dubey and Shubik 1978, Amir, Sahi and Yaho 1990). In contrast, in our approach we use the equilibrium prices corresponding to the quantity strategies utilised by the agents. In this respect, we are in line with the tradition inherited from Cournot and continuously applied in theoretical industrial economics: those prices which are manipulated by the oligopolists are the prices at which market demand for each good equals the aggregate quantity of that good supplied by the oligopolists. This major difference between the two approaches again rests on the fact that they pursue different objectives. While strategic market games serve to circumvent the auctioneer, the theory contained in Part 2 puts emphasis on the general equilibrium implications of market power.

Although not directly related to strategic exchange, there have been other attempts to integrate imperfect competition in the general equilibrium model. These attempts differ from the present one because they consider economies with a productive sector, which is the usual way to proceed in partial equilibrium when strategic agents are envisioned. Unfortunately, the introduction of a productive sector in the model compounds the difficulties already met when only exchange is considered (some of these difficulties are briefly examined in Chapter 7). Among these alternative attempts, one must cite in particular the contributions of Laffont and Laroque (1976) and d'Aspremont, Dos Santos-Ferreira and Gérard-Varet (1997). There are however two streams of contributions which are sufficiently related to the present work to be explicitly considered in this introduction. The first one is the so-called 'subjective approach' initiated by Negishi (1961) in order to introduce imperfect competition in a general equilibrium model with a productive sector. This approach suggests a model of a private ownership economy *à la* Arrow-Debreu in which some firms have monopolistic power on one or several markets. Furthermore Negishi assumes that, given a specific state of the market, each monopolistic firm has, for each good over which it has a monopoly, a *conjecture* concerning the price it could charge for any level of output it would sell in the corresponding market. These conjectures are restricted to being self-fulfilling at any state of the market. This assumption allows the presence of both monopolistic and competitive firms in the markets, since profit-maximising firms at given prices have the particular conjecture that they do not anticipate any change in the price system when they modify their production plan. An equilibrium is then defined as a state of the market where demand equals supply in each market at the corresponding price system, while every consumer maximises utility on his budget set, and every firm makes a production decision which, on the basis of the state of the market and its conjecture, maximises its profit. The major difference between the Negishi subjective approach and the approach proposed in the second part of this volume is that market demand considered in Part 2 by oligopolists is the 'true' or 'objective' demand function, as it follows from the microeconomic behavioural assumptions underlying the decisions of the agents participating in the exchange. Admittedly, and particularly when there are many goods and many agents, it requires a considerable amount of information for the oligopolists to be able to evaluate correctly this 'objective' demand function. Nevertheless, the same criticism applies as well to the usual partial equilibrium analysis in which full knowledge of the market demand function by the oligopolists is also postulated. On

the other hand, the equilibrium position of the economy depends, in the
'subjective approach', on the particular beliefs of each monopolist about
demand behaviour. As a consequence, almost every feasible state of the
economy can be rationalised as an equilibrium for a particular config-
uration of firms' beliefs, thereby weakening the predictive power of the
subjective approach (see Gary-Bobo 1989). As Hart (1985, 107) states:

> the problem is that the very generality of the model gives it very little
> predictive power. Given particular subjective demand functions ... the
> model will of course generate a small number of equilibria (possibly only
> one). However the model does not tell us how these conjectures are formed.
> To an outside observer who is asked to predict the market outcome but
> who does not know what conjectures are, almost anything could be an
> equilibrium.

In the framework considered in the second part of this book, oligopolists are assumed to use *output levels* as strategic variables, as in
Cournot and in Shapley-Shubik strategic market games, while prices are
assumed to be determined by the law of supply and demand. Several
authors have instead followed another route, by assuming that firms'
strategies are *prices*, rather than output levels (Marschak and Selten
1974, Benassy 1988). In particular, Benassy requires that all firms set
prices subject to their objective demand (unlike Negishi) which embeds
all the effects that their prices exert on other agents' supply and demand decisions. This modelling stresses the difference from the competitive paradigm since prices no longer convey all the information required
to make decisions; firms must also account for the other agents' decisions through their demands. Benassy shows that at equilibrium, an
imperfect competitor may not want to serve the total demand which is
addressed to him, preferring to ration consumers. This allows him to
throw a bridge between imperfect competition and fixed-price theories
of market disequilibrium.

Let me now briefly summarise the content of the volume. In the first
part, we analyse multilateral exchange using the cooperative concept of

core. The model in which this analysis is conducted corresponds to a *pure exchange economy*: it constitutes the simplest version able to capture the interdependence among markets. This model is formally introduced in Chapter 1. Most economic contributions related to the concept of core in the framework of exchange economies have concentrated on the relationship between the core and the set of *competitive allocations*. We keep on with this tradition, but adopt a different viewpoint from normal. While most past contributions tend to study the relationship between the core and the set of competitive allocations when *all* economic agents are negligible, we examine it when some agents are explicitly recognised to be 'significant'. This can be the case either because their initial ownership of some goods is large, compared with the amount of the same goods owned by the other traders, or when some agents combine in order to bias the result of exchange. The comparison between the core and the set of competitive allocations with negligible agents has been conducted using two alternative approaches: the 'asymptotic approach' and the 'atomless approach'. In the asymptotic approach, the basic economy is enlarged by replicating it an arbitrarily large number of times, increasing thereby the number of traders without limit. Then it is shown that, under some mild conditions, the core of the replicated economies converges to the set of competitive allocations of the basic economy (Debreu-Scarf theorem). The assumptions of this theorem preclude however the existence of important asymmetries among traders in the initial ownership of goods, or the possibility of collusive moves among traders. In the atomless approach, the set of agents in the economy is represented from the outset by a continuum; each point in this continuum is a particular trader. Since in the traditional theory of integration, changing the integrand at a single point does not affect the value of the integral, this representation implies that the actions of a single trader have no consequence on the aggregate behaviour of the economy: the atomless model itself drives the property that agents are 'negligible'. A remarkable result from Aumann (1964) states that, in atomless economies, the core coincides with the set of competitive allocations (equivalence theorem). This result is the counterpart, for the atomless approach, of the Debreu-

Scarf theorem obtained in the asymptotic approach. As in the latter, the existence of strong asymmetries in initial endowments, or of collusive moves among traders, are removed: this is a direct consequence of the modelling adopted.

In Chapter 2 we examine the relationship between the core and the set of competitive allocations in the asymptotic approach. We open the chapter by recalling the Debreu-Scarf result, in order to contrast this result with the propositions obtained when the assumption precluding the asymmetries initial endowments is discarded. To this end, we introduce a variant of the Debreu-Scarf asymptotic replication procedure which consists of maintaining 'significant' traders, even when the number of traders becomes arbitrarily large, obtaining thereby a set of traders which is a mixture of 'giants' and 'dwarfs' (Drèze, Gabszewicz and Gepts 1969). Finally, we provide an alternative interpretation of the giants, which are then viewed as 'syndicates' of agents resulting from collusive moves organised in order to bias the collective allocation mechanism underlying the concept of core. A similar presentation is adopted in Chapter 3, in which the relationship of the core and the set of competitive allocations is examined in economies embodying an atomless sector. We start by assuming that this sector embodies all traders, which is the model considered by Aumann, and prove that, for this version, the core coincides with the set of competitive allocations. Then we consider the so-called *mixed* model, consisting both of an atomless sector and atoms, which are meant to represent the significant traders present in the exchange of goods. A fundamental result from Shitovitz (1973), characterising the core of such mixed markets, is stated and proved. This result is then applied to study the core when large traders cohabit with the atomless continuum. Finally, an economic interpretation of atoms is provided, which parallels the interpretation provided for the giants in the asymptotic approach.

In the second part of our book, we analyse how the Cournotian non-cooperative approach to oligopoly, initially formulated in a partial equilibrium framework, can be extended to the exchange model. Once more, we have selected this model because it allows a general equilibrium approach to strategic interaction, while escaping the difficulties generally met when the analysis is cast in a model of an economy including a productive sector (see Chapter 7). After a short summary of the Cournot theory, we start our analysis by treating several examples showing how to dispense with two major assumptions of the Cournotian framework, partial equilibrium and asymmetric behaviour of the demand and supply sides of the market, while keeping the assumptions of quantity strategies and non-cooperative behavior. These examples lead spontaneously to a general concept of oligopoly equilibrium which applies to any exchange context with strategic agents (Chapter 4). Then we examine the existence problem posed by this concept, a problem which is complicated by the fact that there always exists an oligopoly equilibrium (the autarkic equilibrium) in the formal sense, but without any economic significance, at least in most interesting cases. Far from being solved, the problem of the existence of an oligopoly equilibrium should constitute a challenging subject for mathematical economists in the future. We report briefly about work in progress on this front (Chapter 5). The next chapter (Chapter 6) provides three economic applications of the concept analysed in the preceding chapters. The first application is borrowed from the theory of international trade: we examine the principle of comparative advantage studied by Ricardo (1848, 1951) when the agents operating in the world market behave strategically. The second application is related to strategic behaviour when agents operate in an intertemporal context in which they can influence future trading through investment. The third application deals with public economics: it examines how taxation can influence strategic behaviour in order to resorb market distortions related to the very existence of this behaviour. Chapter 7 is devoted to the difficulties met when the above analysis is cast into a model including a productive sector.

PART 1

Strategic Multilateral Exchange and the Core

1. Allocations in pure exchange economies

1.1 THE PURE EXCHANGE MODEL

The simplest way to capture the interaction between markets leads to the study of an *exchange economy*. In this context, the only economic activity of agents consists in exchanging the goods available in their endowments. The basic model is as follows. There are n *traders* (or *consumers*), indexed by i, $i = 1, \cdots, n$, and ℓ *goods* (or *commodities*), indexed by h, $h = 1, \cdots, \ell$. A *commodity bundle* $x = (x^1, \cdots, x^h, \cdots, x^\ell)$ is a point of R^ℓ_+, the set of all non-negative vectors in R^ℓ. Trader i is represented by his *initial endowment*, ω_i, $\omega_i > 0$, a vector of R^ℓ_+, and his *preference relation* $\succsim_i$ defined on $R^\ell_+ \times R^\ell_+$: if x and y are two commodity bundles, $x \succsim_i y$ reads as: the commodity bundle x is preferred by consumer i to the commodity bundle y. When $x \succsim_i y$, but not $y \succsim_i x$, then the commodity bundle x is *strictly* preferred to y, and we denote $x \succ_i y$. When $x \succsim_i y$ and $y \succsim_i x$, then x is *indifferent* to y. The following assumptions on $\succsim_i$ will be made throughout: (i) $\succsim_i$ is a complete preordering, which is *transitive*; (ii) $\forall\, y \in R^\ell_+$, the sets $\{x \mid x \succsim_i y\}$ and $\{x \mid y \succsim_i x\}$ are closed in R^ℓ_+ (continuity); (iii) $x > y \Rightarrow x \succ_i y$ (strong desirability) ($x > y$ means: $\forall\, h$, $x^h \geq y^h$, and $\exists\, k, x^k > y^k$); (iv) for all y, the set $\{x \mid x \succsim_i y\}$ is strictly convex in R^ℓ_+ (strong convexity).

Consider the following example of an exchange economy, which will be used repeatedly. Let $n = \ell = 2$: the economy consists of two consumers and two goods. Initial endowments of traders 1 and 2 are, respectively,

$\omega_1 = (4,0)$ and $\omega_2 = (0,4)$. Both consumers $i, i = 1, 2$, have the same preference relation $\succsim_i$, defined by

$$x = (x^1, x^2) \succsim_i (y^1, y^2) = y \Leftrightarrow \sqrt{x^1} + \sqrt{x^2} \geq \sqrt{y^1} + \sqrt{y^2}. \qquad (1.1)$$

The real valued (utility) function $U(x^1, x^2) = \sqrt{x^1} + \sqrt{x^2}$ represents this preference relation, since

$$x \succsim_i y \Leftrightarrow U(x^1, x^2) \geq U(y^1, y^2).$$

It is easy to verify that the preference relation defined by (1.1) satisfies the assumptions (i–iv) listed above.

Another example of an exchange economy is provided by the following situation. There are ℓ traders and ℓ goods, and each trader initially owns one unit of each good, i.e. $\omega_i = (1, \cdots, 1)$, $i = 1, \cdots, \ell$. All consumers have the same preference relation $\succsim_i$ defined by

$$x \succsim_i y \Leftrightarrow \sum_{h=1}^{\ell} (x^h)^2 \geq \sum_{h=1}^{\ell} (y^h)^2. \qquad (1.2)$$

This preference relation satisfies assumptions (i–iii), but not assumption (iv).

In an exchange economy, agents exchange goods with a view to improving their situation through trade. For instance, in the first example of an exchange economy provided above, if agent 1 exchanges with agent 2 two units of good 1 against two units of good 2, both end up with the commodity bundle $(2, 2)$. Accordingly, they move from the utility level reached at their initial endowment, i.e., 2, to the higher utility level $2\sqrt{2}$: the utility of both agents has increased through trade. It is this possibility of reallocating existing goods through trade which explains the existence of commerce. Generally, individual ownership is specialised over a restricted set of goods, and people want to extend their consumption to other goods which are not in their initial endowment; the possibility of exchange allows the desired reallocation among traders.

Formally, exchange drives the economy away from its initial position, represented by the n-tuple of initial endowments, to a new position, represented by the n-tuple of commodity bundles obtained by the agents as a result of multilateral trade. This final position is called an *allocation*. By definition, an *allocation* is an n-tuple of commodity bundles $(x_1, \cdots, x_i, \cdots, x_n)$ such that

$$\sum_{i=1}^{n} x_i = \sum_{i=1}^{n} w_i.$$

A useful geometric representation of the set of allocations existing in an exchange economy consisting of two agents and two goods has been proposed by Edgeworth (1881). To illustrate, consider the first example of an exchange economy defined above. In Figure 1.1, we have drawn a box; the vertical axis represents quantities of the good initially owned by agent 1 (good 1), and the horizontal one, quantities of the good initially owned by agent 2 (good 2). If we measure quantities for agent 1 from the origin 0, then any point in the box informs us not only about the quantities that agent 1 receives through exchange, but also about those that go to agent 2. This should be clear since we know the total endowment of both goods $(4, 4)$ in the economy. Hence agent 1 simply gets through exchange those amounts not included in agent 2's bundle. In other words, given an exchange of goods between the agents, we can consider the quantities obtained by agent 2 as measured from the origin $0'$, as represented in Figure 1.1. No point outside the box could represent a feasible exchange since it would imply a negative allocation of some good to one of the agents. Accordingly, to any allocation of the bundle $(4, 4)$ between the agents, there corresponds a single point in the box, and conversely, the box provides an exact representation of all possible allocations existing in the exchange economy. We have

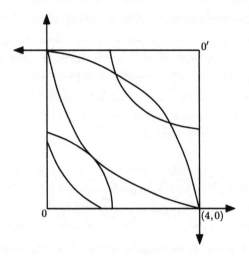

Figure 1.1

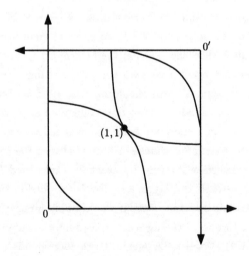

Figure 1.2

also represented in Figure 1.1 the indifference curves of the two agents among the commodity bundles received at the allocations defined in the box (the indifference curves of agent 2 should also be viewed from the origin $0'$).

Figure 1.2 is the Edgeworth box corresponding to the second example of an exchange economy provided above, with $\ell = n = 2$.

1.2 COMPETITIVE ALLOCATIONS

In the next section we shall be interested in comparing two particular mechanisms through which exchange can occur. This comparison will be carried out by examining the relationship between the set of allocations which can obtain as a result of each of these mechanisms. In the first mechanism, agents exchange goods at given prices, and prices are selected by markets in a way which makes supply equal to demand on each market. More precisely, assume that $p = (p^1, \cdots, p^h, \cdots p^\ell)$, is the *price system* operating in the economy, with p^h denoting the price of good h, $p \neq 0$, $p^h \geq 0$. For an agent i, his income (the value of his initial endowment) is then equal to $p \cdot \omega_i = \sum_{h=1}^{\ell} p^h \omega_i^h$. *If he behaves as a price taker*, he can buy any commodity bundle x whose value $p \cdot x$ does not exceed $p \cdot \omega_i$: the *budget set* $B_i(p)$ defines as

$$ B_i(p) = \{x \mid p \cdot x \leq p \cdot \omega_i\}. $$

It is then assumed that each agent i chooses in $B_i(p)$ a maximal element of $\succsim_i$, i.e., a commodity bundle $x_i(p)$ such that, for all $x \in B_i(p)$, $x_i(p) \succsim_i x$. Assumptions (i)–(iv) guarantee that there exists a unique element $x_i(p)$ in $B_i(p)$. The function $p \to x_i(p)$ is the *demand function* of trader i.

When, at given p, the *aggregate excess demand*, defined by $\sum_{i=1}^{n} [x_i(p) - \omega_i]$, is different from 0, the plans of the traders are not compatible: there is aggregate excess demand (aggregate excess supply) on those markets h for which $\sum_{i=1}^{n}\left(x_i^h(p) - \omega_i^h\right) > 0$ $\left(\sum_{i=1}^{n}\left(x_i^h(p) - \omega_i^h\right) < 0\right)$ and some traders must be rationed. It is however assumed that the market mechanism selects the price vector in a way which makes aggregate excess demand equal to zero on all markets.

By definition, a *competitive allocation* is an allocation $(x_1^*, \cdots, x_i^*, \cdots, x_n^*)$ for which there exists a price system p^* such that, for all i, $x_i(p^*) = x_i^*$. A *competitive equilibrium* is a pair $(p^*, (x_1^*, \cdots, x_i^*, \cdots, x_n^*))$ such that $(x_1^*, \cdots, x_i^*, \cdots, x_n^*)$ is a competitive allocation with p^*.

We illustrate the concept of competitive allocation by means of the two examples of an exchange economy provided in Section 1.1. In the simple two-commodity world of these examples we need only one price: we must simply know the rate at which commodity 1 can be exchanged for commodity 2. In the first example, taking commodity 2 as *numéraire* $(p^2 = 1)$, the budget set $B_1(p)$ $(B_2(p))$ of agent 1 (agent 2) is written as $B_1(p) = \{(x^1, x^2) \mid p^1 x^1 + x^2 \leq 4p^1\}$ $(B_2(p) = \{(x^1, x^2) \mid p^1 x^1 + x^2 \leq 4\})$. Assume that the price of commodity 1 is twice the price of commodity 2. Then agent 1 can buy any bundle (x^1, x^2) for which $2x^1 + x^2 \leq 8$ $((x^1, x^2)$ is in the budget set). Choosing the maximal element of $\underset{\tilde{1}}{\succeq}$ (as defined by 1.1) in $B_1(p)$, he buys the bundle which solves

$$\max_{x^1, x^2} \sqrt{x^1} + \sqrt{x^2} \text{ subject to } 2x^1 + x^2 \leq 8,$$

i.e. $\left(\dfrac{4}{3}, \dfrac{16}{3}\right)$, which constitutes the value of the demand function of agent 1 at $p = (2, 1)$. Similarly, at the same price vector, agent 2 can buy any bundle (x^1, x^2) for which $2x^1 + x^2 \leq 4$ $((x^1, x^2)$ is in his budget set). Choosing the maximal element of $\underset{\tilde{2}}{\succeq}$ (as defined by (1.1)) in $B_2(p)$, he chooses the bundle which solves

$$\max_{x^1, x^2} \sqrt{x^1} + \sqrt{x^2} \text{ subject to } 2x^1 + x^2 \leq 4,$$

i.e. $\left(\dfrac{2}{3}, \dfrac{8}{3}\right)$ (which constitutes the value of the demand function of agent

2 at $p = (2,1)$). Accordingly, the aggregate excess demand at p is equal to

$$\left(\frac{4}{3},\frac{16}{3}\right) + \left(\frac{2}{3},\frac{8}{3}\right) - (4,4) = (-2,4),$$

so that there is an aggregate excess supply on market 1 and an aggregate excess demand on market 2: the exchange cannot be carried out. Proceeding as above, but assuming that the exchange rate of commodity 1 against commodity 2 is equal to one, i.e., $p^1 = 1$, would yield $(2,2)$ as the value of the demand function for both traders at $p = (1,1)$. Accordingly, the aggregate excess demand at this price vector obtains as $(2,2) + (2,2) - (4,4) = (0,0)$: $[p^* = (1,1); x_1^* = (2,2), x_2^* = (2,2)]$ is a competitive equilibrium of the exchange economy. Figure 1.3 illustrates the competitive allocation and the corresponding budget sets.

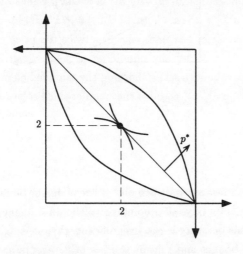

Figure 1.3

In the second example of an exchange economy provided in Section 1.1, there are *two* competitive allocations corresponding to the same price vector $(1,1) = p^*$; namely $[(2,0),(0,2)]$ and $[(0,2),(2,0)]$. Figure 1.4 illustrates the two competitive allocations.

Underlying the concept of competitive allocations are the two basic
assumptions of perfect competition: a large number of agents, and the
equality of supply and demand. The large number of agents assumption
underlies the concept because the definition of the individual demand
function implies that each agent is price-taker.

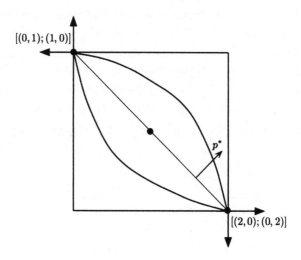

Figure 1.4

Otherwise, with few agents, each one of them should be aware that the
quantity he sells or buys of a commodity should influence equilibrium
prices, since this quantity is not insignificant when it is aggregated with
the quantities bought and sold by the few other agents in the economy.
As for the assumption of equality of demand and supply, it underlies
the concept of competitive allocation, because this allocation is defined
relative to a price system which leads aggregate excess demand to be
equal to zero on each market. Notice that the concept of competitive
equilibrium does not say anything about the manner in which markets
select equilibrium prices. The usual story consists of assuming the existence of an auctioneer – the Walrasian auctioneer – who adjusts the

price system through time in proportion to the discrepancy between demand and supply at the operating prices. This is the so-called 'Walras tâtonnement process'. The assumptions on individual preferences we have introduced in Section 1.1, combined with an assumption of strict positivity of initial endowment vectors ($\omega_i > 0$) are sufficient to guarantee the existence of a competitive equilibrium. But these assumptions guarantee neither the uniqueness of the competitive equilibrium, nor the convergence of the Walrasian tâtonnement process. (On these questions, see Mas-Colell, Whinston and Green 1995.) Finally, a competitive allocation $(x_1^*, \cdots, x_i^*, \cdots, x_n^*)$ is *Pareto-optimal*: there exists no other allocation $(y_1, \cdots, y_i, \cdots, y_n)$ with $y_i \underset{i}{\succsim} x_i^*$ for all $i = 1, \cdots, n$, and some k for whom $y_k \underset{k}{\succ} x_k^*$.

The price mechanism through which a competitive allocation is selected in an exchange economy, is characterised by the double property of *individualism* and *decentralisation*. The mechanism is individualistic since individuals do not take into account the behaviour of the other agents when selecting their commodity bundle at given prices; it is decentralised since the only information needed by an agent to take his decision is the price vector through which his budget set is defined. Furthermore, when the Walras tâtonnement process converges to an equilibrium price vector, the corresponding competitive equilibrium could be reached by letting agents compute for themselves, in a decentralised way, their own demand vectors at each price system.

1.3 THE CORE

The next mechanism through which exchange can occur is, contrary to the price mechanism, essentially based on an interactive cooperation among traders. To be carried out, it does not rely on the use of prices and markets, but is realised through direct barter among traders. To give an idea of how this mechanism works, consider again the first example of an exchange economy defined in Section 1.1 and its Edgeworth *box* representation in Figure 1.1, which is reproduced here in Figure 1.5. The problem of choosing a particular exchange (a point in the box) can be viewed as a collective decision problem in which agents 1 and 2 are simultaneously involved. First, it seems reasonable that no exchange can be collectively acceptable if it affords a utility level to one of the traders which is lower than the utility level he achieves at his initial endowment vector. In that case this trader would object individually to the corresponding allocation, since he would finish up with a worse bundle from his viewpoint than his initial endowment. This means that only those allocations in the 'lens' of Figure 1.5 can be individually acceptable. Does this mean that all allocations in the lens are collectively acceptable? The answer is no, if we accept the simple cooperative assumption that traders will not consider as collectively acceptable an allocation which can be improved upon by further trading among them. Consider for instance the allocation x in Figure 1.5.

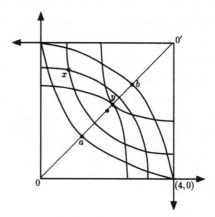

Figure 1.5

If traders were to recontract, and select the allocation y, both of them would obtain a higher utility level (the commodity bundle received by each agent at y lies on a higher indifference curve than the corresponding bundle at x): recontracting has made possible a mutually profitable trade. However, notice that *no* mutually profitable trade is possible by recontracting from y: at least one of the traders would be worse off, and the allocation y is collectively acceptable.

Applying the simple cooperative assumption referred to above eliminates any allocation in the lens which is not a tangency point between two indifference curves; *only those allocations in the lens which are Pareto-optimal are collectively acceptable.* Notice, in particular, that the competitive allocation is collectively acceptable.

It is left to the reader to verify that, in the second example of an exchange economy provided in Section 1.1, the set of collectively acceptable allocations consists of those allocations lying in the corners of the Edgeworth box, as indicated in Figure 1.6.

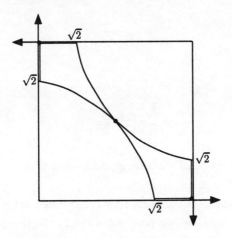

Figure 1.6

All these allocations are again Pareto-optimal, but are no longer characterised as being tangency points between two indifference curves. As in the previous example, we notice that both competitive allocations are collectively acceptable. The set of collectively acceptable allocations in an exchange economy with two agents is usually called the *contract curve.*

How can the cooperative assumption be extended from an economy
with two traders to an economy with an arbitrary number of traders?
The natural extension is to say that any *coalition* of traders can object to
a particular allocation if that coalition, using only the aggregate initial
endowments of its members, can improve upon the utility of each of
them. If, for at least one coalition, its members can do better under
autarky than at the proposed allocation, this allocation is not collectively
acceptable. By definition, the *core* of the exchange economy is the set
of allocations which can be improved upon by no coalition of traders.
Formally, let $(x_1, \cdots, x_i, \cdots, x_n)$ be an allocation and S a *coalition* of
agents, i.e. a subset of $\{1, \cdots, n\}$. The coalition S can *improve upon*
the allocation $(x_1, \cdots, x_i, \cdots, x_n)$ if there exists commodity bundles y_i,
$i \in S$, such that

$$y_i \underset{i}{\succ} x_i$$

and

$$\sum_{i \in S} y_i = \sum_{i \in S} \omega_i.$$

The *core* is the set of all allocations which cannot be improved upon by
any coalition S.

Notice immediately that *all* coalitions are allowed to form in the definition of the core we have just provided. In real collective bargaining, it is
usual however that some coalitions are prevented from forming because
individuals have made agreements among themselves before negotiating
with the other parties. A trade union, for example, would not allow
some of its members to negotiate wages with entrepreneurs independently of the union as a whole. Similarly, a subset of cartel members in
an industry cannot pass price agreements with some customers, unless
all members of the cartel adhere to the agreement. As a consequence,
coalitions which would include a subset of a trade union, or a subset
of a cartel are institutionally forbidden. Thus, the assumption that all

coalitions are allowed to form precludes the possibility of institutional collusive agreements which might exist prior to the collective decision process leading to an allocation in the core.

On the other hand, the selection of a core allocation implies that each agent is fully informed not only about his own preference ordering and initial endowment, but also about the preference orderings and initial endowments of the remaining agents. This knowledge is necessary in order to exploit all the possibilities of recontracting. This is in contrast to the competitive mechanism for selecting an allocation: as we have noted above, each agent needs only to know his own preferences and initial endowment. Information gathering necessary to realise an allocation in the core can be considerable when the number n of agents is large: remember that there are 2^n coalitions and all of them should be taken into consideration if no opportunity of recontracting is to be abandoned, as required by the core concept.

Furthermore, note that the concept of core does not rely on the existence of prices and markets, but rests entirely on the idea of a direct cooperative barter among agents. One should not be surprised, therefore, that the notion of core can be applicable to a class of game-theoretic structures much broader than those generated by an exchange economy.

Finally, the conditions under which an exchange economy has a non-empty core have to be examined. As we shall see in the next chapter, those conditions guaranteeing the existence of a competitive allocation are also sufficient to guarantee the non-emptiness of the core.

2.   The asymptotic approach

2.1 THE ASYMPTOTIC APPROACH TO PERFECT COMPETITION

The main purpose of Part 1 of this book is to examine the relation between competition and cooperation in the circumstances of imperfect competition. When *perfect* competition is assumed, this relationship has been extensively analysed (see, for instance, Hildenbrand 1974), and this analysis will be our reference point to examine how market imperfections create departures from it. More precisely we shall now analyse the relationship between the set of competitive allocations and the core of an exchange economy. First of all, we have already noticed that in both the examples considered above, the competitive allocations are in the core. As we show now, this is a very general property.

Theorem 2.1.

The set of competitive allocations is contained in the core.

Proof Let p^* be a price system for which the allocation $(x_1^*, \cdots, x_i^*, \cdots, x_n^*)$ is competitive. Suppose, contrary to Theorem 2.1, that there exists a coalition S and commodity bundles y_i, $i \in S$, such that

$$y_i \underset{i}{\succ} x_i^*$$

and

$$\sum_{i \in S} y_i = \sum_{i \in S} \omega_i. \tag{2.1}$$

Then y_i is not in $B_i(p^*)$, so that $p^* \cdot y_i > p^* \cdot \omega_i$ for all $i \in S$. Accordingly we must have

$$p^* \cdot \sum_{i \in S} y_i > p^* \cdot \sum_{i \in S} \omega_i,$$

a contradiction to (2.1).

In spite of its simplicity, Theorem 2.1 is extremely important. It guarantees, indeed, that the competitive mechanism does not neglect any opportunity that recontracting would have allowed: at a competitive allocation, no mutually profitable trade can exist not only for the set of all traders, but also for any subset of them. Theorem 2.1 also allows us to draw a conclusion concerning the non-emptiness of the core: as stated at the end of Chapter 1, the assumptions under which a competitive allocation exists, are sufficient to guarantee that the core is non-empty since it contains at least the set of competitive allocations. But generally, it contains many other allocations which are not competitive, as revealed by our two examples.

As argued above, the concept of competitive allocation requires many traders to be meaningful: why would agents otherwise accept prices as being beyond their individual influence? The concept of core does not require this prerequisite: it is as meaningful in an economy with two agents as with a myriad of agents. Nevertheless, the *size* of the core is related to the number of agents, as revealed by the following intuitive argument. Remember that an allocation is in the core if there exists no coalition which can improve upon that allocation. Since an increase in the number of agents increases the number of coalitions in a combinatorial manner, it also increases in the same way the number of possibilities for improving upon a particular allocation.

Accordingly, for an allocation to be in the core, it must pass proportionally more and more tests as the number of coalitions increases as a result of an increase in the number of agents. This suggests that the core must shrink when this number increases. Of course, this reasoning is not fully rigorous because, at first sight, it makes little sense to compare an allocation in an economy with n agents with an allocation in an economy with a number of agents different from n. As stated by Hildenbrand and Kirman (1988), 'how can we decide whether a set of allocations for a two-man economy is bigger or smaller than a set for a three man economy?' Nevertheless, if we succeed in making these sets comparable for different values of n, the above reasoning should be, in fact, meaningful, and the core shrinks with n, as depicted in Figure 2.1.

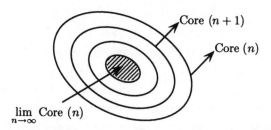

Figure 2.1

In this figure, we have represented the 'limit core' by the shaded area, as n tends to infinity, which is the set of allocations which are in the core for *all* n.

Now remember Theorem 2.1: the set of competitive allocations – denoted by $\mathcal{C}$ – is *always* included in the core, and thus belongs to the set of allocations which are in the core for all n. Accordingly, this set must be a subset of the shaded area in Figure 2.1, as represented in Figure 2.2. It was one of the basic conjectures in mathematical economics since Edgeworth that a situation as depicted in Figure 2.2, with $\mathcal{C}$ strictly contained in $\lim_{n\to\infty} \text{Core}(n)$, should never happen in a competitive environment.

The so-called 'Edgeworth conjecture' (see Bewley 1973) states, on the contrary, that the limit core $\lim_{n\to\infty} \text{Core}(n)$ must coincide with the set $\mathcal{C}$ of competitive allocations. This conjecture was rigorously demonstrated by Debreu and Scarf (1963) for a particular way of increasing the size of the exchange economy and later generalised by Hildenbrand (1974) to a broader class of economies.

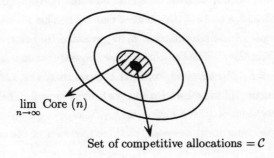

$$\lim_{n\to\infty} \text{Core}(n)$$

Set of competitive allocations $= \mathcal{C}$

Figure 2.2

To illustrate the above considerations and introduce the Debreu-Scarf theorem, let us return for a moment to the first example of a two-agents, two-good exchange economy introduced in Section 1.1. Consider again Figure 1.5 in which the core of this exchange economy is depicted (the set of allocations between a and b on the diagonal of the box), with the competitive allocation $x_1^* = x_2^* = (2,2)$ in the middle of it. Now imagine that we increase the number of agents by considering a new exchange economy with *two* agents similar to agent 1 and *two* agents similar to agent 2. By 'similar' we mean that the two 'twins' of agents 1 and 2 have identical preferences and identical initial endowments to those of their counterparts. Formally, this new exchange economy now embodies *four* agents, namely agents 11, 12 and agents 21, 22, defined by

$$\omega_{11} = \omega_{12} = (4,0)$$
$$\omega_{21} = \omega_{22} = (0,4)$$
$$u_{ij}(x^1, x^2) = \sqrt{x^1} + \sqrt{x^2}, \qquad i,j = 1,2.$$

The new exchange economy – denoted $\mathcal{E}_2$ – is an exact duplicate of the economy considered in the first example of Section 1.1, which we denote by $\mathcal{E}_1$. First we notice that the competitive allocation in $\mathcal{E}_2$ is also an exact duplicate of the competitive allocation in $\mathcal{E}_1$, namely $x_{11}^* = x_{12}^* = x_{21}^* = x_{22}^* = (2,2)$, which is competitive for the same price system $p^* = (1,1)$. Now let us examine the core of $\mathcal{E}_2$ and consider, in particular, the allocation which assigns the commodity bundle $(1,1)$ to agents 11 and 12, and $(3,3)$ to agents 21 and 22. This allocation is the exact duplicate of the allocation in $\mathcal{E}_1$ represented by point a in Figure 1.5, which is in the core of $\mathcal{E}_1$. Let us show, however, that it is no longer in the core of $\mathcal{E}_2$. To this end, consider the coalition $\{11, 12, 21\}$, made of the two agents of type 1 and a single agent of type 2. The aggregate initial endowment of this coalition is $2\omega_{11} + \omega_{21} = (8,4)$. If we split the aggregate endowment between the three members of the coalition by assigning $(\frac{5}{2}, \frac{1}{2})$ to agents 11 and 12, and $(3,3)$ to agent 21, all of them are at least as well off while agents 11 and 12 are strictly better off at $(\frac{5}{2}, \frac{1}{2})$ than at $(1,1)$ (see Figure 2.3).

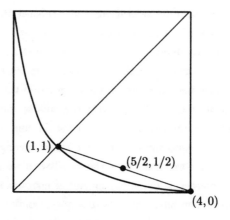

Figure 2.3

This coalition can thus improve upon the replica of allocation a in $\mathcal{E}_2$ and, as stated above, this allocation is no longer in the core of $\mathcal{E}_2$. The core has shrunk when increasing the number of agents in the economy from 2 to 4. This increase has created the possibility of coalitions consisting of *three* agents, which were not available in the economy $\mathcal{E}_1$, and which were needed to remove the allocation a, or its duplicate, from the core. Of course, the presence of these coalitions is not sufficient to be able to remove *all* allocations in the core of $\mathcal{E}_1$ (except, of course, the competitive one which we know, by Theorem 2.1, to be always in the core). Other coalitions are necessary which, in turn, require a further increase in the number of agents. The natural way to proceed in that direction consists in defining, for all integers r, an exchange economy $\mathcal{E}_r$ with r agents of type 1 and r agents of type 2, all agents of type 1 (type 2) having the same preferences and the same initial endowment as those of their counterparts in $\mathcal{E}_1$. The economy $\mathcal{E}_r$ embodies $2r$ agents and is an exact r^{th} replicate of $\mathcal{E}_1$. It is clear that the competitive allocation $\mathcal{C}$ in $\mathcal{E}_r$ is the rth replicate of the competitive allocation in $\mathcal{E}_1$. If we denote by $\text{Core}(\mathcal{E}_r)$ the core of the economy $\mathcal{E}_r$, Edgeworth's conjecture applied to our example can be formulated as $\lim_{r \to \infty} \text{Core}(\mathcal{E}_r) = \mathcal{C}$. That this is indeed true in our example follows from the general statement of the Debreu-Scarf theorem.

To prove rigorously Edgeworth's conjecture, Debreu and Scarf (1963) have considered the same general model of an exchange economy with n agents as the one defined in Section 1.1, endowed with the same assumptions about preferences $\succsim_i$, $i = 1, \cdots, n$. By analogy with the example presented in the previous section, let us denote this economy $\mathcal{E}_1$. Then, for any integer r, we define by $\mathcal{E}_r$ the exchange economy obtained by replicating r-times the economy $\mathcal{E}_1$. The economy $\mathcal{E}_r$ embodies nr agents, each agent i of $\mathcal{E}_1$ being replicated r times; i.e. having the same initial endowment ω_{iq}, $\omega_{iq} = \omega_i$, $q = 1, \cdots, r$, and the same preferences $\succsim_{iq} = \succsim_i$ as agent i in $\mathcal{E}_1$; we call the agents who replicate agent i, the agents 'of type i'. Now consider an allocation $(x_1, \cdots, x_i, \cdots, x_n)$ in $\mathcal{E}_1$ and define, in $\mathcal{E}_r$, x_{iq}, $q = 1, \cdots, r$, by

$$x_{iq} = x_i.$$

Since $(x_1, \cdots, x_i, \cdots, x_n)$ is an allocation in $\mathcal{E}_1$, we have

$$\sum_{i=1}^{n} x_i = \sum_{i=1}^{n} \omega_i$$

so that

$$\sum_{q=1}^{r} \sum_{i=1}^{n} x_{iq} = r \sum_{i=1}^{n} x_i = r \sum_{i=1}^{n} \omega_i,$$

which shows that the nr-tuple of vectors $(x_{11}, \cdots, x_{1r}; x_{21}, \cdots, x_{2r}, \cdots, x_{n1}, \cdots, x_{nr})$ is an allocation in $\mathcal{E}_r$: it is the r-replica of the allocation $(x_1, \cdots, x_n)$ in $\mathcal{E}_1$.

Lemma 2.1.
The core of $\mathcal{E}_r$ consists only of allocations which are r-replicas of allocations in $\mathcal{E}_1$.

Proof Suppose, on the contrary, that for some r, an allocation $(x_{11}, \cdots, x_{1r}; \cdots, x_{n1}, \cdots, x_{nr})$ is in the core of $\mathcal{E}_r$ and that $x_{\hat{i}\nu} \neq x_{\hat{i}q}$ for some $\hat{i}$ and $\nu, q \in \{1, \cdots, r\}$. For each type i, choose a consumer q_i for which $x_{is} \succsim x_{iq_i}$ for all $s \in \{1, \cdots, r\}$, and consider the coalition $S = \{q_1, \cdots, q_i, \cdots, q_n\}$. Also define y_i by

$$y_i = \frac{1}{r} \sum_{s=1}^{r} x_{is}.$$

For all $q_i \in S$, y_i is a convex combination of preferred bundles, relative to the preferences $\succsim$ common to all agents of type i. Accordingly, by strict convexity of $\succsim_{\hat{i}}$, we have, for all $q_i \in S$, $y_i \succsim_{\hat{i}} q_i$, and for $i = \hat{i}$, $y_{\hat{i}} \succ_{\hat{i}} x_{\hat{i} q_{\hat{i}}}$. Furthermore

$$\sum_{i=1}^{n} y_i = \sum_{i=1}^{n} \frac{1}{r} \sum_{s=1}^{r} x_{is} = \frac{1}{r} \sum_{i=1}^{n} \sum_{s=1}^{r} x_{is}$$
$$= \frac{1}{r} \sum_{i=1}^{n} \sum_{s=1}^{r} \omega_{is} = \sum_{i=1}^{n} \omega_{is} = \sum_{i=1}^{n} \omega_{i q_i},$$

so that the coalition S can improve upon the allocation in the economy $\mathcal{E}_r$, a contradiction to the fact that this allocation is supposed to be in the core of $\mathcal{E}_r$.

The preceding lemma shows that, for the particular method chosen to increase the number of agents in the economy (replica procedure), we may compare the allocations in the cores corresponding to an increase in the number of agents: for all r, an allocation in the core of $\mathcal{E}_r$ is necessarily an allocation of $\mathcal{E}_1$ replicated r times. Of course, the *set* of allocations in the core of $\mathcal{E}_r$ depends on r. In particular, it is easy to see that the core of $\mathcal{E}_{r+1}$ is included in the core of $\mathcal{E}_r$, for a coalition which can improve upon an allocation of $\mathcal{E}_1$ replicated r times in $\mathcal{E}_r$ can *a fortiori* improve upon the same allocation replicated $r + 1$ times in $\mathcal{E}_{r+1}$. By Theorem 2.1, we know however that a competitive allocation of $\mathcal{E}_1$ replicated r times is in the core of $\mathcal{E}_r$. Accordingly, as a function of r, the cores of the economies $\mathcal{E}_r$ constitute a decreasing sequence of sets, each of which contains the set of competitive allocations of $\mathcal{E}_1$. The Debreu-Scarf theorem states that there is no other allocation in the core of $\mathcal{E}_r$ for all r.

Theorem 2.2.
If an allocation $(x_1, \cdots, x_i, \cdots, x_n)$ of $\mathcal{E}_1$ replicated r times is in the core of $\mathcal{E}_r$, for all r, then it is competitive in $\mathcal{E}_1$.

Proof Let $(x_1, \cdots, x_i, \cdots, x_n)$ be in the core of $\mathcal{E}_r$ for all r. Define the sets F_i and G_i, $i = 1, \cdots, n$, by

$$F_i = \{x \mid x \succsim_{\tilde{i}} x_i\}$$
$$G_i = \{x \mid x + \omega_i \in F_i.\}$$

Define also Γ by $\Gamma = $ convex hull of $\cup_{i=1}^n G_i$: since G_i is convex and non-empty, Γ consists of the set of all vectors z which can be written as $z = \sum_{i=1}^n \alpha_i z_i$, $z_i \in G_i$ and $\sum_{i=1}^n \alpha_i = 1$. Let us first prove that $0 \notin \Gamma$. Suppose on the contrary that there exist positive numbers $\alpha_1, \cdots, \alpha_n$, with $\sum_{i=1}^n \alpha_i = 1$, and vectors z_i, $z_i \in G_i$, such that $\sum_{i=1}^n \alpha_i z_i = 0$. For each integer k, let us denote by a_i^k the smallest integer larger or equal to $k\alpha_i$. Furthermore, define y_i^k by

$$y_i^k = \frac{k\alpha_i}{a_i^k} z_i + w_i.$$

Notice that

$$\sum_{i=1}^n a_i^k y_i^k = k \sum_{i=1}^n \alpha_i z_i + \sum_{i=1}^n a_i^k \omega_i$$
$$= \sum_{i=1}^n a_i^k \omega_i. \tag{2.2}$$

Since $z_i \in G_i$, $y_i^k \in F_i$ when k is large enough: indeed, when $k \to \infty$, $\frac{k\alpha_i}{a_i^k} \to 1$, so that $\frac{k\alpha_i}{a_i^k} z_i + \omega_i$ must belong to F_i, by continuity of $\succsim_{\tilde{i}}$, when k is chosen sufficiently large. Choose k so that y_i^k belongs to F_i for all $i = 1, \cdots, n$. Then $y_i^k \succ_i x_i$ for all i. Assign y_i^k to a_i^k agents in the economy $\mathcal{E}_{r^*}$, with $r^* = \max_i\{a_i^k\}$. It follows from (2.2) that the coalition S consisting of the a_i^k agents of type i receiving y_i^k, can improve upon the allocation $(x_1, \cdots, x_i, \cdots, x_n)$ replicated r^*-times in the economy $\mathcal{E}_{r^*}$, contrary to the assumption that this allocation is in the core for all r. This proves that $0 \notin \Gamma$.

Since Γ is convex, it follows from the hyperplane theorem that there exists a vector p, $p \neq 0$, such that $p \cdot x \geq 0$ for all $x \in \Gamma$ and, consequently, for all $x \in G_i$, $i = 1, \cdots, n$. By definition of F_i, $p \cdot x \geq 0$ for all $x \in G_i \Rightarrow$

$$p \cdot x \geq p \cdot \omega_i, \text{ for all } x \in F_i. \tag{2.3}$$

Since x_i is in the closure of F_i, the continuity of $\succsim_i$ implies that, for all $i = 1, \cdots, n,$

$$p \cdot x_i \geq p \cdot \omega_i. \tag{2.4}$$

From the fact that $(x_1, \cdots, x_i, \cdots, x_n)$ is an allocation, we find also that

$$p \cdot \sum_{i=1}^{n} x_i = p \cdot \sum_{i=1}^{n} \omega_i. \tag{2.5}$$

Combining (2.4) and (2.5), we get that, for all $i = 1, \cdots, n,$

$$p \cdot x_i = p \cdot \omega_i. \tag{2.6}$$

So far, we have shown that, if we consider p as a price system, any point preferred to x_i is as expensive as ω_i (see (2.3)) and that x_i is in $B_i(p)$ (see (2.6)). To prove that $(x_1, \cdots, x_i, \cdots x_n)$ is a competitive allocation for p, it remains to show that any *strictly* preferred point to x_i is strictly more expensive than ω_i in terms of p. This is proved as follows. First, it is easy to see that strict desirability of $\succsim_i$ implies that p has all its components strictly positive. Assume then that there exists x, with $x \succ_i x_i$ and $p \cdot x = p \cdot \omega_i$. By continuity, $x - \varepsilon \succ_i x_i$ when ε is chosen sufficiently small and subtracted from all the strictly positive components of x. Accordingly, by (2.3), we have

$$p \cdot (x - \varepsilon) = p \cdot x - p \cdot \varepsilon \geq p \cdot \omega_i. \qquad (2.7)$$

If we had $p \cdot x = p \cdot \omega_i$, it would follow from (2.7) that $p \cdot (x - \varepsilon) < p \cdot \omega_i$. But $x - \varepsilon \underset{i}{\succ} x_i$ and $p \cdot (x - \varepsilon) < p \cdot \omega_i$ violates (2.3). The proof of the theorem is complete.

The Debreu-Scarf theorem seems to indicate that increasing the number of agents in the exchange economy reduces progressively the possibility for each one of them to get a bundle *in the core* preferred to those obtained at a competitive allocation. To illustrate, let us come back to our initial example (Section 1.1) with two traders and two goods. The collective choice of a particular allocation *in the core* depends on the ability of each trader to enforce a point on the segment $[a, b]$ (see Figure 1.5) providing him with a higher utility level than the competitive bundle (2,2). However, as revealed by the reasoning underlying Figure 2.3, duplicating by $\mathcal{E}_2$ the exchange economy $\mathcal{E}_1$ already suffices to throw out of the core $[a, b]$ those allocations which are close to the two extreme points a and b in the core. For further replicas, the subsets of allocations in the segment $[a, b]$ remaining in the corresponding cores form a decreasing sequence of intervals centered on the competitive allocation $(x_1^* = x_2^* = (2, 2))$: the possibility for the traders to enforce an allocation which dominates in utility the competitive outcome is progressively reduced as the number of replicas increases.

Finally, when the number of replicas tends to infinity, it starts to produce equivalent results whether the agents accept trading individually at competitive prices or recontract proposed allocations through the whole mechanism of coalition formation. Thus we may conclude from the Debreu-Scarf theorem that under those conditions which make meaningful the competitive solution – a large number of agents – the complicated process of choosing an allocation in the core is almost equivalent to the decentralised competitive mechanism. As shown in the next section, we should however avoid hastiness when we formulate this conclusion, and examine closely the underlying assumptions of Debreu-Scarf's result.

2.2 THE ASYMPTOTIC APPROACH TO IMPERFECT COMPETITION: 'GIANTS' AND 'DWARFS'

To enlighten this investigation, it is useful to come back to our two-agent, two-commodity example of an exchange economy, as defined in Section 1.1. Let us once more replicate the exchange economy $\mathcal{E}_1$ in a manner analogous to the replication considered in Section 2.1, with one exception however: the economy replicated r times, – call it $\mathcal{E}'_r$ – now includes $r + 1$ agents, all agents having the same preferences as before, all agents of type 1 having the same initial endowment $\omega_{ij} = \left(\frac{4}{r}, 0\right)$, $j = 1, \cdots, r$, while a single agent – agent $r + 1$ – has now an initial endowment $\omega_{r+1} = (0, 4)$. The economy $\mathcal{E}'_r$ is the same as $\mathcal{E}_r$, except that the ownership of commodity 2 is fully concentrated in the hands of a single agent. In contrast, the total amount of commodity 1 is now spread over a number of agents which increases with r. Notice that the method used by Debreu and Scarf to increase by replication the number of agents in the economy not only guarantees that this increase is effective, *but also that the ownership of each commodity is spread over*. In contrast, the replication of $\mathcal{E}_1$ by $\mathcal{E}'_r$ undoubtedly also guarantees that the increase in the number of agents is effective, but it does not spread the ownership of each commodity over an increasing number of agents: agent $r + 1$ remains, as in $\mathcal{E}_1$, a monopolist of commodity 2.

The competitive allocation in $\mathcal{E}'_r$ is easily seen to be given by

$$x^*_{ij} = \left(\frac{2}{r}, \frac{2}{r}\right); \qquad j = 1, \cdots, r$$
$$x^*_{r+1} = (2, 2),$$

with the price system (1,1). Now, let the number r increase *ad infinitum*. Since the number of agents increases without limit, one would think that the basic condition under which the competitive solution is meaningful – a large number of agents – would entail at the limit that the competitive allocation is the sole allocation remaining in the limit core. Let us check however *that the allocation* $x = (x_{11}, \cdots, x_{1r}; x_{r+1})$ *defined by*

$$x_i = x_{1j} = \left(\frac{1}{r}, \frac{1}{r}\right), \qquad 1j = 1, \cdots, r$$
$$x_{r+1} = (3, 3)$$

remains in the core for all r. Suppose indeed on the contrary that this allocation is not in the core of an economy $\mathcal{E}'_r$ for some value of r. Let S be the coalition which can improve upon this allocation and y_i, $i \in S$, the commodity bundles for which $y_i \underset{i}{\succ} x_i$ and

$$\sum_{i \in S} y_i = \sum_{i \in S} \omega_i, \qquad (2.8)$$

with x_i denoting the commodity bundle obtained by agent i in the allocation x. First notice that S cannot be the coalition of all agents. It is clear, indeed, that the proposed allocation is Pareto-optimal, so that it cannot be improved upon by all agents together. The coalition S cannot be either a coalition consisting solely of agents of type 1: these agents only own initially commodity 1, and they could not increase their utility level from the bundle $\left(\frac{1}{r}, \frac{1}{r}\right)$ without some amount of commodity 2. Accordingly, the coalition S which is assumed to improve upon the allocation x is made of a *proper* subset of agents of type 1 *and* agent $r + 1$. Let us show that this is impossible. At the price system $p = (1, 1)$, for each agent $i \in S$, we have

$$y_i \underset{i}{\succ} x_i \Rightarrow p \cdot y_i > p \cdot x_i$$

which implies that

$$p \cdot \sum_{i \in S} y_i > p \cdot \sum_{i \in S} x_i. \qquad (2.9)$$

Furthermore, for all $i \in \{11, \cdots, 1j, \cdots, 1r, r+1\} \setminus S$, we get

$$p \cdot x_i = \frac{2}{r} < p \cdot \omega_i = \frac{4}{r}, \qquad (2.10)$$

since the set $\{11, \cdots, 1r, r+1\} \setminus S$, which is non-empty, contains only agents of type 1. Of course (2.10) implies that

$$p \cdot \sum_{i \in \{11, \cdots, 1r; r+1\} \setminus S} \omega_i > p \cdot \sum_{i \in \{11, \cdots, 1r; r+1\} \setminus S} x_i. \qquad (2.11)$$

Accordingly, it follows from (2.9), (2.11) and the fact that x is an allocation that

$$p \cdot \sum_{i \in S} y_i + p \cdot \sum_{i \in \{11, \cdots, 1r; r+1\} \setminus S} \omega_i > p \cdot \sum_{i \in S} x_i + p \cdot \sum_{i \in \{11, \cdots, 1r; r+1\} \setminus S} x_i$$

$$= p \cdot \sum_{i=1}^{r+1} \omega_i = p \cdot \sum_{i \in S} \omega_i + p \cdot \sum_{i \in \{11, \cdots, 1r; r+1\} \setminus S} \omega_i,$$

an inequality which contradicts (2.8).

Consequently, the alternative procedure used for increasing the number of agents in the economy $\mathcal{E}'_r$ does not remove the allocation x from the core, while this allocation is already removed from the core of $\mathcal{E}_2$ when the Debreu-Scarf replication procedure is used (see the reasoning underlying Figure 2.3, p. 32: the 'image' of the allocation x in the Edgeworth box is the point a on Figure 1.5, p. 24). Notice that not only the allocation x remains in the core for all r but also any allocation $z = (z_{11}, \cdots, z_{1j}, \cdots, z_{1r}; z_{r+1})$ which can be written as

$$z_{1j} = \left(\frac{2-\alpha}{r}, \frac{2-\alpha}{r} \right) \qquad 0 \le \alpha \le 1, j = 1, \cdots, r;$$
$$z_{r+1} = ((2+\alpha), (2+\alpha)):$$

A proof similar to the one we have just used for the allocation x can be repeated to reach this conclusion for allocations z (the allocation x obtains when $\alpha = 1$). This discrepancy in the consequences of increasing the number of agents finds its source in the fact that the Debreu-Scarf procedure guarantees that this increase is accompanied by a dissemination of the ownership of each good over an increasing number of people. On the contrary, for the alternative procedure considered here, and in spite of the increase in the number of agents, trader $r+1$ 'keeps a corner' on commodity 2, however large the number r.

The above version of our example shows that the interpretation of the Debreu-Scarf result should be made with caution. In particular, the initial distribution of the ownership of goods seems to play an important role, beyond the existence of a large number of agents. This is not surprising since economists know very well that pure competition is not *a priori* compatible with market situations in which only a few traders sell or buy a particular good. But even when the ownership of each good is adequately spread over a large number of agents, the agents can, by *their own decision*, destroy this *a priori* competitive environment. We are referring here to the possibility, opened to the agents, of colluding and thereby influencing the collective choice of an allocation in the exchange economy. We have already alluded to this possibility when evoking the existence of trade unions, cartels and syndicates.

To illustrate, suppose that all agents of type 2 in the economy $\mathcal{E}_r$, with r agents of each type, decide together *that they will not enter into broader coalitions including some or all agents of type 1, except in unison.* What is the effect of such a group decision on the core? Henceforth, any coalition which included a *proper* subset of $\{21, \cdots, 2j, \cdots, 2r\}$ is forbidden, so that the class of coalitions which can improve upon a particular allocation is considerably reduced. The astute reader will immediately notice that the collusive decision reduces the class of available coalitions in the economy $\mathcal{E}_r$ to exactly the same class of coalitions which is available to improve upon an allocation in the economy $\mathcal{E}'_r$: the r agents of type 2 acting in unison form a single decision unit identical to the monopolist agent $r+1$ in the economy $\mathcal{E}'_r$. Accordingly, the consequence on the core of the collusive move can be described by the passage from the core of $\mathcal{E}_r$ to the core of $\mathcal{E}'_r$, a dramatic change indeed.

The existence of large economies which either do not meet the distributive requirements on initial endowments, or are subject to voluntary collusive moves of the agents, raises the difficult problem of the core behaviour in these imperfectly competitive environments. This behaviour has been studied from two directions. The first one aims at extending the Debreu-Scarf asymptotic result to a much wider class of economies than those obtained by the replica procedure considered by these authors. This approach is well illustrated in Hildenbrand (1974). The second approach tries to tackle directly the study of the core in some specific non-competitive contexts which are well known in partial equilibrium analysis, like situations of oligopoly with concentrated ownership of some goods.

One way to represent non-competitive contexts consists of considering the following delegation procedure, proposed in Drèze, Gabszewicz and Gepts (1969), which is an analog of the Debreu-Scarf replication procedure. Let us define the economy $\mathcal{E}_r$ from the economy $\mathcal{E}_1$ by considering an exchange situation where each agent i *delegates* to r intermediaries iq, $i = 1, \cdots, n$, $q = 1, \cdots, r$, the responsibility of trading on his behalf. To this effect, he transfers to intermediary ij the rth part of his initial endowment ω_i, i.e. $\frac{\omega_i}{r}$, and instructs him to trade according to the preference ordering $\underset{ij}{\succsim}$ defined by $x \underset{ij}{\succsim} y \Leftrightarrow rx \underset{i}{\succsim} ry$. Then trading takes place among the nr intermediaries. If an agent agrees to participate in the exchange in this manner, *no matter how large the number r may be*, it is natural to conclude that he is willing to give up whatever influence he may have on the collective choice – since he agrees to dilute that influence over an arbitrarily large number of anonymous intermediaries, each of which will trade in arbitrarily small quantities. It is clear that the model which we have just constructed is perfectly analogous to that of Debreu-Scarf. Thus, it must carry the same properties, namely, (i) for an allocation x in the core of $\mathcal{E}_r$, all intermediaries of type i must get the same bundle $\frac{x_i}{r}$, and (ii) if an allocation $(x_1, \cdots, x_i, \cdots, x_n)$ of $\mathcal{E}_1$

is such that, for all r, this allocation $\left(\frac{x_1}{r}, \cdots, \frac{x_i}{r}, \cdots, \frac{x_n}{r}\right)$ replicated r times belongs to the core of $\mathcal{E}_r$, then $(x_1, \cdots, x_i, \cdots, x_n)$ is a competitive allocation of $\mathcal{E}_1$ (for a formal proof, see Drèze, Gabszewicz and Gepts 1969, p. 103 and 104).

Now imagine that *some, but not all agents*, agree to delegate their trading in the manner described above, to an arbitrarily large number of anonymous intermediaries; while the former agree to dilute their influence, the latter wish to keep the possibility of influencing the collective choice of the allocation in the core. It is possible to represent this situation formally by considering an economy $\mathcal{E}_1'$ with ℓn agents, namely ℓ agents ($\ell > 1$) for each one of n types; it is assumed that $n\ell - \ell$ agents agree to delegate while ℓ do not; the proportion of the number of those who do not delegate to the size ℓn of the economy is exactly equal to $\frac{1}{n}$. Of course, the ongoing analysis would still hold if this proportion were strictly less than $\frac{1}{n}$. Also we assume that at least one agent of each type agrees to delegate. We build the economy $\mathcal{E}_r'$ from $\mathcal{E}_1'$, by letting the $\ell(n-1)$ 'competitive' traders delegate their trading each to r intermediaries. Accordingly the economy $\mathcal{E}_r'$ embodies $r\ell(n-1) + \ell$ agents, consisting of the $r\ell(n-1)$ intermediaries – the *dwarfs* – and the ℓ agents who do not delegate – the *giants*. The set of agents is subdivided into n types i, $i = 1, \cdots, n$, where the agents of type i consist of λ_i giants, $\lambda_i < \ell$, $\sum_{i=1}^{n} \lambda_i = \ell$, with initial endowment ω_i and the preferences $\underset{i}{\succsim}$, and $r(\ell - \lambda_i)$ dwarfs, with initial endowment $\omega_i = \frac{\omega_i}{r}$ and preferences $\underset{i'}{\succsim}$, such that $x \underset{i'}{\succsim} y \Leftrightarrow rx \underset{i}{\succsim} ry$. Let us prove the following:

Lemma 2.2.

If an allocation is in the core of $\mathcal{E}_r'$, then all dwarfs of type i receive the same bundle – say $x_{ij} = \frac{y_i}{r}$, and all giants of that type receive the bundle y_i.

Proof Let x be an allocation in the core. It is convenient to index the agents of type i by $j = 1, \cdots, r\ell$, with one index assigned to each dwarf and r consecutive indices assigned to each giant; if j refers to a dwarf, let x_{ij} be the commodity assigned to him by the allocation x. If j is one of the indices assigned to a giant, let x_{ij} denote $\frac{1}{r}$ times the vector that he obtains in the allocation x. Furthermore, the indexing also satisfies the following property:

$$x_{ij} \underset{i'}{\succsim} x_{ik}, \qquad j = 1, \cdots, r\ell - 1; k = j + 1, \cdots, r\ell.$$

The lemma says that $x_{ij} = x_{ik}$, $i = 1, \cdots, n; j, k = 1, \cdots, r\ell$. Under this indexing procedure, there is always a positive integer $\rho < r\ell$ such that, for all $i = 1, \cdots, n$, either the index ρ refers to a dwarf, or if ρ belongs to the set of r consecutive indices assigned to some giant, then $\rho + 1$ does not belong to that set; in other words, there is always an index ρ such that the set of indices $\{j \mid j \leq \rho\}$ and $\{j \mid j > \rho\}$ partition the agents into two groups, with no giant 'split' across the two groups. The existence of such a ρ is guaranteed by the fact that *at most* $(r - 1)\ell$ integers between 1 and $r\ell$ can belong to the set of indices assigned to one of the ℓ giants (remember that $\lambda_i < \ell$) *and* be such that the highest index also belongs to the same set – whereas there are $r\ell - 1$ integers to choose from in selecting ρ.

Then let

$$\overline{x}_i \overset{\text{def}}{=} \frac{1}{r\ell - \rho} \sum_{j=\ell+1}^{r\ell} x_{ij}.$$

It follows from convexity and from our indexing convention that $\overline{x}_i \underset{i}{\succsim} x_{i\rho}$. Suppose that, contrary to the lemma, $x_{ij} \neq x_{ik}$ for some i, j and $k > j$. Take $i = 1$. Then, by strict convexity, $\overline{x}_1 \underset{i}{\succ} x_{11}$. Consider the coalition S formed by all traders whose indices do not exceed ρ; such a coalition exists and, in view of the definition of ρ, it does not include any 'split' giant. Consider also the commodity bundles x'_{ih} defined by

$$x'_{ih} = \frac{\rho x_{ih} + (r\ell - \rho)\overline{x}_i}{r\ell}, \quad i = 1, \cdots, n; h = 1, \cdots, \rho.$$

By convexity, $x'_{ih} \underset{\overline{i}}{\succeq} x_{ih}$, $h = 1, \cdots, \rho$; $i = 1, \cdots, n$. Furthermore, for $i = 1$,

$$x'_{11} \underset{1}{\succ} x_{11}.$$

Notice also that

$$\sum_{i=1}^{n} \left(\sum_{h=1}^{\rho} x'_{ih} \right) = \frac{\rho}{r\ell} \sum_{i=1}^{n} \sum_{h=1}^{\rho} x_{ih} + \rho \frac{r\ell - \rho}{r\ell} \sum_{i=1}^{n} \overline{x}_i$$

$$= \frac{\rho}{r\ell} \left[\sum_{i=1}^{n} \sum_{h=1}^{\rho} x_{ih} + \sum_{i=1}^{n} \sum_{h=\rho+1}^{r\ell} x_{ih} \right]$$

$$= \frac{\rho}{r\ell} \left[\sum_{i=1}^{n} \sum_{h=1}^{r\ell} \frac{\omega_i}{r} \right].$$

Therefore the coalition S can improve upon the allocation x, contrary to the assumption that x is in the core.

From Lemma 2.2, we conclude that the agents in $\mathcal{E}_1$ who refuse to delegate their trading do not get a better treatment in the core than those who have accepted it: the latter receive from their r intermediaries r times the vector $\frac{y_i}{r}$, while the former get the bundle y_i. Accordingly, as in the replica procedure, any allocation in the core of $\mathcal{E}'_r$ may be described by an n-tuple of vectors $(y_1, \cdots, y_i, \cdots, y_n)$, it being understood that a trader of type i receives either y_i or $\frac{y_i}{r}$ according to whether he is a giant or a dwarf. Now, we prove the following.

Theorem 2.3.
Let $(y_1, \cdots, y_i, \cdots, y_n)$ be an allocation in $\mathcal{E}_1$ which is, for all r, in the core of $\mathcal{E}'_r$, being understood that dwarfs of type i get $\frac{y_i}{r}$, and giants y_i. Then $(y_1, \cdots, y_i, \cdots, y_n)$ is a competitive allocation in $\mathcal{E}_1$.

Proof Let $(y_1, \cdots, y_i, \cdots, y_n)$ be in the core of $\mathcal{E}'_r$ for all r. Since $\lambda_i < \ell$, there exists at least one agent of type i who agrees to delegate his trading to r intermediaries. Accordingly, there exists, for each type i, r intermediaries getting $\frac{y_i}{r}$ with $\sum_{i=1}^{n} y_i = \sum_{i=1}^{n} \omega_i$. Consider the subeconomy consisting of these nr intermediaries. The allocation $\left(\frac{y_1}{r}, \cdots, \frac{y_i}{r}, \cdots, \frac{y_n}{r}\right)$, assigning $\frac{y_i}{r}$ to the r intermediaries of type i, should be, for all r, in the core of this subeconomy for otherwise the coalition which would have improved this allocation in the subeconomy, would also improve upon the allocation $(y_1, \cdots, y_i, \cdots, y_n)$ in the economy $\mathcal{E}'_r$, contrary to the assumption of the theorem. As noticed above (see p. 46), it follows that the allocation $(y_1, \cdots, y_i, \cdots, y_n)$ is competitive in the subeconomy consisting of one agent of each type i. But then it is easy to see that it is also competitive in $\mathcal{E}'_1$.

The preceding asymptotic study of the core, with dwarfs and giants, shares with the Debreu-Scarf approach the property that the number of agents in each type increases without limit in the economy $\mathcal{E}'_r$ when r increases. Remember, indeed, that at least one agent of each type agrees to delegate trading to r intermediaries. This implies in particular that, as a function of r, there are more and more sellers and buyers of each good. Even if this is not enough to guarantee the asymptotic result with the presence of giants (remember that we have assumed that the proportion of the number of giants to the size ℓn of the economy does not exceed $\frac{1}{n}$), it meets however a basic requirement for competition: when r increases, each good starts to be owned by a large number of agents, precluding any monopolistic or oligopolistic structure in markets. Is this a necessary condition to restore competition? As we shall see, this is not the case: competition can also be driven by rivalry among giants when they exchange with a large number of dwarfs (see Gabszewicz 1977). To show this, consider the exchange economy $\mathcal{E}''_r$ defined as follows. There are $r+2$ traders: one trader with initial endowment $w_{1r} = (1 - \frac{1}{r})w, w \gg 0$, another trader with initial endowment $w_{2r} = \frac{w}{r}$ (the two giants) and r traders with initial endowments $w_i = \frac{w'}{r}$ each, $i = 3, \ldots, r+2$, $w' \gg 0$ (the dwarfs). Assume also that traders $1r$ and $2r$ have preference orderings denoted by $\underset{1r}{\succsim}$ and $\underset{2r}{\succsim}$, respectively, derived from a given preference ordering $\succeq_r$ by the conditions

$$x \succeq_r y \Leftrightarrow x(1 - \frac{1}{r}) \underset{1r}{\succeq} y(1 - \frac{1}{r}) \Leftrightarrow \frac{x}{r} \underset{2r}{\succeq} \frac{y}{r}. \tag{2.12}$$

Furthermore, we assume that all traders in $\{3, \ldots, r+2\}$ have the same preference ordering $\succeq_r$ derived from a given preference ordering $\succeq$ by

$$x \succeq y \Leftrightarrow \frac{x}{r} \underset{r}{\succeq} \frac{y}{r}. \tag{2.13}$$

Beyond the assumptions stated in Section 1.1, the following assumptions are made on $\succeq_r$ and $\succeq$: (i) $\succeq_r$ and $\succeq$ are both representable by C^1-utility functions with non-vanishing gradients and (ii) if x is on the boundary of R^ℓ_+, $x \underset{1}{\sim} 0$ and $x \sim 0$.

To illustrate, consider an example of an economy $\mathcal{E}''_r$ of the type described above derived from our example in Section 1.1 as follows. There are two goods and $r + 2$ traders with identical utility functions $U(x^1, x^2) = \sqrt{x^1} + \sqrt{x^2}$. *Two* traders share the same initial bundle $w = (0, 4)$ as endowment, with one of them owning a share $(1 - \frac{1}{r})$ of this bundle, while the other owns a share $\frac{1}{r}$ of it, namely

$$w_{1r} = (0, (1 - \frac{1}{r})4)$$
$$w_{2r} = (0, \frac{4}{r}).$$

The r remaining traders have $w_i = (\frac{4}{r}, 0)$ each, as initial endowment, $i = 3, \ldots, r + 2$. The economy $\mathcal{E}''_r$ is almost identical to the economy $\mathcal{E}'_r$ defined on page 42, except that the ownership of commodity 2 is no longer concentrated in the hands of a single agent. This ownership is now shared between the two agents $1r$ and $2r$; eventually, this sharing would reinforce the competitive position of the dwarfs owning commodity 1, due to the rivalry between the two giants in commodity 2. We shall see, indeed, that this rivalry has dramatic effects on the behaviour of the core. To analyse these effects, let us prove the following:

Lemma 2.3.

If $(x_{1r}, x_{2r}, x_3, \ldots, x_{r+2})$ is an allocation in the core of $\mathcal{E}_r''$, then there exist two commodity bundles, x and x' such that $x_{1r} = x(1 - \frac{1}{r})$, $x_{2r} = \frac{x}{r}$ and $x_i = \frac{x'}{r}$, $i = 3, \ldots, r+2$.

Proof Let $(x_{1r}, x_{2r}, x_3, \ldots, x_{r+2})$ be in the core of $\mathcal{E}_r''$ for all r. First we show that $\frac{x_{1r}}{r-1} \underset{2r}{\succsim} x_{2r}$. Suppose indeed, on the contrary, that we had $x_{2r} \underset{2r}{\succ} \frac{x_{1r}}{r-1}$. Then, by (2.12),

$$(r-1)x_{2r} \underset{1r}{\succ} x_{1r}.$$

We find, indeed, that $x_{2r} \underset{2r}{\succ} \frac{x_{1r}}{r-1}$, which implies $rx_{2r} \underset{1}{\succ} r\left(\frac{x_{1r}}{r-1}\right)$ since $x \underset{1}{\succ} y$ $\Leftrightarrow \frac{x}{r} \underset{2r}{\succ} \frac{y}{r}$ (see (2.13)). But, it follows from (2.13) that $rx_{2r} \underset{1}{\succ} r\left(\frac{x_{1r}}{r-1}\right)$, which implies $\frac{r-1}{r}(rx_{2r}) \underset{1r}{\succ} \frac{r-1}{r}\left(\frac{rx_{1r}}{r-1}\right)$, or $(r-1)x_{2r} \underset{1r}{\succ} x_{1r}$. Since $\underset{1r}{\succsim}$ is strictly convex, we get

$$y_{1r} \overset{\text{def}}{=} \frac{1}{r}(r-1)x_{2r} + \frac{(r-1)}{r}x_{1r} \underset{1r}{\succ} x_{1r}.$$

Let i^* be a trader in $\{3, \ldots, r+2\}$ such that $x_{i^*} \underset{r}{\succsim} x_i$ for all $i \in \{3, \ldots, r+2\}$. Consider the coalition S defined by $S = \{1 \cup \{3, \ldots, r+2\} \setminus \{i^*\}\}$ and define y_i for $i \in S$ by

$$y_{1r} = \frac{r-1}{r}(x_{2r} + x_{1r})$$

$$y_i = \frac{1}{r}y_i^* + (1 - \frac{1}{r})x_{ir}, \quad i = 3, \ldots, r+2, i \neq i^*.$$

Clearly, by strict convexity of $\underset{2r}{\succsim}$, $y_i \underset{2r}{\succsim} x_i$ for all $i \in \{3, \ldots, r+2\}$, $i \neq i^*$.

Furthermore,

$$\sum_{i \in S} y_i = \frac{r-1}{r}(x_{1r} + x_{2r}) + \frac{r-1}{r}x_{i^*} + \frac{r-1}{r}\sum_{\substack{i=3 \\ i \neq i^*}}^{r+2} x_i$$

$$= \frac{r-1}{r}\left[\sum_{i=3}^{n+2} x_i + x_{1r} + x_{2r}\right]$$

$$= \frac{r-1}{r}(w + w') = \sum_{i \in S} w_i,$$

so the coalition S can improve upon the allocation, a contradiction to the fact that this allocation is in the core of $\mathcal{E}_r''$.

Now we shall show that $x_{2r} \underset{\underset{2r}{\sim}}{\succeq} \frac{x_{1r}}{r-1}$ and $x_i \underset{r}{\sim} x_k$ for all $i, k \in \{3, \dots, r+2\}$. Suppose indeed that we had either (i) $\frac{x_{1r}}{r-1} \underset{\underset{2r}{}}{\succ} x_{2r}$ or, (ii) $\exists\, i$ and k for whom $x_k \underset{r}{\succ} x_i$, or (iii) both (i) and (ii) hold at the same time. Define i^* by the condition that $x_i \underset{r}{\succeq} x_{i^*}$ for all $i \in \{3, \dots, r+2\}$. Consider the coalition S defined by $S = \left\{\{2r\} \cup \{i^*\}\right\}$ and define

$$y_{2r} = \frac{1}{r}x_{2r} + \left(1 - \frac{1}{r}\right)\frac{x_{1r}}{r-1};$$

$$y_{i^*} = \frac{1}{r}\sum_{i=3}^{r+2} x_i.$$

We observe that

$$y_{2r} + y_{i^*} = \frac{1}{r}(x_{1r} + x_{2r}) + \frac{1}{r}\sum_{i=3}^{r+2} x_i$$

$$= \frac{1}{r}(w + w') = w_{2r} + w_{i^*}.$$

Furthermore, by strict convexity of $\underset{2r}{\succeq}$ and $\underset{r}{\succeq}$, should one of the alternatives (i), (ii) or (iii) hold, the coalition S would improve upon the allocation, a contradiction. Thus we have proved that

$$\frac{x_{1r}}{r-1} \underset{2r}{\succsim} x_{2r} \quad \text{and} \quad x_{2r} \underset{2r}{\succsim} \frac{x_{1r}}{r-1},$$

which implies $\frac{x_{1r}}{r-1} \underset{2r}{\sim} x_{2r}$. By (2.12), we also have $x_{1r} \underset{1r}{\sim} x_{2r}(r-1)$. In-deed, $\frac{x_{1r}}{r-1} \underset{2r}{\sim} x_{2r} \Rightarrow \frac{rx_{1r}}{r-1} \underset{1}{\sim} rx_{2r} \Rightarrow \frac{r-1}{r}\left(\frac{rx_{1r}}{r-1}\right) \underset{1r}{\sim} rx_{2r}\frac{r-1}{r}$; the conclusion $x_{1r} \underset{1r}{\sim} (r-1)x_{2r}$ follows. Finally, let us show that we have $x_{1r} = x(1-\frac{1}{r})$, $x_{2r} = \frac{x}{r}$ for some bundle x. Suppose on the contrary that $\frac{x_{1r}}{r-1} \underset{2r}{\sim} x_{2r}$ and $x_{1r} \underset{1r}{\sim} (r-1)x_{2r}$ could hold without meeting this conclusion. Then, by strict convexity, we have

$$y_{2r} = \frac{1}{r}x_{2r} + (1-\frac{1}{r})\left(\frac{x_{1r}}{r-1}\right) \underset{2r}{\succ} x_{2r}$$

and

$$y_{1r} = \frac{r-1}{r}x_{1r} + \frac{1}{r}x_{2r}(r-1) \underset{1r}{\succ} x_{1r}.$$

Notice however that $y_{1r} + y_{2r} = x_{1r} + x_{2r}$. But this implies that the allocation $(x_{1r}, x_{2r}, x_3, \ldots, x_{r+1})$ is not Pareto-optimal, contradicting the fact that it belongs to the core of $\mathcal{E}_r''$. Finally, $x_k \underset{r}{\sim} x_i$ for all $i, k \in \{3, \ldots, r+1\}$ implies, with strict convexity of $\succsim$, that $x_i = \frac{x'}{r}$ for all $i, k \in \{3, \ldots, r+2\}$, if x' is defined by $x' = \sum_{i=3}^{r+2} x_i$.

By Lemma 2.3, any allocation in the core of $\mathcal{E}_r''$ can be represented by two vectors x and x'. Clearly all competitive allocations of $\mathcal{E}_r''$ share this property. We establish now that only the competitive allocations remain in the core of $\mathcal{E}_r''$ for all r.

Theorem 2.4.
Let (x, x') be an allocation which is, for all r, in the core of $\mathcal{E}_r''$. Then (x, x') is a competitive allocation of $\mathcal{E}_r''$ for all r.

Proof Let (x, x') be in the core of $\mathcal{E}''_r$ for all r. First, it is clear that x and x' are both in the interior of R^ℓ_+. Suppose indeed, for instance, that x' is on the boundary of R^ℓ_+. Then, by assumption (ii), x' is indifferent to 0. However we must have $x' \succsim w' \succ 0$, where $x' \succsim w'$ follows from the fact that (x, x') is in the core of $\mathcal{E}''_r$ for all r, and $w' \succ 0$ follows from $w' \gg 0$ and monotonicity. Since $\succsim_1$ and $\succeq$ are furthermore strictly convex and representable by C^1-utility functions (see assumption (i), p. 51), there exists a unique price vector p such that

$$y \underset{1}{\succ} x \Rightarrow p \cdot y > p \cdot x \qquad (2.14)$$

and

$$y \succ x' \Rightarrow p \cdot y > p \cdot x'. \qquad (2.15)$$

First the price vector p also sustains (x, x') in $\mathcal{E}''_r$ for all r. Indeed suppose for instance that, in $\mathcal{E}''_r$, $z \underset{r}{\succ} \frac{x'}{r}$. Then, by (2.13),

$$rz \succ x',$$

which implies, by (2.15), that $p \cdot (rz) > p \cdot x'$, or $p \cdot z > p \cdot \frac{x'}{r}$. Accordingly, if we prove that, for all r, we must have $p \cdot \frac{x'}{r} = p \frac{w'}{r}$ and $p \cdot \frac{x}{r} = p \cdot \frac{w}{r}$ (which implies $p \cdot x(1 - \frac{1}{r}) = p \cdot w(1 - \frac{1}{r})$), we shall have completed the proof that the pair $(p, (x, x'))$ is a competitive equilibrium. So assume first that $p \cdot \frac{x'}{r} < p \cdot \frac{w'}{r}$. Then $p \cdot x' < p \cdot w'$. Since x' is interior to R^ℓ_+ and $x' \succsim w'$, the differentiability assumption implies that there exists an integer ρ such that $(1 - \frac{1}{\rho})x' + \frac{1}{\rho}w' \succ x'$. Then, it follows from (2.13) that in the economy $\mathcal{E}''_\rho$, we have

$$\frac{1}{\rho}\left[(1 - \frac{1}{\rho})x' + \frac{1}{\rho}w'\right] \underset{\rho}{\succ} \frac{x'}{\rho}.$$

Consider then the coalition V in $\mathcal{E}''_\rho$ consisting of $\{3, \ldots, \rho+2\}$ and trader 1. Define

$$y^1 = \left(1 - \frac{1}{\rho}\right) x;$$

$$y_i = \left(1 - \frac{1}{\rho}\right) \frac{x'}{\rho} + \frac{1}{\rho}\frac{w'}{\rho}, \quad i = 3, \ldots, \rho+2.$$

We verify that

$$\sum_{i \in V} y_i = \left(1 - \frac{1}{\rho}\right) x + \left(1 - \frac{1}{\rho}\right) x' + \frac{w'}{\rho}$$

$$= \left(1 - \frac{1}{\rho}\right) (w + w') + \frac{w'}{\rho} = \sum_{i \in V} w_{i\rho},$$

so that V can improve upon (x, x'), a contradiction to the fact that (x, x') is in the core of $\mathcal{E}''_\rho$. Consequently, we have proved that $p \cdot \frac{x'}{r} \geq p \cdot \frac{w'}{r}$. Assume now that $p \cdot \frac{x}{r} < p \cdot \frac{w}{r}$. Using an argument similar to the one considered above, we get $x \underset{1}{\succsim} w$ and $p \cdot x < p \cdot w \Rightarrow \exists \ \rho$ such that $(1 - \frac{1}{\rho})x + \frac{1}{\rho}w \underset{1}{\succ} x$. Then it follows from (2.13) that, in the economy $\mathcal{E}''_\rho$,

$$y_1 \overset{\text{def}}{=} \frac{\rho - 1}{\rho} \left[\left(1 - \frac{1}{\rho}\right) x + \frac{1}{\rho}w\right] \underset{1\rho}{\succ} \frac{\rho - 1}{\rho}x = x_{1\rho};$$

$$y_2 \overset{\text{def}}{=} \frac{1}{\rho} \left[\left(1 - \frac{1}{\rho}\right) x + \frac{1}{\rho}w\right] \underset{2\rho}{\succ} \frac{x}{\rho} = x_{2\rho}.$$

Define

$$y_i = \frac{x'}{\rho}, \quad i = 3, \ldots, \rho+1.$$

Consider the coalition V in $\mathcal{E}''_\rho$ consisting of $\{3, \ldots, \rho+1\}$ and traders 1 and 2. We easily verify that

$$\sum_{i \in V} y_i = \left(1 - \frac{1}{\rho}\right) x + \frac{w}{\rho} + \left(1 - \frac{1}{\rho}\right) x' = \sum_{i \in V} w_{i\rho},$$

so that V can improve upon (x, x'), a contradiction. Consequently, for all r,

$$p \cdot \frac{x}{r} \geq p \cdot \frac{w}{r}.$$

Since (x, x') is an allocation, $p \cdot \frac{x}{r} \geq p \cdot \frac{w}{r}$ and $p \cdot \frac{x'}{r} \geq p \cdot \frac{w'}{r}$ together imply that, for all r

$$p \cdot \frac{x'}{r} = p \cdot \frac{w'}{r} \quad \text{and} \quad p \cdot \frac{x}{r} = p \cdot \frac{w}{r},$$

which completes the proof that $[p, (x, x')]$ is a competitive equilibrium.

The result we have just proved shows that, in spite of the presence of giants, competition can be restored asymptotically, not only when the ownership of each good is spread over a large number of dwarfs as in the first case considered in this section. It can also follow from *competition among the giants*, as long as they exchange with a sufficiently large number of dwarfs. Even more surprisingly, this conclusion holds whatever the relative sizes of the giants. Notice indeed that, in the last asymptotic version considered above, the exchange economy with dwarfs tends, when $r \to \infty$, to a pure monopolistic economy consisting of a single giant, as in the economy corresponding to the example provided on p. 43 and 44. However large the number r may be, the resulting large giant cannot get a better outcome in the core than the competitive one. Nevertheless, as proved on p. 43 and 44, for $r = \infty$, the core suddenly enlarges so as to contain many allocations which are not competitive.

In the next section, we provide an alternative interpretation of the asymptotic approach to imperfect competition based on *collusion*. This is done in the simpler framework of a constant returns-to-scale productive economy.

2.3 COLLUSION AND THE ASYMPTOTIC BEHAVIOUR OF THE CORE

In order to show the wide applicability of the core concept, and further illustrate the asymptotic approach to imperfect competition, we shall now study how collusive moves can affect the set of outcomes in a simple constant returns-to-scale productive economy. Thus we leave temporarily the framework of pure exchange economies and consider a situation akin to the problem of the competitive imputation of social output, in which production is shared among factor owners at their marginal product. The analysis which follows is based on Gabszewicz and Hansen (1972). Assume for simplicity, that there are two types of *factor owners* (landowners and workers), consisting each of r individuals ij, $i = 1, 2$, $j = 1, \ldots, r$. We denote by $I_i = \{i1, \ldots, ij, \ldots, ir\}$ the set of factor owners of type i, $i = 1, 2$, and we assume that each factor owner of type i owns exactly one unit of factor j. The economy is characterised by a constant returns-to-scale production function $F(z_1, z_2)$, which we normalise by assuming

$$F(1, 1) = 1 :$$

the combination of one unit of each factor produces one unit of output. Furthermore, we suppose that the first and second derivatives of F exist, and that $\frac{\partial^2 F}{\partial z_i^2} < 0$, $i = 1, 2$ (decreasing marginal productivities).

Let us initially assume that, in order to realise the output out of their factor endowment, all coalitions have access to the above productive technology. For a given coalition S, $S \in \mathcal{P}(I_1 \cup I_2)$, the amount of output it can produce is equal to

$$F(|S \cap I_1|, |s \cap I_2|),$$

since each member of $S \cap I_i$ owns exactly one unit of factor $i, i = 1, 2$.
(The notation $|A|$ means the number of elements included in the set A.)
In particular, we obtain

$$F(|I_1|, |I_2|) = F(r, r) = r,$$

where the last equality follows from the fact that F is constant returns-to-scale. Consequently, the total amount which can be produced out of
the cooperation of all factor owners is equal to r units of output. We call
an *imputation* a $2r$-dimensional vector $x = (x_{11}, \ldots, x_{1j}, \ldots x_{1r}; x_{21}, \ldots,$
$x_{2j}, \ldots x_{2r})$ corresponding to a distribution of this total amount among
the factor owners, namely,

$$\sum_{1j \in I_1} x_{1j} + \sum_{2j \in I_2} x_{2j} = r.$$

A coalition S can *improve upon* an imputation x if

$$F(|S \cap I_1|, |S \cap I_2|) > \sum_{1j \in S} x_{1j} + \sum_{2j \in S} x_{2j}.$$

The core is the set of all imputations which cannot be improved upon
by any coalition S; namely, the core is the set

$$\{x \mid \forall S \in \mathcal{P}(I_1 \cup I_2) : \sum_{1j} x_{1j} + \sum_{2j} x_{2j} \leq F(|S \cap I_1|, |S \cap I_2|)\}.$$

It is easy to see the analogy existing between the core concept defined
above, and the concept proposed on p. 26 for the framework of a pure
exchange economy. The only difference lies in the fact that, in our production economy, utility is transferable among agents (factor owners)
while this is not assumed to be the case in the exchange economy.

The *competitive imputation* is the distribution of the total output r, at which each factor owner of type i receives his marginal product, namely

$$x^*_{ij} = \left.\frac{\partial F}{\partial z_i}\right|_{(r,r)}. \tag{2.16}$$

The distribution x^* is an imputation since the production function F is homogeneous of degree one (constant returns-to-scale) which implies, with Euler's theorem, that

$$F(r,r) = r\left.\frac{\partial F}{\partial z_1}\right|_{(r,r)} + r\left.\frac{\partial F}{\partial z_2}\right|_{(r,r)},$$

so that

$$rx^*_{1j} + rx^*_{2j} = r.$$

The imputation x^* is called competitive because it would spontaneously follow from a market mechanism in which agents take factor prices as given, with factor prices resulting from equality of supply and demand in the markets of the two factors. Assume, indeed, that factor owners sell their factor units on markets in which a profit maximising firm buys these units at prices p_1 and p_2 respectively. Then profit maximisation implies

$$\frac{\partial F}{\partial z_i} = p_i,$$

$i = 1, 2$. Supposing that the supply of factors is inelastic, the equality of supply and demand on the market of each factor implies

$$\left.\frac{\partial F}{\partial z_i}\right|_{(r,r)} = p^*_i,$$

with p_i^* denoting the equilibrium price on market i, $i = 1, 2$. Since each factor owner of type i owns exactly one unit of factor i, he gets accordingly x_{ij}^* as the result of his factor unit's sale at price p_i^*.

Now, let us come back to the core concept, and assume that a *collusive move* takes place among some of the factor owners of type i. Denote by J_i, $J_i \subseteq I_i$, the set of factor owners of type i who are involved in this collusive move and by $k_i r$, $k_i \in [0, 1]$, the size of this set, namely $k_i r = |J_i|$. The set J_i itself is called hereafter the *syndicate of type i*.

The members of the syndicate of type i are assumed to agree on the following collusive rules: (i) the amount of output received at any imputation by the members of the syndicate J_i are uniformly spread among its members; (ii) if the syndicate J_i decides to participate in a given coalition, then all of its members must simultaneously participate in that coalition. This collusive process entails two important implications. First, only imputations assigning the same amount of output to all syndicate members of J_i, $i = 1, 2$, are to be taken into account in the definition of the core. Second the set of coalitions which are still allowed to improve upon a given imputation is now reduced to the set $\mathcal{C}$ defined by

$$\mathcal{C} = \{S \mid S \in \mathcal{P}(I_1 \cup I_2); \text{either } S \cap J_i = \emptyset, \text{ or } S \cap J_i = J_i, i = 1, 2\}.$$

Consequently, after a collusive move has led to a syndicate structure $\{J_1, J_2\}$, the core has to be redefined as the set of imputations which are constant on J_i, $i = 1, 2$, and which cannot be improved upon by any coalition in $\mathcal{C}$. The preceding adjustment of the core concept to the possibility of institutional collusive agreements reveals how flexible this concept is in order to represent the consequences of syndicates' – or cartels' – formation. Now we can look at the core corresponding to various syndicate structures.

First we establish an important proposition, which is the natural counterpart of Lemma 2.1 (p. 37) for the case of our production economy.

Proposition 2.1.

If $k_i < 1$, $i = 1, 2$, and x is an imputation in the core, then, for any pair of factor owners $ij \in I_i \setminus J_i$ and $ik \in I_i \setminus J_i$,

$$x_{ij} = x_{ik}.$$

Proof Define $x_{i\min} = \min_{ij \in I_i \setminus J_i} \{x_{ij}\}$ and $x_{i\max} = \max_{ij \in I_i \setminus J_i} \{x_{ij}\}$. First, we notice that

$$x_{1\min} + x_{2\min} \geq 1 \qquad (2.17)$$

for, otherwise, a coalition consisting of one non-syndicate factor owner of each type receiving $x_{i\min}$ could improve upon the imputation x, contrary to the fact that x is in the core and that such a coalition belongs to $\mathcal{C}$. Similarly,

$$x_{1\max} + x_{2\max} \leq 1. \qquad (2.18)$$

On the contrary, the coalition S consisting of all factor owners except the two non-syndicate members receiving $x_{i\max}$, could improve upon the imputation x. This coalition belongs to $\mathcal{C}$ since it includes the two syndicates J_i. Furthermore, it can produce $F(r - 1, r - 1) = r - 1$, so that it could improve upon the imputation x if the reverse of inequality (2.17) held, a contradiction. Consequently, it follows from (2.17) and (2.18) that

$$(x_{1\max} - x_{1\min}) + (x_{2\max} - x_{2\min}) \leq 0,$$

an inequality which holds if, and only if, $x_{i\min} = x_{i\max}, i = 1, 2$.

First notice that if $J_1 = J_2 = \emptyset$, Proposition 2.1 implies that *all* factor owners of type i must receive the same amount of output at a core imputation. Furthermore, it follows from Proposition 2.1 that an imputation x in the core corresponding to a syndicate structure $\{J_1, J_2\}$ with $J_1 \neq \emptyset$ and $J_2 \neq \emptyset$ is entirely described by *four* numbers $x = (x_1^s, x_1^{ns}; x_2^s, x_2^{ns})$ with x_i^s and x_i^{ns} denoting, respectively, the amounts of output received by a syndicate member in J_i and a non-syndicate factor owner of type $i, i = 1, 2$. This property invites a comparison between these two amounts: do syndicate members get an amount of output in the core which exceeds the amount received by their non-syndicate companions? This looks like a desirable feature of the core for, otherwise, why should syndicate members be inclined to remain faithful to their syndicate? However, as the next lemma shows, this property is *never* satisfied at a core imputation.

Proposition 2.2.

If $k_i < 1$, $k_i \neq 0$, $i = 1, 2$, there exists no imputation x in the core such that $x_i^s \geq x_i^{ns}$, $i = 1, 2$ with $x_h^s > x_h^{ns}$ for at least one index h.

Proof Contrary to Proposition 2.2, suppose, without loss of generality, that there exists an imputation x in the core with $x_1^s \geq x_1^{ns}$ and $x_2^s > x_2^{ns}$. Since x is an imputation, we have

$$k_1 r x_1^s + (1 - k_1) r x_1^{ns} + k_2 r x_2^s + (1 - k_2) r x_2^{ns} = r,$$

which reduces to

$$k_1(x_1^s - x_1^{ns}) + k_2(x_2^s - x_2^{ns}) = 1 - (x_1^{ns} + x_2^{ns}) > 0,$$

where the last strict inequality follows from the fact that $x_1^s \geq x_1^{ns}$ and $x_2^s > x_2^{ns}$. But then a coalition in C consisting of one non-syndicate member of each type can improve upon the imputation x, a contradiction.

Thus, if the cohesion of a syndicate structure relies on the possibility of their members getting a larger share of the cake in the core than their similar companions who are not syndicate members, we must conclude that no core imputation can satisfy this prerequisite. In other words, whenever a core imputation discriminates between syndicate and non-syndicate members, discrimination always occurs against the members of at least one syndicate. Does it mean that any syndicate structure is inherently unstable? This statement goes too far. Rather than being interested in comparing the amount of output they receive with the amount received by their non-syndicate companions, syndicate members are probably willing to compare the amount they receive with the amount they would receive *if the syndicate structure did not exist!*

Before examining what could be the result of such a comparison, it is interesting to single out a further property satisfied by a core allocation when the total number of syndicate members $(k_1 + k_2)r$ is strictly smaller than r, namely

Proposition 2.3.
If $k_1 + k_2 < 1$, and x is an imputation in the core, then $x_i^s = x_i^{ns}$, $i = 1, 2$.

Proof Suppose, contrary to Proposition 2.3, that $x_i^s \neq x_i^{ns}$ for at least one index i and, without loss of generality, let $i = 1$. Then, it follows from Proposition 2.2 that if $x_1^s > x_1^{ns}$, we must necessarily have $x_2^s < x_2^{ns}$. Consider then a coalition S consisting of the $k_2 r$ factor owners members of J_2 and of an equal number of non-syndicate factor owners owning factor 1. First, notice that such a coalition exists since, by assumption, we have $k_1 + k_2 < 1$, which implies $k_2 r < (1 - k_1)r$. Furthermore, this coalition belongs to the set $\mathcal{C}$, and may accordingly serve to improve upon an imputation. Let us show that it can, indeed, improve upon the imputation x, contrary to the assumption that x is in the core. This coalition can produce an amount of output equal to $F(k_2 r, k_2 r) = k_2 r$. Assign $k_1 x_1^s + (1 - k_1)x_1^{ns}$ to each of the $k_2 r$ non-syndicate factor owners of type 1 and $k_2 x_2^s + (1 - k_2)x_2^{ns}$ to each of the $k_2 r$ syndicate factor owners of type 2 who are members of the coalition S. Given that $x_1^s > x_1^{ns}$ and $x_2^s < x_2^{ns}$, each member of S receives accordingly an amount of output which exceeds the amount of output he had received under the imputation x. We notice however that

$$k_2 r[k_1 x_1^s + (1 - k_1)x_1^{ns}] + k_2 r[k_2 x_2^s + (1 - k_2)x_2^{ns}] = k_2 r$$

where the last equality follows from the fact that x is an imputation. Accordingly, the above assignment does not exceed the production possibilities of coalition S so that S can improve upon the imputation x, a contradiction.

As shown in Proposition 2.2, any imputation in the core which discriminates between syndicate and non-syndicate members must be at the expense of at least one syndicate. This raises the question of maintaining syndicate cohesion, in spite of the envy that this property could generate among the members of that syndicate who are deprived of the advantageous treatment assigned to their non-syndicate companions. This question was raised above, and it was suggested that a better criterion to appreciate syndicate stability would be to compare the amount received by syndicate members at an imputation in the core with the amount they would receive if the syndicate structure collapsed. This is reminiscent of the position taken by the leader of a price cartel who aims at achieving cartel stability by convincing its members that deviation from cartel discipline could bring about the competitive price, the worst situation to be envisaged by them. Notice however that a major difficulty arises when comparing the amount received by syndicate members at a given core imputation with the amount they would receive without a syndicate: the latter is not uniquely defined since the core generally includes many imputations. Accordingly, there is not a unique outcome in the core which could serve as a reference, should the syndicate structure collapse. Nevertheless, there exists one case in which this type of comparison becomes meaningful, and does not suffer from any ambiguity: namely, when the number r of factor owners is very large. Let us show indeed that the core tends asymptotically to assign to *non-syndicate members* of type i the amount of output they would receive at the competitive imputation, i.e., their marginal product. To prove this assertion, let us denote by Core (r) the set of imputations in the core when there are r factor owners of each type and syndicates J_i include a number $k_i r$ of syndicate members, $i = 1, 2$. Similarly, denote by $({}^r x_i{}^{ns}, {}^r x_i{}^s)$ any imputation in Core (r).

Proposition 2.4.
If $k_i < 1$, $i = 1, 2$ and, for all r, the imputations $({}^r x_i{}^{ns}, {}^r x_i{}^s)$ belong to Core (r), then

$$\lim_{r \to \infty} \left\{ {}^r x_i{}^{ns} \right\} = \left. \frac{\partial F}{\partial z_i} \right|_{(1,1)} = x_i^*, \qquad i = 1, 2.$$

Proof Let the imputation $({}^r x_i{}^{ns}, {}^r x_i{}^s)$ be in Core (r) for all r. First, notice that, for all r, we have

$$ {}^r x_1{}^{ns} + {}^r x_2{}^{ns} \geq 1; $$

otherwise a coalition consisting of a non-syndicate member of each type (such a coalition belongs to C) could improve upon the imputation $({}^r x_i{}^{ns}, {}^r x_i{}^s)$, a contradiction. Accordingly, we get

$$\lim_{r \to \infty} \left\{ {}^r x_1{}^{ns} \right\} + \lim_{r \to \infty} \left\{ {}^r x_2{}^{ns} \right\} \geq 1. \qquad (2.19)$$

Furthermore consider, for all r, the coalition S consisting of all factor owners but one non-syndicate factor owner of type 1. This coalition belongs to C and can produce $F(r-1, r)$. Consequently, if the inequality

$$ F(r-1, r) > r - {}^r x_1{}^{ns} $$

held for some value of r, then the coalition S could improve upon the imputation $({}^r x_i{}^s, {}^r x_i{}^{ns})$ in the economy consisting of r factor owners of each type, which would contradict the assumption that $(^r x_i{}^s, {}^r x_i{}^{ns})$ belongs to Core (r) for all r. Accordingly, for all r, we have

$$F(r-1, r) \leq r - {}^r x_1{}^{ns}$$

or, due to constant returns-to-scale of F, for all r,

$$F(1, 1) - F\left(1 - \frac{1}{r}, 1\right) \geq {}^r x_1{}^{ns}.$$

Passing to the limit on both sides of this inequality, we get

$$\left.\frac{\partial F}{\partial z_1}\right|_{(1,1)} \geq \lim_{r \to \infty} \{{}^r x_1{}^{ns}\}. \qquad (2.20)$$

A similar reasoning, using a coalition S consisting of all factor owners but one non-syndicate member of type 2, leads to the conclusion that

$$\left.\frac{\partial F}{\partial z_2}\right|_{(1,1)} \geq \lim_{r \to \infty} \{{}^r x_2{}^{ns}\}. \qquad (2.21)$$

Combining (2.19), (2.20) and (2.21), we obtain

$$\left.\frac{\partial F}{\partial z_1}\right|_{(1,1)} + \left.\frac{\partial F}{\partial z_2}\right|_{(1,1)} \geq \lim_{r \to \infty} \{{}^r x_1{}^{ns}\} + \lim_{r \to \infty} \{{}^r x_2{}^{ns}\} \geq 1. \qquad (2.22)$$

Since it follows from Euler's theorem that $\left.\frac{\partial F}{\partial z_1}\right|_{(1,1)} + \left.\frac{\partial F}{\partial z_2}\right|_{(1,1)} = 1$, (2.22) implies that

$$\left.\frac{\partial F}{\partial z_1}\right|_{(1,1)} + \left.\frac{\partial F}{\partial z_2}\right|_{(1,1)} = \lim_{r \to \infty} \{{}^r x_1{}^{ns}\} + \lim_{r \to \infty} \{{}^r x_2{}^{ns}\},$$

an equality which, combined with (2.20) and (2.21), leads to the desired conclusion.

It is now easy to comment on the stability of a syndicate structure $\{J_1, J_2\}$ when the number r of factor owners is large. As shown in Proposition 2.4, an imputation in the core assigns to non-syndicate members approximately their marginal product. On the other hand, if the corresponding imputation discriminates between syndicate and non-syndicate members, we know from Proposition 2.2 that the syndicate members of at least one type obtain necessarily in this imputation a smaller amount of output than the non-syndicate members owning the same factor. Since from Proposition 2.4, the latter get approximately their marginal product, we deduce from the above that the former obtain in this imputation less than their marginal product, that is, *less than they would obtain if they left the syndicate*. It is then natural to conjecture that this syndicate will disaggregate, so that the condition $k_1 + k_2 < 1$ will realise, entailing, according to Proposition 2.2, that *all* factor owners of the same type must obtain approximately their competitive outcome. Thus this analysis leads us to predict that, for large values of r, the tendency to syndicate formation is countervailed by competitive forces which guarantee under constant returns-to-scale that non-syndicate members obtain their marginal product. In such a situation, if a syndicate succeeds in providing its members with more than their competitive outcome, it is necessarily at the expense of the other syndicate, whose members receive less than their marginal product.

To illustrate the above, it is useful to examine the asymptotic behaviour of the core for the particular case of a Cobb-Douglas production function F, say

$$F(z_1, z_2) = \sqrt{z_1}\sqrt{z_2}.$$

When $k_1 + k_2 < 1$, the asymptotic core consists only of the competitive imputation $x^* : x_i^{*ns} = x_i^{*s} = \frac{1}{2}$, $i = 1, 2$. When $k_1 + k_2 > 1$, the non-syndicate members each receive at the limit their marginal product $\frac{1}{2}$. As for the syndicates, a core imputation $x = (x_i^s, x_i^{ns})$ must necessarily satisfy the following constraints:

$$k_1 x_1^s + k_2 x_2^s = \frac{k_1 + k_2}{2};$$

$$x_1^s \geq \min\{x_1^s\} = \frac{\sqrt{k_1}\sqrt{1 - k_2} - \frac{1}{2}(1 - k_2)}{k_1};$$

$$x_2^s \geq \min\{x_2^s\} = \frac{\sqrt{k_2}\sqrt{1 - k_1} - \frac{1}{2}}{(1 - k_1)}.$$

The first constraint follows from the fact that $x_i^{ns} = x_i^*$ and from the equality $k_1 x_1^s + k_2 x_2^s + (1 - k_1)x_1^{ns} + (1 - k_2)x_2^{ns} = 1$. The second and third constraints follow from the fact that a coalition made of syndicate i and the non-syndicate members of the other type could otherwise improve upon the corresponding imputation. Table 2.1 illustrates the values of $\min\{x_i^s\}$ corresponding to different values of $k_1 = k_2$.

Table 2.1

$\min\{x_i^s\}$	$k_1 = k_2$
0.5	0.52
0.440	0.7
0.278	0.9
0.095	0.99

Two assumptions have been used to characterise the imputations in the core resulting from the collusion of factor owners. The first assumption guarantees that no syndicate owns a monopoly on the total amount of a given factor ($k_i < 1, i = 1, 2$). Let us substitute for this assumption the alternative hypothesis according to which one production factor

i is fully monopolised by the corresponding syndicate J_i while no syndicate exists for the other factor $(J_k = \emptyset, k \neq i)$. Then we obtain a simplified, but suggestive, representation of a situation which has been repeatedly considered by Marxist theorists: capital ownership concentration with an institutionally organised dispersion of the labour force (laws forbidding syndicate formation, like the Le Chatelier law). Under this alternative hypothesis it can be shown that the asymptotic core consists of all imputations which assign to syndicate members of J_i an amount of output which exceeds their marginal product, while all similar imputations, which would assign more than their marginal product to the owners of factor k, are excluded from the core. This property gives a precise content to the idea of labour force exploitation resulting from the concentration of capital when syndicate formation is forbidden. The second assumption used in the above core characterisation with collusion is constant returns-to-scale of the production function F. This assumption is crucial since even the 'equal treatment' property of Proposition 2.1 does not hold otherwise, as shown by the following example involving increasing returns-to-scale. Consider a firm using a single factor z in the production of a good according to the production function F defined by

$$F(z) = z^2.$$

Suppose there are five factor owners each owning one unit of the production factor. The firm can then produce 25 units, and the core consists of all imputations of these units among the five factor owners which cannot be improved upon by any subset of them. It is not difficult to check that the imputation

$$x_1 = 1, x_2 = 3, x_3 = 5, x_4 = 7, x_5 = 9$$

with x_i denoting the amount received by the ith factor owner, is in the core.

In the next chapter we tackle a similar study of the core of imperfectly competitive economies, using however an alternative way of representing market power, which is based on a pathbreaking idea proposed by Aumann (1964).

3.   Markets with an atomless sector

3.1 AN APPROACH TO PERFECT COMPETITION USING ATOMLESS ECONOMIES

The asymptotic approach to perfect competition studied in Section 2.1 consists of increasing the size of the economy, thereby reducing the core to the set of its competitive allocations. This approach gives support to the existence of a logical link relating price-taking behaviour to the large number of participants in the economy: nothing is to be gained by manipulating prices since, according to the Debreu-Scarf theorem, the alternative barter mechanism which underlies the core concept can only bring about a competitive allocation when the number of agents is large. Notice however that this statement is true only 'at the limit': however large the number of replicas, each participant still has the possibility of changing equilibrium prices by manipulating his individual supply of goods. As stated by Aumann:

> Though writers on economics equilibrium have traditionally assumed perfect competition, they have, paradoxically, adopted a mathematical model that does not fit this assumption. Indeed, the influence of an individual participant on the economy cannot be mathematically negligible, as long as there are only finitely many participants (Aumann 1964, p. 39).

Furthermore, Sections 2.2 and 2.3 have illustrated that the Debreu-Scarf result is far from being universal. In particular, its validity is strongly limited by the specific replication procedure used in order to increase the number of agents.

One way to circumvent these difficulties consists in proposing from the outset a mathematical model of the economy which is more appropriate to the intuitive notion of perfect competition. This is the proposal made by Aumann:

we submit that the most natural model for this purpose contains a *continuum* of participants, similar to the continuum of points on a line or the continuum of particles in a fluid. Very succintly, the reason for this is that one can integrate over a continuum, and changing the integrand at a single point does not affect the value of the integral, that is, the actions of a single individual are negligible (Aumann 1964, p. 39).

The mathematical model using a 'continuum of traders' is based on Lebesgue measure and integration, but only their most elementary aspects are needed to understand the approach. It translates into the 'continuum' version the exchange model defined above, for the asymptotic approach (see Section 1.1). There are ℓ goods, or commodities, indexed by h, $h = 1, \cdots, \ell$, and the set of *commodity bundles* is R_+^ℓ. The set of *traders* is the closed unit interval $[0, 1]$, denoted by T. The *space of traders* is the measure space $(T, \mathcal{T}, \mu)$, with μ the Lebesgue measure defined on $\mathcal{T}$, the set of all Lebesgue-measurable subsets of T, which is identified with the class of *coalitions*. It is well known that the class $\mathcal{T}$ has no atom; in other words, the class $\mathcal{T}$ does not include any set of strictly positive measure dwhich would include another set of strictly positive measure, like a 'mass point', i.e. a single point that carries positive measure. As will become clear later, the non-atomicity of $\mathcal{T}$ plays a crucial role in the proof of the central result of this approach.

As in the finite exchange model, we shall assume that for each agent $t \in T$, there exists a preference relation, denoted by $\succ_t$, defined on $R_+^\ell \times R_+^\ell$, satisfying the following assumptions: (i) $x > y \Rightarrow x \succ_t y$ (strong desirability) and (ii) for $y \in R_+^\ell$, the sets $\{x \mid x \succ_t y\}$ and $\{x \mid y \succ_t x\}$ are open relative to R_+^ℓ (continuity). Notice that, contrary to the finite exchange model, no indifference relation is defined and no assumption of strict convexity is consented on $\succ_t$. An *assignment* x (of commodity bundles to traders) is a Lebesgue integrable function from T to R_+^ℓ. For simplicity, we shall denote by $\int_T \mathbf{x}$ the expression $\int_T \mathbf{x}(t)d\mu(t)$. Furthermore we assume that (iii) if $\mathbf{x}$ and $\mathbf{y}$ are assignments, the set $\{t \mid \mathbf{x}(t) \succ_t \mathbf{y}(t)\}$ is Lebesgue measurable in T, i.e. it belongs to T. There is a fixed *initial assignment* $\mathbf{w}$, with $\mathbf{w}(t)$ denoting the initial endowment of trader t. An *allocation* is an assignment $\mathbf{x}$ which satisfies

$$\int_T \mathbf{x} = \int_T \mathbf{w}.$$

A price system is a non-null vector $p \in R_+^\ell$. A *competitive allocation* is an allocation $\mathbf{x}$ for which there exists a price system p such that $\mathbf{x}(t)$ is maximal with respect to $\succ_t$ in the set $\{x \mid p \cdot x \leq p \cdot \mathbf{w}(t)\}$ for almost every trader t. A *competitive equilibrium* is a pair $(p, \mathbf{x})$ consisting of a price system p and a competitive allocation $\mathbf{x}$ for p. A coalition S can *improve upon* an allocation $\mathbf{x}$ via an assignment $\mathbf{y}$ if there exists an assignment $\mathbf{y}$ with $\mathbf{y}(t) \succ_t \mathbf{x}(t)$ for almost all $t \in S$, and $\int_S \mathbf{y} = \int_s \mathbf{w}$. The *core* is the set of all allocations which cannot be improved upon by any coalition S of strictly positive measure. As stated above, both the notion of competitive equilibrium and the core are defined with respect to a set of *full* measure in T, i.e. a set of measure equal to 1: their properties must hold *almost everywhere*, with the exception, possibly, of a set of measure zero. Notice also, that the definition of a competitive allocation provided above coincides with the definition of such an allocation provided for the case of a finite exchange economy when the preference relation $\succ_t$ satisfies the assumptions stated for this model (see Section 1.1). In this case, if $(p, \mathbf{x})$ is a competitive equilibrium, $\mathbf{x}(t)$ is the value of *trader t-demand function* $\underset{\sim}{x}(t, p)$, i.e., $\underset{\sim}{x}(t)$ is the maximal element for $\succ_t$ in the budget set $B(t, p) = \{x \mid p \cdot x \leq p \cdot \mathbf{w}(t)\}$.

Now we prove the following fundamental result.

Theorem 3.1.

The core coincides with the set of competitive allocations.

Proof First, we prove that a competitive allocation is in the core. Let $(p, \mathbf{x})$ be a competitive allocation and assume, on the contrary, that $\mathbf{x}$ is not in the core. Let S be the non-null coalition and $\mathbf{y}$ the assignment through which the coalition S can improve upon the allocation $\mathbf{x}$. Then $\mathbf{y}(t) \underset{t}{\succ} \mathbf{x}(t) \Rightarrow p \cdot \mathbf{y}(t) > p \cdot \mathbf{x}(t)$ for almost every trader t in the coalition S. Accordingly, $p \cdot \int_S \mathbf{y} > p \cdot \int_S \mathbf{w}$, which contradicts $\int_S \mathbf{y} = \int_S \mathbf{w}$, as required by the fact that S can improve upon $\mathbf{x}$ via $\mathbf{y}$.

Now, we prove that, for any allocation $\mathbf{x}$ in the core, there exists a price system p such that $(p, \mathbf{x})$ is a competitive equilibrium. To this end, we shall first prove a lemma based on the following definitions. Let $\mathbf{x}$ be in the core and define, for each $t \in T$, the following sets: $F(t) = \{x \mid x \underset{t}{\succ} \mathbf{x}(t)\}$, $G(t) = \{x - \mathbf{w}(t) \mid x \in F(t)\}$, $G^{-1}(x) = \{x \mid x + \mathbf{w}(t) \underset{t}{\succ} \mathbf{x}(t)\}$: the set $F(t)$ is the set of all commodity bundles prefered by agent t to what he receives at the allocation $\mathbf{x}$, while $G(t)$ is the translation of this set by his initial endowment. As for the set $G^{-1}(x)$, it is a subset of the unit interval which consists of traders t for which the commodity bundle x belongs to $G(t)$. Furthermore define Z as the set of rational numbers in $[0, 1]$ and R by $R = \{r \mid r \in Z; \mu[G^{-1}(r)] = 0\}$. Finally, define by U the set $T \setminus \cup_{r \in R} G^{-1}(r)$ and by $\Delta(U)$ the convex hull of the set U. It is clear that $\mu(U) = 1$ (U is full) since $\mu(\cup_{r \in R} G^{-1}(r)) = 0$ as a measure of a denumerable union of sets of measure 0.

Lemma 3.1.

$0 \notin \Delta(U)$.

Proof The proof is *ab absurdum*. Suppose on the contrary that $0 \in \Delta(U)$. Then there exists a vector $x \in R_+^{\ell}$, $x \gg 0$ and traders $t_i \in U$, $i = 1, \cdots, k$, such that $-x = \sum_{i=1}^{k} \beta_i x_i \ll 0$, $x_i \in G(t_i)$ and $\sum_{i=1}^{k} \beta_i = 1$. By the continuity assumption (ii), we may replace the vectors x_i by rational vectors $r_i \in G(t_i)$ (vectors whose components are rational numbers) and the numbers β_i by rational numbers γ_i so that we still have $-r = \sum_{i=1}^{k} \gamma_i r_i \ll 0$. Consequently, the vector r has all its components strictly positive and, by strong desirability (i), we can find a trader t_0 in U such that $\alpha r + \mathbf{w}(t_0) \underset{t_0}{\succ}$ if α is chosen sufficiently large. Hence $\alpha r \in G(t_0)$ and $\alpha r + \mathbf{w}(t_0) \in F(t_0)$. Let $r_0 = \alpha r$, $\alpha_0 = \frac{1}{\alpha+1}$, $\alpha_i = \frac{\alpha\gamma_i}{\alpha+1}$ for $i = 1, \cdots, k$. Then $\alpha_i > 0$ for all i and $\sum_{i=0}^{k} \alpha_i = 1$. Furthermore,

$$\sum_{i=0}^{k} \alpha_i r_i = \frac{\alpha}{\alpha+1} r + \frac{\alpha}{\alpha+1} \sum_{i=1}^{k} \gamma_i r_i = 0,$$

with $r_i \in G(t_i)$ for all i. Then $t_i \in G^{-1}(r_i)$ and, since $t_i \in U$, $r_i \notin R$ so that $\mu[G^{-1}(r_i)] > 0$. Since μ has no atom, we may choose δ sufficiently small in order to find disjoint subsets S_i, $S_i \subseteq G^{-1}(r_i)$ so that $\mu(S_i) = \delta\alpha_i$. Define $S = \cup_{i=0}^{k} S_i$ and the assignment $\mathbf{y}$ by

$$\mathbf{y}(t) = r_i + \mathbf{w}(t) \underset{t}{\succ} \mathbf{x}(t), \quad t \in S_i$$
$$= \mathbf{w}(t), t \notin S.$$

$(r_i + \mathbf{w}(t) \succ_t \mathbf{x}(t)$, for $t \in S_i$, since $r_i \in G(t)$ so that $r_i + \mathbf{w}(t) \in F(t))$. It is clear that $\mathbf{y}(t) \in R_+^\ell$ for $t \notin S$ and, for $t \in S$, it follows from the fact that $r_i \in G(t)$ since $t \in S_i \subset G^{-1}(r_i)$. Furthermore,

$$\int_S \mathbf{y} = \sum_{i=0}^{k} \delta\alpha_i r_i + \int_S \mathbf{w} = \int_S \mathbf{w}.$$

Since $\mathbf{y}(t) = \mathbf{w}(t)$ for $t \notin S$, $\mathbf{y}$ is an assignment. But then the coalition S can improve upon the allocation $\mathbf{x}$, contradicting the assumption that $\mathbf{x}$ is in the core.

To continue the proof of Theorem 3.1, let U be as in the lemma. In the remainder of the proof, statements about traders will refer to $t \in U$. This is sufficient since U is full. Lemma 3.1 and the hyperplane theorem imply that there exists a vector p, $p \neq 0$, such that for all x in the convex set $\Delta(U)$, $p \cdot x \geq 0$. $t \in U$ and $x \in G(t) \Rightarrow x \in \Delta(U)$, so that $x \in G(t) \Rightarrow p \cdot x \geq 0$ and, by definition of $G(t)$,

$$p \cdot x \geq p \cdot \mathbf{w}(t), \tag{3.1}$$

for $x \in F(t)$. By strong desirability (i), $F(t)$ includes a translation of R_+^{ℓ}, which implies that $p > 0$. Now we prove that $(p, \mathbf{x})$ is a competitive equilibrium. By strong desirability (i) again, there are points arbitrarily close to $\mathbf{x}(t)$ which are in $F(t)$; accordingly $\mathbf{x}(t)$ is in the closure of $F(t)$ and, by continuity, we obtain

$$p \cdot \mathbf{x}(t) \geq p \cdot \mathbf{w}(t), \qquad \forall \, t \in U.$$

Furthermore, since U is full, the last inequality implies

$$p \cdot \int_t \mathbf{x} \geq p \cdot \int_T \mathbf{w}.$$

If, for a non-null subset of U, we had

$$p \cdot \mathbf{x}(t) > p \cdot \mathbf{w}(t),$$

then $p \int_T \mathbf{x} > p \int_T \mathbf{w}$, contrary to the assumption that $\mathbf{x}$ is an allocation. Consequently, $p \cdot \mathbf{x}(t) = p \cdot \mathbf{w}(t)$ for all $t \in U$, so that $\mathbf{x}(t)$ is in the budget set defined by p for all $t \in U$. Now let us show that $x \succ_t \mathbf{x}(t) \Rightarrow p \cdot x > p \cdot \mathbf{w}(t)$. Suppose on the contrary that, for a set of positive measure we had $x \succ_t \mathbf{x}(t)$ and $p \cdot x \leq p \cdot \mathbf{w}(t)$. Then, by continuity of $\succ_t$ (assumption (ii)), there exists a neighbourhood of x such that for any point z in this neighbourhood $z \succ_t \mathbf{x}(t)$. The vector $z = x - \delta$ is in this neighbourhood when δ is chosen sufficiently small and is subtracted from any strictly positive coordinate of x (such coordinates must exist, for otherwise we would not have $x \succ_t \mathbf{x}(t)$). Consequently, $z = x - \delta \succ_t \mathbf{x}(t)$ so that $z \in F(t)$. However, if δ is chosen sufficiently small, we get

$$p \cdot z = p \cdot x - p \cdot \delta < p \cdot \mathbf{w}(t). \tag{3.2}$$

But it follows from (3.1) that $z \in F(t)$ implies $p \cdot z \geq p \cdot \mathbf{w}(t)$, which contradicts (3.2). This completes the proof that $(p, \mathbf{x})$ is a competitive equilibrium, which is the statement of the second part of Theorem 3.1.

Let us illustrate the equivalence Theorem 3.1 by applying it to the continuous version of the first example, with two goods and two agents, which we have introduced in Section 1.1. This continuous representation obtains as follows. Let $T = [0, 2]$ be the set of traders and $\mathcal{T}$ the class of coalitions, namely, the set of all Lebesgue measurable subsets of T endowed with the Lebesgue measure μ. Define the initial assignment as the simple function $\mathbf{w}$ from T to R_+^2:

$$
\begin{aligned}
\mathbf{w}(t) &= (4, 0); && \forall t \in [0, 1] \\
&= (0, 4); && \forall t \in]1, 2].
\end{aligned}
$$

For all $t \in T$, the preference relation $\succ_t$ defined on $R_+^2 \times R_+^2$, obtains as

$$
x = (x^1, x^2) \underset{t}{\succ} (y^1, y^2) = y \Leftrightarrow \sqrt{x^1} + \sqrt{x^2} > \sqrt{y^1} + \sqrt{y^2}.
$$

This exchange economy is the exact continuous counterpart of the example introduced in Section 1.1, *except that each 'atomic' trader in the finite example has been split into a continuum of small traders identical to him*, namely, the traders in $[0, 1]$ representing trader 1 and, similarly, the traders in $]1, 2]$ representing trader 2. It can be checked that this exchange economy has a unique competitive equilibrium, namely, the pair $(p, \mathbf{x})$ with $p = (1, 1)$ and $\mathbf{x}(t) = (2, 2)$ for all $t \in T$. As expected, the competitive equilibrium is the same in the finite and the continuous versions of the exchange economy. What about the core? As shown in Section 1.3, the core of the finite version consists of all allocations existing between points a and b in the Edgeworth box depicted in Figure 1.5 (p. 26). By the equivalence Theorem 3.1, *we know that the core in the continuous version now consists only of the competitive allocation* $\mathbf{x}$: the contract curve of the atomless version has shrunk to the sole competitive outcome. The intuition underlying this result is clear: by splitting the two atomic traders (of mass equal to 1) of the finite version into two atomless sets of small traders, we have enriched the class of potential coalitions T to such an extent that any allocation which is not competitive can be improved upon by some coalition in this class. The asymptotic approach to perfect competition studied in Section 2.1 was an alternative method to enrich progressively the class of coalitions by increasing the number of replicas of the exchange economy. As shown in Theorem 2.2, this alternative method also leads asymptotically to the same result for this replication procedure: an allocation which is in the core of all replicas, is necessarly competitive.

Nevertheless, the idea of perfect competition has traditionally been viewed by economists as representing an extreme case, which mainly serves as a reference point in order to contrast real market phenomena: far from being perfect, real competition is often the expression of market power exercised by one or several agents who are not insignificant. First, even if market places often embody an 'ocean' of small anonymous traders, some merchants who are *not* anonymous may be present as well. This turns out to be the case when their endowment of some commodities is large, compared with the amount of the same good owned by the other traders. The most extreme case corresponds of course to a situation of monopoly, when the whole market endowment of a good is concentrated in the hands of a single trader. Intermediate cases refer to the various forms of oligopolistic market structures in which the initial ownership of resources, although concentrated, is however spread over a small number of competitors.

Marxian economists have seen in the concentration of capital ownership, accompanied by the dispersion of the labour force, the basis for economic exploitation in capitalistic economies. There is no doubt that, for large values of n, the bargaining position of a single capitalist owning x units of capital and facing n nonunionised workers is far stronger than the position of the same capitalist, if he owns one unit of capital and faces a single worker. Ownership concentration and market power are intimately related

(Gabszewicz and Shitovitz 1992, p. 460)

On the other hand, even if the ownership of goods is not initially concentrated, but on the contrary spread over a large number of small economic units, it is possible for these units to combine among themselves in order to bias the collective decision outcome. This possibility was already stressed by von Neumann and Morgenstern 1944:

The classical definitions of free competition all involve further postulates besides the greatness of the number (of participants). E.g. it is clear that, if certain great group of participants act together, then the great number of participants may not become effective; the decisive exchanges may take place directly between large "coalitions" (such as trade unions, cooperatives, ...), and not between individuals, many in number, acting independently.

When ownership of goods is concentrated, or when collusion takes place, the ideal state of perfect competition is not effective since its conditions are violated by such market realities. Consequently, the continuous atomless model – designed to represent this ideal state – is no longer appropriate if it is not amended in order to handle the imperfectly competitive ingredients evoked above. Undoubtedly, the model is still adequate to represent the 'oceanic sector' of the economy, that is, the large number of market participants with negligible influence. But the non-negligible participants – monopolists, oligopolists, cartels, syndicates, etc. – can no longer be represented as points with null measure in the continuum: otherwise, the actions of these participants would be *mathematically* negligible when clearly they are not. These participants need a specific formal counterpart in the model, distinct from the one used to represent the oceanic sector. We submit that the most appropriate formal model consists in representing them as *atoms*, i.e. subsets with strictly positive mass containing no proper subset of strictly positive measure. In this alternative representation, changing the integrand of an atom does affect the value of the integral, so that the actions of the economic unit represented by an atom are not mathematically negligible.

Such markets, including both an atomless continuum of traders and atoms, have been called 'markets with an atomless sector' or 'mixed markets'.

3.2 MIXED MARKETS AND THE 'BUDGETARY EXPLOITATION' THEOREM

We introduce the formal model of a mixed market by considering again the first example of an exchange economy with two traders introduced in Section 1.1 and its continuous counterpart which has been defined on p. 74. The version with two traders can be viewed as a purely 'atomic' economy, with two atoms of measure 1. Its continuous version is, on the contrary, a purely 'atomless' economy in which all individual agents are insignificant. Let us now build a 'mixed' version of the same example by considering the exchange economy consisting of the set of traders T defined as $T = T_0 \cup T_1$ with $T_0 = [0,1]$ and $T_1 = \{2\}$. Furthermore, letting μ be the Lebesgue measure on T_0 and $\mathcal{T}$ the set of all Lebesgue measurable subsets of T_0, define the measure ν by

$$\nu(R) = \mu(R) \text{ if } R \in \mathcal{T} \text{ and } \{2\} \notin R;$$
$$= \mu(R \setminus \{2\}) + 1 \text{ if } \{2\} \in R \text{ and } R \in \mathcal{T}.$$

Then the point $\{2\}$ is an atom for the measure ν defined on the σ-field $\mathcal{T}'$ consisting of all Lebesgue measurable subsets which include, or do not include, the point $\{2\}$. On the contrary, the set T_0 endowed with the Lebesgue measure μ has no atom. Extend the definition of the example by introducing the initial assignment **w** as

$$\mathbf{w}(t) = (4,0) \quad \forall\, t \in [0,1] = T_0$$
$$= (0,4) \quad t = \{2\},$$

and the preference relation $\underset{t}{\succ}$ defined on $R_+^2 \times R_+^2$, for all $t \in T$, by

$$(x^1, x^2) \underset{t}{\succ} (y^1, y^2) \Leftrightarrow \sqrt{x^1} + \sqrt{x^2} > \sqrt{y^1} + \sqrt{y^2}.$$

The above exchange economy defines a mixed market which appears as a compromise between the purely atomic example considered in Section 1.1 and its purely atomless version defined on p. 75. The latter version was meant to represent an economy in which the two atoms of the former were each split into a continuum of insignificant traders. The mixed market examplified here represents an economy in which *one* of the atoms (agent 1) has been split into a continuum of insignificant agents, while the other remains significant (agent 2). The counterpart of this mixed model in the asymptotic approach analysed in Chapter 2 has to be found in the example considered on pp. 39 and 40, for which, in the economy $\mathcal{E}_r'$ replicated r-times, the ownership of commodity 2 is fully concentrated in the endowment of agent 2, while the ownership of commodity 1 is spread over the endowments of r different agents. We have shown for this example that the allocation which is the least favourable in the core for the latter when the economy consists of two agents, remains in the core of the economies $\mathcal{E}_r'$ whatever the number r of replicas. As will be shown later, a similar result obtains in the mixed market we have just defined. To this end, we need however to use a fundamental result proved by Shitovitz (1973). To state and establish this result, we rely on the following modelling, which adapts the continuous model defined on pp. 70 and 71 in order to accommodate the presence of atoms among the traders. The space of *agents* is the measure space $(T, \mathcal{T}, \nu)$; T_1 denotes the set of atoms in T, while $T_0 = T \setminus T_1$ denotes the atomless part of T. All assumptions on preferences are extended to atoms (strong desirability (i) and continuity (ii)). Furthermore, we also assume that the convexity assumption holds for the atoms' preferences. Several classes of coalitions derived from the class $\mathcal{T}$ will be considered, in particular the classes $\mathcal{T}_0, \mathcal{T}_1$ and $\mathcal{T}_2$ defined by

$$T_0 = \{S \mid S \in T, S \subseteq T_0\},$$
$$T_1 = \{S \mid S \in T; T \setminus S \subseteq T_0\}, \text{ and}$$
$$T_2 = T_0 \cup T_1.$$

Intuitively, T denotes the set of *coalitions*, T_0 the set of *atomless coalitions*, T_1 the set of coalitions which include all the atoms and T_2 the set of coalitions which either do not include any atom, or include all of them. It is easily checked that T_1 and T_2 are σ-fields.

Beyond the definitions given on p. 71, we introduce the following specifications on *allocations*. An allocation $\mathbf{x}$ is *individually rational* if, for almost every $t \in T$, $\mathbf{w}(t) \not\succ_t \mathbf{x}(t)$. An allocation $\mathbf{x}$ is *Pareto-optimal* if it cannot be improved upon by the coalition T consisting of all agents. An allocation $\mathbf{x}$ is a *price equilibrium* if there exists a price system p such that, for almost every $t \in T$,

$$\{y \mid y \underset{t}{\succ} \mathbf{x}(t)\} \cap \{y \mid p \cdot y \le p \cdot \mathbf{x}(t)\} = \emptyset.$$

Given an allocation $\mathbf{x}$, we denote by $\mathbf{x}\big|_{T_0}$ the function defined on T_0 by

$$\mathbf{x}\big|_{T_0}(t) = \mathbf{x}(t);$$

$\mathbf{x}\big|_{T_0}$ is called the *allocation* $\mathbf{x}$ *restricted* to T_0, or its *restriction to* T_0. An individually rational allocation assigns to every trader a bundle which is not less preferred than his initial endowment. An allocation is Pareto-optimal when another allocation cannot be found which would assign to (almost) every trader a commodity bundle preferred to the bundle received at that allocation. A price equilibrium $(p, \mathbf{x})$ differs from a competitive equilibrium $(p', \mathbf{x}')$ because the former requires $\mathbf{x}(t)$ to be a maximal element in $\{y \mid p \cdot y \le p \cdot \mathbf{x}(t)\}$ while the latter requires the bundle $\mathbf{x}'(t)$ to be a maximal element in $\{y \mid p' \cdot y \le p' \cdot \mathbf{w}(t)\}$. Accordingly, a price equilibrium does not refer to the initial assignment $\mathbf{w}$, while a competitive equilibrium does. Figure 3.1 illustrates how a commodity bundle $\mathbf{x}(t)$ being part of a price equilibrium $(p, \mathbf{x})$ differs from a commodity bundle $\mathbf{x}'(t)$ being part of a competitive equilibrium $(p', \mathbf{x}')$.

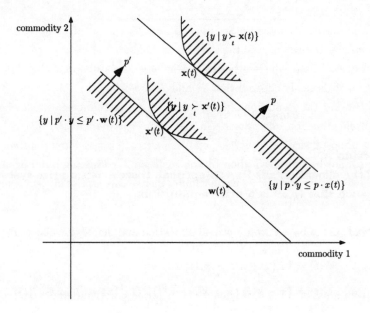

Figure 3.1

It is easily seen that, with the convexity assumption on preferences, any Pareto-optimal allocation in a two-commodities, two-traders, exchange economy is a price equilibrium, using the price system defined by the slope of the line which is the common tangency line to indifference curves through the corresponding allocation, as depicted in the Edgeworth box represented in Figure 3.2. In fact, this property holds in any finite exchange economy, with an arbitrary number of goods and traders, as long as traders' preferences satisfy the convexity assumption (see, for instance, Debreu 1959). As the following lemma shows, it also holds in a mixed market if, as we have assumed, atoms' preferences are convex.

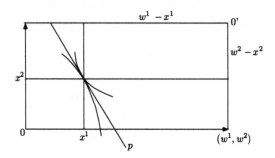

Figure 3.2

Lemma 3.2.

If the allocation x is Pareto-optimal, there exists a price system p such that $(p, \mathbf{x})$ is a price equilibrium.

Proof Let $\mathbf{x}$ be a Pareto-optimal allocation and define, for all $t \in T$,

$$F(t) = \{x \mid x + \mathbf{x}(t) \underset{t}{\succ} \mathbf{x}(t)\}$$

$$\text{and } G(t) = \{x - \mathbf{x}(t) \mid x + \mathbf{x}(t) \underset{t}{\succ} \mathbf{x}(t)\}, G^{-1}(x) = \{t \mid x \in G(t)\}.$$

$F(t)$ is a correspondence defined on T with values in the set of subsets of R_+^ℓ. Define also

$$\mathcal{L}_F = \{\mathbf{f} \mid \mathbf{f} \text{ is } \nu - \text{integrable and } \mathbf{f}(t) \in F(t), \text{ a.e. in } T\}$$

and

$$\int_T F = \{x \in R_+^\ell \mid x = \int_T \mathbf{f}; \mathbf{f} \in \mathcal{L}_F\}.$$

Let $\int_{T_0} F_0$ and $\int_{T_1} F_1$ denote the restrictions of F to T_0 and T_1 respectively. It follows from Richter (1963) that $\int_{T_0} F_0$ is convex, since T_0 is atomless. Furthermore, $F(t)$ is convex for all $t \in T_1$ by assumption, so that $\int_{T_1} F_1$ is convex. Consequently the set $\int_T F = \int_{T_0} F_0 + \int_{T_1} F_1$

is also convex, as the sum of two convex sets. Moreover $0 \notin \int_T F$, for otherwise there would exist $\mathbf{f}$ with $\int_T \mathbf{f} = 0$ and $\mathbf{f}(t) + \mathbf{x}(t) \succ_t \mathbf{x}(t)$ almost everywhere in T. Defining $\mathbf{y}$ by $\mathbf{y}(t) = \mathbf{f}(t) + \mathbf{x}(t)$, we would then have $\mathbf{y}(t) \succ_t \mathbf{x}(t)$ for almost all $t \in T$ and $\int_T \mathbf{y} = \int_T \mathbf{x} = \int_T \mathbf{w}$. But then the allocation $\mathbf{x}$ is not Pareto-optimal, a contradiction. Consequently, it follows from the separating hyperplane theorem that there exists a vector p, $p \neq 0$, such that, for all $x \in \int_T F$,

$$p \cdot x \geq 0. \tag{3.3}$$

Now we show that (3.3) implies that, for all $x \in G(t)$,

$$p \cdot x \geq 0. \tag{3.4}$$

To this end define

$$Z = \{r \mid r \in R^\ell, r \text{ rational and } \mu[G^{-1}(r)] = 0\}$$

and

$$U = T \setminus \cup_{r \in Z} G^{-1}(r);$$

it is easily seen that $\nu(U) = 1$. Suppose that, contrary to (3.4), there existed a trader t, $t \in U$, and a vector x, $x \in G(t)$, such that

$$p \cdot x < 0.$$

Then, by continuity, there would exist a vector r, $r \in Z$, such that $r \in G(t)$ and $p \cdot r < 0$. Since $t \in U$, we get $\nu(G^{-1}(r)) > 0$. Define $\mathbf{f}_\varepsilon$ by

$$\mathbf{f}_\varepsilon = r \; \forall t \in G^{-1}(r)$$
$$= \varepsilon \; \forall \, t \in U \setminus G^{-1}(r).$$

For all $\varepsilon > 0$, $\mathbf{f}_\varepsilon \in F$ since, for $t \in G^{-1}(t)$, $\mathbf{f}_\varepsilon(t) \in G(t)$ and, for $t \in U \setminus G^{-1}(r)$, $\mathbf{f}_\varepsilon(t) \in F(t)$ by strong desirability (i). Consequently $\int_T \mathbf{f}_\varepsilon \in \int_T F$, so that, for all $\varepsilon > 0$,

$$p \int_T \mathbf{f}_\varepsilon \geq 0,$$

or

$$p \cdot r\nu(G^{-1}(r)) + \varepsilon\nu(U \setminus G^{-1}(r)) \geq 0. \qquad (3.5)$$

However, since $r < 0$ and $\varepsilon\nu(U \setminus G^{-1}(r)) \to 0$ when $\varepsilon \to 0$, the inequality (3.5) must fail to hold when ε is chosen sufficiently small, a contradiction which completes the proof of (3.4). Thus (3.4) and the definition of $G(t)$ imply that

$$x \underset{t}{\succ} \mathbf{x}(t) \Rightarrow p \cdot x \geq p \cdot \mathbf{x}(t). \qquad (3.6)$$

The proof of the lemma would then be complete if we can reinforce (3.6) in

$$x \underset{t}{\succ} \mathbf{x}(t) \Rightarrow p \cdot x > p \cdot \mathbf{x}(t). \qquad (3.7)$$

Suppose, contrary to (3.7), that there exists $x \in G(t)$ with

$$p \cdot x = p \cdot \mathbf{x}(t);$$

then, by continuity (ii), $z = x - \varepsilon \succ_t \mathbf{x}(t)$ when ε is chosen sufficiently small. Accordingly we have $p \cdot z = p \cdot x - p \cdot \varepsilon < p \cdot \mathbf{x}(t)$ and $z \in G(t)$. But this contradicts (3.6).

Before proceeding to the main price characterisation of core allocations in mixed markets, we introduce the following assumption which considerably simplifies the proof of the 'budgetary exploitation theorem' provided by Shitovitz (1973).

Assumption A

Let $S \subseteq T_0$, $p \neq 0$ and **x** an allocation. If x is a commodity bundle such that, for almost each trader t in S, $p \cdot x > p \cdot \mathbf{x}(t)$, then there exists ε, $\varepsilon > 0$, such that, for almost every t in S, $\mathbf{x}(t) + \varepsilon x \succ_t \mathbf{x}(t)$.

In Figure 3.3.a, the preference relation $\succ_t$ is such that $p \cdot x > p \cdot \mathbf{x}(t)$ $\Rightarrow \exists \varepsilon : \mathbf{x}(t) + \varepsilon x \succ_t \mathbf{x}(t)$ which is not the case for the preference relation $\succ_t$ depicted in Figure 3.3.b.

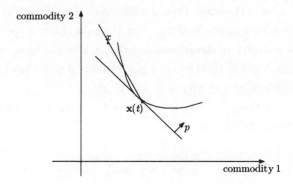

Figure 3.3.a

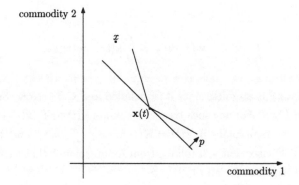

Figure 3.3.b

Now we prove the following result, known as the *budgetary exploitation theorem* (Shitovitz 1973).

Theorem 3.2.

If an allocation x is in the core, there exists a price system p such that, for almost every trader $t \in T_0$,

$$p \cdot \mathbf{x}(t) \le p \cdot \mathbf{w}(t). \tag{3.8}$$

Proof Let $\mathbf{x}$ be in the core. Then the allocation $\mathbf{x}$ is necessarily Pareto-optimal for otherwise the coalition $S = T$ would improve upon the allocation $\mathbf{x}$, contrary to the assumption that $\mathbf{x}$ is in the core. It follows from Lemma 3.2 that there exists a price system p such that $(p, \mathbf{x})$ is a price equilibrium, or $x \succ_t \mathbf{x}(t) \Rightarrow p \cdot x > p \cdot \mathbf{x}(t)$.

Now assume that, contrary to Theorem 3.2, there existed a non-null set of traders $S, S \subseteq T_0$, for which

$$p \cdot \mathbf{x}(t) > p \cdot \mathbf{w}(t). \tag{3.9}$$

By Lyapounov's theorem, $\forall \varepsilon > 0$, there exists a subset εS, $\varepsilon S \subseteq S$, such that

$$\int_{\varepsilon S} [\mathbf{x}(t) - \mathbf{w}(t)] d\nu = \varepsilon \int_S [\mathbf{x}(t) - \mathbf{w}(t)] d\nu. \tag{3.10}$$

Notice that εS is atomless since it is included in $S \subseteq T_0$. Now consider a trader t in $T \backslash \varepsilon S$. For any such trader, the vector $\mathbf{x}(t) + \varepsilon \int_S [\mathbf{x}(t) - \mathbf{w}(t)] d\nu$ lies above the hyperplane $p \cdot \mathbf{x}(t) = K(t)$ since $p \cdot \int_{\varepsilon S} [\mathbf{x}(t) - \mathbf{w}(t)] d\nu > 0$ (see (3.9)). Consequently, it follows from Assumption A that there exists ε, $\varepsilon > 0$, such that, for all $t \in T \backslash \varepsilon S$,

$$\mathbf{y}(t) = \mathbf{x}(t) + \frac{\varepsilon}{\nu(T \backslash \varepsilon S)} \int_S [\mathbf{x}(t) - \mathbf{w}(t)] d\nu \succ_t \mathbf{x}(t).$$

Furthermore, it follows from (3.10) that

$$\int_{T\setminus\varepsilon S} \mathbf{y}(t)d\nu = \int_{T\setminus\varepsilon S} \mathbf{x}(t)d\nu + \varepsilon \int_S [\mathbf{x}(t) - \mathbf{w}(t)]d\nu;$$

$$= \int_{T\setminus\varepsilon S} \mathbf{x}(t)d\nu + \int_{\varepsilon S} [\mathbf{x}(t) - \mathbf{w}(t)]d\nu.$$

Since $\mathbf{x}$ is an allocation, we have

$$\int_{\varepsilon S} [\mathbf{x}(t) - \mathbf{w}(t)]d\nu = \int_{T\setminus\varepsilon S} [\mathbf{w}(t) - \mathbf{x}(t)]d\nu,$$

so that

$$\int_{T\setminus\varepsilon S} \mathbf{y}(t)d\nu = \int_{T\setminus\varepsilon S} \mathbf{x}(t)d\nu + \int_{T\setminus\varepsilon S} \mathbf{w}(t)d\nu - \int_{T\setminus\varepsilon S} \mathbf{x}(t)d\nu$$

$$= \int_{T\setminus\varepsilon S} \mathbf{w}(t)d\nu.$$

But then the coalition $T\setminus\varepsilon S$, – which is of strictly positive measure since it contains all the atoms – improves upon the allocation $\mathbf{x}$, contrary to the assumption that $\mathbf{x}$ is in the core.

As a preliminary comment on the above result, notice that Theorem 3.1 is the special case of Theorem 3.2 corresponding to $T_1 = \emptyset$. Then $\int_T (\mathbf{x}(t) - \mathbf{w}(t))d\nu = \int_{T_0} (\mathbf{x}(t) - \mathbf{w}(t))d\nu = 0$, where the last equality follows from the fact that $\mathbf{x}$ is an allocation and $p \cdot \mathbf{x}(t) \leq p \cdot \mathbf{w}(t)$ for all $t \in T_0$ by Theorem 3.2. Since it follows from the same theorem that $\mathbf{x}(t)$ is a maximal element for $\succ_t$ in $\{x \mid p \cdot x \leq p \cdot \mathbf{w}(t)\}$, $t \in T_0 = T$, $(p, \mathbf{x})$ is a competitive equilibrium, as stated in Theorem 3.1

To illustrate the strength of Theorem 3.2, it is useful to apply its main conclusion to the example of the mixed market introduced at the beginning of this section. This exchange economy has a unique competitive allocation that assigns (2,2) to all traders. Now let us show that, as a consequence of Theorem 3.2, the core also includes all allocations $\mathbf{x}$ which can be written as $\mathbf{x}(t) = (\mathbf{z}(t), \mathbf{z}(t))$ for almost all t, where $1 \leq \mathbf{z}(t) \leq 2$ for $t \in T_0$ and $2 \leq \mathbf{z}(t) \leq 3$ for $t \in T_1$, with $\int_T \mathbf{z}(t)d\nu = 4$. Indeed, any such allocation is Pareto-optimal since it assigns to each trader a commodity bundle lying on the main diagonal, as required by the symmetric preferences of the agents. Furthermore, at any allocation $\mathbf{x}$ defined by $\mathbf{x}(t) = (\mathbf{z}(t), \mathbf{z}(t))$ as above, we observe that

$$p \cdot \mathbf{x}(t) \leq p \cdot \mathbf{w}(t)$$

for all traders $t \in T_0$ at the Pareto-optimal price vector $p = (1,1)$, which sustains that allocation (in our example, any Pareto-optimal allocation is sustained by the same price vector $(1,1)$). Consequently, it follows from Theorem 3.2 that all these allocations are in the core of our mixed market. In particular, the allocation $\mathbf{x}_0$ defined by

$$\begin{aligned} \mathbf{x}_0(t) &= (1,1) & t \in T_0 \\ &= (3,3) & t \in T_1 = \{2\} \end{aligned}$$

is in the core, as already noticed in the asymptotic version of this example (cf. page 40). At $\mathbf{x}_0$, the small traders (in T_0) are 'budgetarily exploited', i.e., we have

$$p \cdot \mathbf{x}_0(t) = p \cdot (1,1) < p \cdot (4,0) = p \cdot \mathbf{w}(t)$$

where the unique Pareto-optimal price system for all points in the core is $p = (1,1)$. Moreover notice that in this example the utility of every small trader at the allocation $\mathbf{x}_0$ is exactly the same as that of his initial endowment bundle $(4,0)$. It is also true that, for all allocations $\mathbf{x}(t) = (\mathbf{z}(t), \mathbf{z}(t))$ described above, their utility is smaller than their utility at the competitive allocation assigning $(2,2)$ to each one of them. Consequently, the small traders are not only budgetarily exploited at these core allocations, but also exploited in utility: their utility level at these allocations is always smaller than their utility level at the competitive allocation. Later we shall see that this property is not always satisfied: budgetary exploitation does not necessarily imply utility exploitation.

3.3 COMPETITIVE ALLOCATIONS AND THE CORE OF MIXED MARKETS

We continue our investigation of the cores in mixed markets by identifying some situations in which, in spite of the existence of atoms, the equivalence theorem holds. Interestingly enough, these situations reveal that, in spite of their size, large traders can be engaged in an intense competition because other traders are similar to them in the economy. These can either be other large traders or small traders when they are sufficiently numerous. In Section 3.3.1 the case of similar large traders is considered, while in Section 3.3.2 we consider the core when large traders correspond to similar small traders.

3.3.1. The Core when Large Traders are Similar

A significant result in Shitovitz (1973) is his 'Theorem B', which appears as an extension of the equivalence Theorem 3.1 to oligopolistic mixed markets. It states that in a market in which there are at least two large traders, and all the large traders are similar, all core allocations are competitive. Two traders s and t are said to be of the same *type* or *similar* if $\mathbf{w}(s) = \mathbf{w}(t)$ and, for all $x, y \in R_+^\ell, x \succ_s y$ if and only if $x \succ_t y$. Note that when $s \in T_1$ is of the same type as t (not necessarily in T_1), then both s and t have the same utility function $u_s(x) = u_t(x)$.

Theorem 3.3.
Assume that there are at least two large traders, and that all large traders are similar. Then, the core coincides with the set of competitive allocations.

A straightforward proof of this equivalence theorem can be found in Shitovitz (1973). Thus such a market is essentially indistinguishable from a perfectly competitive market; if all the large traders were to split into a continuum of small traders of the same type as the original large traders, there would be no change in the core. In this case, therefore, the presence of several large traders engenders such intense competition among them that the effect of the larger traders' size is nullified.

Here, we provide only a heuristic argument. For simplicity, in this description, let us assume that there are just two large traders A_1 and A_2, and they are of the same type with equal measure, and let $\mathbf{x}$ be an allocation in the core. Obviously, both large traders are indifferent between $\mathbf{x}(A_1)$ and $\mathbf{x}(A_2)$. In fact, we may go further; assume that both traders actually get the same bundle, i.e. that $\mathbf{x}(A_1) = \mathbf{x}(A_2)$. Therefore, by Lyapunov's theorem there exist two disjoint coalitions S_1 and S_2 of small traders trading with A_1 and A_2, respectively, i.e. $\int_R \mathbf{x} = \int_R \mathbf{w}$ for $R = S_1 \cup A_1$ and $R = S_2 \cup A_2$. Intuitively, also, it is not unreasonable to assume that two identical large traders will split the market evenly between them. This means that the market is actually composed of two monopolistic submarkets whose traders are $S_1 \cup A_1$ and $S_2 \cup A_2$, respectively. Let $\mathbf{p}(t) = p \cdot \mathbf{x}(t) - p \cdot \mathbf{w}(t)$ be the budgetary profit of trader t at the market prices p. By Theorem 3.2 we know that each small trader t has a non-positive profit. Suppose now that one of the large traders, say A_1, has a positive profit. Then, since the total profit of each submarket is zero, there are small traders in S_1 who have been budgetarily exploited. Therefore, by adding a sufficiently small part of these traders to the other submarket, and by distributing the excess $\mathbf{w}(t) - \mathbf{x}(t)$ of the part (whose value at the market prices is positive) among themselves and the traders of the other submarket, we obtain a new submarket whose traders t receive a new bundle in the neighbourhood of $\mathbf{x}(t)$ whose value at the market prices is more than the value of $\mathbf{x}(t)$. Therefore, the traders of this new submarket can improve upon $\mathbf{x}$, in contradiction to the assumption that x is in the core.

In very simple terms, what is happening is that if some of the customers of A_1 are losing money, then it is worthwhile for A_2 to steal at least a small number of these customers from A_1 (while keeping his own customers). Therefore, none of A_1's customers can lose money, and so, by the symmetry of the situation, nobody does.

3.3.2. The Core when Large Traders Correspond to Similar Small Traders

Theorem 3.3 asserts that when all large traders are competitors of the same type, the core is equivalent to the set of competitive allocations. Our next theorem (Theorem 3.4 below) asserts that the same must hold whenever there is a corresponding set of *small* traders of the same type for each large trader, *and* a constraint on the size of the atoms is satisfied. Let $A_1, A_2, \cdots, A_k, \cdots$ denote the set of atoms and, for each atom A_k consider the class

$$T_k \stackrel{\text{def}}{=} \{t \in T \mid \mathbf{w}(t) = \mathbf{w}(A_k); \forall (x,y) \in R_+^\ell \times R_+^\ell : x \succeq_t y \Leftrightarrow \mathbf{x} \succeq_{A_k} y\};$$

the class T_k is the set of all traders who are of the same type as the atom A_k. Denote by $\succeq_k$ the common preferences of traders in T_k and by A_{hk} the hth atom of type k, $h \in N^*$. We then obtain a partition of the set of agents into at most countably many classes T_k, and an atomless part $T \backslash \cup_{k \in N^*} T_k$. Gabszewicz and Mertens (1971) have proved the following:

Theorem 3.4.
If

$$\sum_k \left(\sum_h \frac{\nu(A_{hk})}{\nu(T_k)} \right) < 1, \tag{3.11}$$

then, the core coincides with the set of competitive allocations.

The inequality (3.11) says that the sum over all types of the atomic proportions of the types should be less than one. This result implies in particular that if there is only a single atom in the economy, *any* non-null set of small traders similar to the atom nullifies the effect of the large trader's size. The proof of Theorem 3.4 is too long to be reported in full detail. Let us however give an idea of the proof, which the reader can find in Gabszewicz and Mertens (1971, p. 714). This proof essentially rests on a lemma which states that, under condition (3.11), *all* traders in T_k – the large and the small ones – must get a consumption bundle in the core which is in the same indifference class relative to their common preferences $\succeq_k$. Indeed, the equivalence theorem is an immediate corollary of this lemma when combined with Theorem 3.1. As for the lemma, the idea of the proof is as follows. Let x be in the core. Suppose that traders in each type are represented on the unit interval, with Lebesgue measure ν, atoms of that type being subintervals: Figure 3.4 provides a representation of the economy where, for all pairs of traders in a given type, one trader is below another if, and only if, under an allocation x he prefers the other's consumption to his own. The set D represents the atomless part $T \setminus \cup_k T_k$.

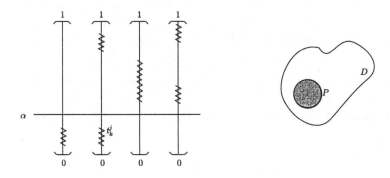

Figure 3.4

If, contrary to the lemma, all traders in some type are not in the same indifference class, then the condition of Theorem 3.4 implies that there exists a number α, $\alpha \in]0, 1[$, such that if a horizontal straight line is drawn in Figure 3.4 at level α through the types, no atom is split by this line. Then the agents below this line are worse off in all types, and they will, supplemented by some subcoalition P in D, form a coalition which can improve upon the allocation **x**. The idea is to choose, by Lyapunov's theorem, a subset P of D such that the agents below α together with the subset form an α-reduction of the initial economy. Of course, the agents of a given type are not originally defined as the above reasoning suggests, and the main difficulty of the proof of the lemma consists in rearranging traders in such a way that the above reasoning can be applied.

Theorems 3.3 and 3.4 reveal that, in spite of the existence of atomic traders, it is sometimes possible to extend the equivalence theorem between the core and the set of competitive allocations. This is true in particular, when these large traders are similar to each other, or when for each such large trader there is a corresponding set of small traders which are similar to him. Such conditions suggest that when large traders find competitors similar to them in the economy, it may well imply the dilution of their market power; this is reminiscent of Bertrand price competition in a non-cooperative context.

3.4 RESTRICTED COMPETITIVE ALLOCATIONS AND THE CORE OF MIXED MARKETS

The budgetary exploitation theorem asserts that core allocations in mixed markets are sustained by efficiency prices such that, for any trader, a consumption preferable to what he gets under that allocation would also be more expensive; furthermore the values, at these prices, of the consumption received in that allocation by any *small* trader cannot exceed the value of his initial endowment. As the example in Section 3.2 shows, one should generally expect the latter to be *strictly* larger than the former, implying strict budgetary exploitation (i.e., $p \cdot \mathbf{x}(t) < p \cdot \mathbf{w}(t), t \in T_0$). Nonetheless, under the additional assumptions introduced in Section 3.3, the equivalence property is restored: efficiency prices are also competitive prices.

Without requiring as much as the equivalence property for core allocations in mixed markets, one could be interested in a weaker property of price decentralisation for such allocations, namely, that all small traders should be, at that allocation, in a situation corresponding to a competitive equilibrium with respect to the efficiency price system p. More precisely, define a *restricted allocation* $x|_{T_0}$ to be *competitive* if there exists a price system p such that, for almost all $t \in T_0$, $p \cdot \mathbf{x}(t) = p \cdot \mathbf{w}(t)$ and $y \succ_t \mathbf{x}(t) \Rightarrow p \cdot y > p \cdot \mathbf{w}(t)$. That is, a competitive restricted allocation carries the property that all small traders are in a competitive allocation with respect to a price vector p: $\mathbf{x}(t)$ is a maximal element for $\succ_t$ of the budget set $\{y \mid p \cdot y \leq p \cdot \mathbf{w}(t)\}$. But it does not follow that $\mathbf{x}|_{T_0}$ is the restriction to T_0 of a competitive allocation, for the large traders need not be in a competitive equilibrium with respect to p; and it does not follow that $\mathbf{x}|_{T_0}$ is an allocation for the subeconomy consisting of the atomless sector T_0 alone, since the equality of supply and demand (over T_0) may be violated (it is not required that $\int_{T_0} \mathbf{x} = \int_{T_0} \mathbf{w}$). However, if at a particular core allocation $\mathbf{x}$ no *strict* budgetary exploitation against the small traders is observed at efficiency prices p, i.e. if $p \cdot \mathbf{x}(t) = p \cdot \mathbf{w}(t)$ for $t \in T_0$, the restriction $\mathbf{x}|_{T_0}$ would then be competitive. Moreover, note that small traders of the same type must get, at a restricted competitive allocation, equivalent bundles.

In this section we study sufficient conditions under which an allocation in the core of a mixed market has a competitive restriction on the atomless sector. To this end it is useful to introduce the notion of a split market. The market is said to be *split* with respect to a core allocation $\mathbf{x}$ if there exists a coalition S (called the *splitting coalition*) such that $\int_S \mathbf{x} = \int_S \mathbf{w}$ and $0 < \nu(S) < \nu(T)$. For the two following theorems, from Shitovitz (1982), we assume that core allocations are in the interior of the commodity space and that indifference curves generated by $\succ_t$ are C_1.

Theorem 3.5.
If the market is split with respect to a core allocation x, $\mathbf{x}|_{T_0}$ is a restricted competitive allocation.

In the literature on mixed markets, several conditions have been identified under which the market can be split with respect to each core allocation, implying, with Theorem 3.5, that such core allocations are restricted competitive allocations. The first condition stated below involves only the set of atoms and has been introduced by Shitovitz (1973). Define two large traders (atoms) to be of the same *kind* if they are of the same type and have the same measure. Thus every market may be represented by $(T_0; A_1, A_2, \cdots)$, where T_0 is the atomless sector and $A_1, A_2, \cdots$ is a partition of the set of all atoms such that two atoms belong to the same A_k, if they are of the same kind. Denote the number of atoms in A_k by $|A_k|$.

Theorem 3.6.
Given a market $(T_0 : A_1, A_2, \cdots)$, let m denote the greatest common divisor of $|A_k|, k = 1, 2, \cdots$; if $m \geq 2$, all core allocations are restricted competitive allocations.

An alternative condition, implying an identical result, has been introduced in Drèze, Gabszewicz, Schmeidler and Vind (1972); this condition involves only the atomless sector. It states that, for each commodity, there exists a non-null subset of the atomless sector, the initial endowment of which is made only of that commodity. Assuming also that indifference surfaces generated by $\succ_t$ are C_1, these authors prove

Theorem 3.7.
If, for each commodity h, $h = 1, \cdots, \ell$, there exists a non-null coalition S_h, $S_h \subset T_0$, for which $\int_{S_k} \mathbf{w}^k = 0$, $k \neq h$, and $\int_{S_h} \mathbf{w}^h > 0$, then the market can be split and all core allocations are restricted competitive allocations.

Finally, the following condition, introduced by Gabszewicz (1975), concerns both the set of atoms and the atomless part of the economy. Assume that there is a finite number of atoms A_j, $j = 1, \cdots, m$, and that for all j, $\mathbf{w}_j(A_j) = w$. Further, assume that, for all j, $\succ_{A_j}$ is derived from a homogeneous utility function and that there exists S_j, $S_j \subset T_0$, $\nu(S_j) > 0$, with, for all $t \in S_j$, $\succ_t = \succ_{A_j}$ and $\mathbf{w}(t) = w$.

Theorem 3.8.
Under the preceding assumptions, any allocation x in the core is a restricted competitive allocation.

Not only can a restricted competitive allocation which is in the core be fully decentralised by efficiency prices on the atomless sector, but such a core allocation can also be transformed in a competitive allocation for the same prices under an appropriate redistribution of the initial resources *of the atoms among themselves* $(p \cdot \int_{T_0} \mathbf{x} = p \cdot \int_{T_0} \mathbf{w} \Rightarrow p \cdot \int_{T_1} \mathbf{x} = p \cdot \int_{T_1} \mathbf{w})$. Accordingly any discrimination among traders introduced by an allocation in the core which is restricted competitive – as compared with a competitive allocation – is a phenomenon affecting the atoms only; within the atomless sector, no discrimination takes place. It may still be true, however, that the efficiency prices discriminate against the whole atomless sector when compared with the price system corresponding to a fully competitive allocation for the same economy; on this subject, see Gabszewicz and Drèze (1971).

3.5 BUDGETARY EXPLOITATION VERSUS UTILITY EXPLOITATION

As promised at the end of Section 3.2, we now treat the idea of exploitation of the small traders, which is fundamental in our analysis of oligopoly in mixed markets. We have expressed this idea in terms of a value criterion, using Pareto prices. Actually, however, each trader is concerned with his preferences rather than with any budgetary criterion. There exist classes of markets in which budgetary profit expresses the relative situations of some traders in terms of their preferences (see Section 3.5.2 below). But in general this is not the case, and there exist markets (even monopolistic markets) in which, although budgetarily exploited in the sense of Theorem 3.1, *all* small traders are actually better off than at any competitive equilibrium. We now examine this question in the narrow sense of a monopoly, from the viewpoint of the atom.

3.5.1. Advantageous and Disadvantageous Monopolies

In his 'disadvantageous monopolies', Aumann (1973) presents a series of examples (Examples A, B and C) showing that budgetary exploitation does not necessarily imply utility exploitation. In these examples there is a single atom $\{a\}$ and a non-atomic part (the 'ocean'). All examples are two-commodity markets, with all of one commodity initially concentrated in the hands of the atom and all of the other commodity initially held by the ocean. Thus a is a monopolist both in the sense of being an atom and in the sense that he initially holds a 'corner' on one of the two commodities. We omit the other details of the examples.

In Example A, the core is quite large, there is a unique competitive allocation, and from the monopolist's viewpoint, the competitive allocation is approximately in the middle of the core (see Figure 3.5.a).

Example B is a variant of Example A. Here, the core is again quite large, there is a unique competitive allocation, and from the monopolist's viewpoint, the competitive allocation is the *best* in the core (see Figure 3.5.b). Thus the monopoly is disadvantageous and the monopolist would do well to 'go competitive', i.e. split itself into a continuum of small traders.

Perhaps the most disturbing aspect of these examples is their utter lack of pathology. One is almost forced to the conclusion that monopolies which are not particularly advantageous are probably the rule rather than the exception. The conclusion is rather counterintuitive since one would conjecture that the monopoly outcome should be advantageous for the monopolist when compared with its competitive outcome. Although Aumann's examples disprove this conjecture, Greenberg and Shitovitz (1977) have been able to show:

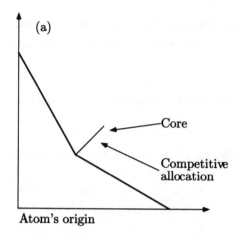

Figure 3.5.a

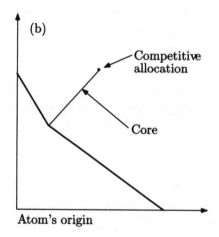

Figure 3.5.b

Theorem 3.9.

In an exchange economy with one atom, and one type of small traders, for each core allocation x there is a competitive allocation y whose utility to the atom is smaller than that of x whenever either x is an equal treatment allocation, or all small traders have the same homogeneous preferences.

3.5.2. When Budgetary Exploitation Implies Utility Exploitation

That budgetary exploitation implies utility exploitation for the small traders has been established for two particular classes of markets, namely homogeneous and monetary markets. A *homogeneous market* is a market in which all traders t have the same homogeneous preference relation, namely a relation derived from a concave utility function $u(x)$ that is homogeneous of degree 1 and has continuous derivatives in the neighbourhood of $\int_T \mathbf{w}$. It is easy to see that a Pareto-optimal allocation $\mathbf{x}$ can be written as $\mathbf{x}(t) = \mathbf{z}(t) \cdot \int_T \mathbf{w}$, with $\int_T \mathbf{z}(t) = 1$. Hence, the efficiency prices p are the same for all Pareto-optimal allocations. There is also a unique competitive allocation $\mathbf{x}^*$. Let $\mathbf{p}(t) = p \cdot \mathbf{x}(t) - p \cdot \mathbf{w}(t)$ be the 'budgetary profit' of trader t. Then we have $\mathbf{p}(t) \geq 0$ if and only if $u(\mathbf{x}(t)) \leq u(\mathbf{x}^*(t))$. For $\mathbf{x}$ in the core, therefore, it follows that small traders are at most as satisfied (in the sense of preferences) as they are at the competitive equilibrium, and in split markets the small traders receive the same bundle in the core that they receive at the competitive equilibrium.

In a *monetary market*, the consumption set of each trader is $R \times R_+^\ell$, i.e. a commodity bundle (ξ, x) consists of an amount ξ of money and a vector $x \in R_+^\ell$ of commodities. The utility function $U_t(\xi, x)$ of trader t is assumed to be linear in money, i.e.

$$U_t(\xi, x) = \xi + V_t(x).$$

Furthermore, the initial amount of money of each trader in T_1 is supposed to be zero, while trader t holds commodities $\mathbf{w}(t) \gg 0$. Note that a price vector for a monetary economy which constitutes an efficiency equilibrium with some allocation $\mathbf{x}$ is of the form $(1, p)$ where, for each t, $V_t(\mathbf{x}(t) - p \cdot \mathbf{x}(t)) = \max_{x \in R_+^\ell} (V_t(x) - p \cdot x)$. Using a generalisation of Theorem 3.1 (see Shitovitz 1982 and Champsaur and Laroque 1976) it can be proved that for each core allocation $\mathbf{x}$, there exists $p \gg 0$ in R^ℓ, which constitutes an efficiency equilibrium with $(1, p)$ and $\xi(t) + p \cdot \mathbf{x}(t) \leq p \cdot \mathbf{w}(t) \ \forall t \in T_0$. But, defining $\xi^*(t)$ in such a way that, for almost all $t \in T$

$$\xi^*(t) + p \cdot \mathbf{x}(t) = p \cdot \mathbf{w}(t),$$

we find that $(1, p), (\xi^*, \mathbf{x})$ is a competitive equilibrium. Hence it follows that, for almost all $t \in T_0$, $\xi(t) \leq \xi^*(t)$ and therefore we obtain $U_t(\xi(t), \mathbf{x}(t)) \leq U_t(\xi^*(t), \mathbf{x}(t))$. Thus, budgetary exploitation implies utility exploitation (Samet and Shitovitz, unpublished).

3.6 SYNDICATES

In Section 2.3, we provided an interpretation of the asymptotic approach to imperfect competition based on *collusion*. In this section, we consider in the same manner the possibility of interpreting an atom as a syndicate of traders formed in an initially atomless economy. Accordingly, the following analysis mirrors, in the framework of a mixed model of pure exchange, the study performed in Section 2.3 for the asymptotic approach. Assume that $(T, \mathcal{T}, \mu)$ is an atomless measure space, where the set T is to be interpreted as the set of traders, and $\mathcal{T}$ as the set of possible coalitions of traders in the same economy. Imagine that, for any reason whatsoever, all traders in some *non-null* subset A in $\mathcal{T}$ decide to act only in unison, for instance by delegating to a single decision unit the task of representing their economic interests in the trade. Whenever effective, such a binding agreement definitely prevents the formation of any coalition of traders, including a *proper* subset of A: while such coalitions were allowed before the collusive agreement, they are henceforth forbidden. Formally, the σ-field $\mathcal{T}$ no longer represents the class of acceptable coalitions; this class is now reduced to the σ-field $\mathcal{T}_A = \{S \in \mathcal{T} \mid$ either $S \cap A = \emptyset$, or $S \cap A = A\}$, i.e. the subset A now constitutes an *atom* in $\mathcal{T}_A$. In the following we elaborate on the above interpretation by investigating the effectiveness and the stability of binding agreements among traders in the context of a pure exchange economy. To this end, it is convenient to work with a simplified version of our general exchange model. Consider an atomless exchange economy with a continuum T of traders falling into r types, $T_k, k = 1, \cdots, r$, i.e. all traders t in T_k have the same preferences $(\succeq_t = \succeq_k; t \in T_k, k = 1, \cdots, r)$ and the same initial assignment $(\mathbf{w}(t) = w_k; t \in T_k; k = 1, \cdots, r)$. For simplicity, let T_k be the right open interval $[k-1, k[$ and T_r the closed interval $[r-1, r]$ so that $T = [0, r]$. Also let $\mathcal{T}$ denote the class of Lebesgue measurable subsets of T and μ the Lebesgue measure defined on $\mathcal{T}$. *Syndicates* of traders are defined informally as follows: let $A_{hk}, h = 1, \cdots, j_k$, be a measurable subset of T_k and imagine that all traders in A_{hk} agree that (i) no *proper* subset of them will form a coalition with traders outside A_{hk}, so that only the group as a whole will enter into broader coalitions, (ii) only those allocations which assign an identical consumption vector to all $t \in A_{hk}$ will be accepted by the group. Denote by A the set $\cup_{k=1}^{r}[\cup_{h=1}^{j_k} A_{hk}]$; the set A contains all agents in A who are members of a syndicate; the set A will also be referred to as a *syndicate structure*. The formal consequences of this definition of the syndicates A_{hk} are the following:

1. The set of potential coalitions is now reduced to a subclass of the original σ-field $\mathcal{T}$, namely the subclass $\mathcal{T}_A$ defined by

$$\mathcal{T}_A = \{S \in \mathcal{T} \mid \forall k = 1, \cdots, r, \forall h = 1, \cdots, j_k,$$
$$S \cap A_{hk} = \emptyset \text{ or } S \cap A_{hk} = A_{hk}\};$$

2. The set of admissible allocations in the economy is now restricted to those allocations which are constant-valued on $A_{hk}, k = 1, \cdots, r$;

$h = 1, \cdots, j_k$, i.e. which are T_A-measurable;

3. The core must be redefined in terms of the new class of coalitions and the new set of admissible allocations; the T_A-core $C(T_A)$ is the set of all T_A-measurable allocations that are not dominated, via any non-null coalition in T_A, by some T_A-measurable allocation;

4. On the other hand, it is readily verified that the set $\mathcal{E}$ of competitive allocations is invariant with respect to the process of syndicate formation.

The formal analogy between a syndicate in an atomless measure space and an atom in an atomic measure space is thus complete. Accordingly, general results established for an exchange economy with atoms are directly applicable to our special case. This is true in particular for Theorems 3.3 and 3.4 which now become, respectively:

Proposition 3.1.
Assume that, for some k and for all $k' \neq k$, there is no syndicate included in $T_{k'}$, while there are at least two non-null syndicates included in T_k. Then $C(T_A) = \mathcal{E}$.

Proposition 3.2.
$$\mu(A) < 1 \Rightarrow C(T_A) = \mathcal{E}.$$

Proposition 3.1 states that if all existing syndicates are of the same type, the equivalence theorem must hold. Proposition 3.2 shows that the process of syndicate formation must involve a sufficiently broad class of traders before it can become effective in enlarging the core of the economy.

In the absence of syndicates, the core of our (atomless) exchange economy coincides with $\mathcal{E}$; this set consists of T_A-measurable allocations only, and thus belongs to the T_A-core. If syndicates are to be *effective*, they must bring about an allocation that is not competitive; assuming that only allocations in the T_A-core can emerge, we are led to investigate allocations in $C(T_A) \setminus \mathcal{E}$, i.e. non-competitive core allocations. Any such allocation could be improved upon by some coalition involving a *proper* subset of at least one syndicate; that is, it could be blocked if some syndicate members could be persuaded to break the agreement which binds them to the syndicate. Under a non-competitive allocation, one must accordingly reckon with a permanent temptation for some traders either to leave their syndicate or to break its rules (by secretly recontracting with outsiders). How can the syndicates achieve stability in the face of such temptations? To simplify the discussion, we shall assume that there is only one syndicate in each type k, and denote it by A_k. One can think of two types of economic considerations that may preserve the stability of syndicates, namely: (i) comparison of the consumption of syndicate members (t in A_k) with that of unorganised traders of the same type (t in $T_k \setminus A_k$), and (ii) comparison of the consumption of syndicate members with what they would receive under competitive allocations. A natural requirement for the stability of a syndicate A_k under the first type of comparison, given an allocation $\mathbf{y}$, would be the existence of a non-null set of unorganised traders of the same type who are not better off than the members of the syndicate A_k. This leads to the concept of *marginal stability*. Given a syndicate structure $A = (A_1, \cdots, A_r)$ with $\mu(A_k) < 1$, $\forall k$, an allocation $\mathbf{y} \in \mathcal{C}(T_A)$ is *marginally stable* if, for all k with $\mu(A_k) > 0$, there exists $S_k, S_k \subseteq T_k \setminus A_k$, $\mu(S_k) > 0$ and $\mathbf{y}(t) \succeq_k \mathbf{y}(\tau)$, $\tau \in A_k$, $t \in S_k$.

Clearly any competitive allocation satisfies marginal stability, but no other allocations in $\mathcal{C}(T_A)$ do, as indicated in the following proposition (see Gabszewicz and Drèze (1971)):

Proposition 3.3.
Let A be a syndicate structure with $\mu(A_k) < 1, k = 1, \cdots, r$; then no allocation in $\mathcal{C}(T_A) \setminus \mathcal{E}$ is marginally stable.

Having reached this negative conclusion, we turn to the other type of comparison, in which an allocation $\mathbf{y} \in \mathcal{C}(T_A) \setminus \mathcal{E}$ is compared with allocations in $\mathcal{E}$. A natural requirement for the stability of a syndicate A_k under this type of comparison, given an allocation $\mathbf{y}$, $\mathbf{y} \in \mathcal{C}(T_A) \setminus \mathcal{E}$, would be that the members of A_k are better off under $\mathbf{y}$ than they would be under every competitive allocation. Given a syndicate structure A, an allocation $y \in C(T_A) \setminus \mathcal{E}$ carries the property of *total stability* whenever, for all $t \in A$ and all $\mathbf{x} \in \mathcal{E}$,

$$\mathbf{y}(t) \succeq_t \mathbf{x}(t).$$

Proposition 3.4.
There exist exchange economies for which the class of syndicate structures A, with $\mu(A_k) < 1$, $k = 1, \cdots, r$, such that $C(T_A) \setminus \mathcal{E}$ contains allocations that satisfy total stability, is non-empty.

Propositions 3.3 and 3.4 raise several interesting questions insofar as the stability of syndicates is concerned. Clearly syndicates are relevant only to the extent that they may enforce non-competitive core allocations, i.e. allocations in $C(T_A) \setminus \mathcal{E}$. Such allocations appear at first sight unstable because they never satisfy marginal stability (Proposition 3.3). We must infer from this that the relevant stability concept is one of total stability. Proposition 3.4 tells us that total stability may well hold for all syndicates simultaneously. Combining the two propositions, we are led to recognise the possibility that a syndicate structure may be both relevant and stable, contrary to the conclusion reached above in the framework of the productive economy which was considered in Section 2.3.

We have so far considered that all traders belonging to a particular syndicate are of the same type; this assumption allowed us to restrict our attention to allocations which were uniform on each syndicate (T_A-measurable allocations). In many circumstances, however, more complex forms of syndicates should be envisaged; thus, a large corporation may be regarded as a syndicate of employees and stockholders; then all members are not of the same type and no rule of uniform imputation would be justified. The question then arises whether the above results on syndicate structures would still hold when syndicates might include traders of different types. Unfortunately, Champsaur and Laroque (1976) have shown that the analogs of Propositions 3.1 and 3.3 are no longer valid with such syndicate structures. Clearly much remains to be done on this topic, in which further research would be welcome.

3.7 CONCLUSION

The work we have reported above is only part of the full panoply of research devoted to the study of mixed markets. Other paths have been followed by researchers, and most of our concluding remarks aim at briefly describing the results they have discovered. These include in particular the study of alternative cooperative game-theoretic solution concepts in the framework of mixed markets, and the problem of approximating mixed markets by finite exchange economies. We start, however, with a brief comment about some surprising features of the core's behaviour in such markets. To this end let us return to the example presented in Section 3.2, p. 78. In this example we have assumed that there is a single atom with measure equal to 1. Now consider the same exchange economy, but in which the atom has been replaced by *two* atoms of measure β and $1 - \beta$, respectively, $\beta \in]0, 1[$. While the core with a single atom consisted of all allocations $\mathbf{x}$ of the form $(\mathbf{z}(t), \mathbf{z}(t))$, where $1 \leq \mathbf{z}(t) \leq 2$, for almost all $t \in T_0$ and $2 \leq \mathbf{z}(t) \leq 3$ for the atom (see p. 88), the core now consists of the sole competitive allocation, irrespective of the value of β in $]0, 1[$; this follows immediately from Theorem 3.3. We conclude from this example that, in the abstract setup of a measure space of traders with atoms and an atomless part, the core correspondence is not lower hemicontinuous. Consider indeed the sequence of economies E_r obtained by replacing the single atom of measure 1 by two atoms of measure $1/r$ and $(r-1)/r$, respectively. This sequence of economies converges to the economy E_∞ containing a single atom of measure 1. According to Theorem 3.3, the core of E_r consists, for all r, of the sole competitive allocation. However, for $r = \infty$, the core suddenly enlarges so as to contain a whole segment of allocations which are no longer competitive. Starting from these difficulties, some have questioned the abstract representation of oligopolistic markets via mixed markets. Perhaps the abstract representation itself is responsible for those disturbing results. The question is whether the representation of a mixture of small and large traders via finite, possibly large economies, would dispose of this pathology. It turns out, however, that this is not the case: the same disturbing phenomena may well occur even if one considers *finite* exchange economies. Building a sequence of *finite* duopolistic markets $\mathcal{E}_r$, converging to an economy containing a single monopoly, $\mathcal{E}_\infty$, Gabszewicz (1977) has shown that while the cores of the duopolistic markets $\mathcal{E}_r$, converge to the set of competitive allocations, the core of the limit monopolistic market $\mathcal{E}_\infty$ is much larger and includes many non-competitive allocations; also, in this asymptotic version the core does not behave lower hemicontinuously. Most probably it is the concept of the core itself which is responsible for the discontinuity. Some small coalitions, including the 'small' large trader, are endowed with the possibility of depriving the 'big' large trader of all its power, while intuition would suggest that such coalitions will not act to do so. This seems to indicate that the concept of core must be used with care: core analysis gives qualitative insights rather than exact predictions of market behaviour.

The model of mixed markets has also been used to examine the behaviour of other cooperative concepts, like the von Neumann and Morgenstern (v-N.M.) solutions, the bargaining set, and the transferable Shapley value. The v-N.M. solutions in large markets were analysed by Hart (1974). He considers an atomless market consisting of a finite number of different types of traders, initially owning disjoint sets of goods. It is proved there that if all traders of each type form a cartel and behave like a single (atomic) trader (their representative), then one gets solutions (i.e. v-N.M. stable sets of allocations) of the original nonatomic market from those of the finite market made of the representatives; furthermore, *all* symmetric solutions are obtained in this manner. Another solution concept is the bargaining set, i.e. the set of all allocations with 'no justified objection'. Mas-Colell (1989) has given a uniform modified definition of the bargaining set for atomless economies, and has proved its equivalence with the set of competitive allocations. Applying this concept to mixed markets, Shitovitz (1987) has given an example involving a duopolistic market (with two atoms) where the equivalence theorem between the core and the bargaining set fails to hold. This suggests that, in some contexts, the bargaining set would lead to drastically different outcomes from the core, reflecting more adequately the relationship of market power to the size of the agents. Nevertheless, it can be shown that, when each atom has a corner on some commodities and hence is a veto player, the core and the bargaining set do coincide (Shitovitz 1987). As we have seen in Section 3.5.1, syndicates can be advantageous as well as disadvantageous. The existence of disadvantageous syndicates led Aumann (1973) to the conclusion that 'the game theoretic notion of core is not the proper vehicle for the explanation ... (of the monopolistic advantage)'. He conjectured that perhaps the ideas underlying the concept of the Shapley value could better capture the bargaining power engendered by the harm the monopolist can cause by refusing to trade. Starting from this conjecture and using the asymptotic approach, Guesnerie (1977) has examined the stability of a monopoly from the viewpoint of Shapley's non-transferable utility value. He gives examples with no pathological features where the monopoly is unstable from this viewpoint as well, thus disproving Aumann's conjecture. Hence the Shapley value does not seem at first sight a more appropriate concept than the core for capturing the bargaining power of syndicates or monopolies.

PART 2

Strategic Multilateral Exchange and Oligopoly
Equilibrium

4.   The notion of oligopoly equilibrium

4.1 AN HISTORICAL BACKGROUND

Cournot (1838) was the first to analyse non-cooperative behaviour in an economic decision context. At the time he wrote his celebrated essay, no general equilibrium formulation of an economy — like the pure exchange model considered in Part 1 – was available to economic scientists. More surprisingly, no model at all existed yet to represent the price formation mechanism, even for the case of an isolated market. This is why Cournot had first to elaborate the building blocks of the theory under the form of a *partial equilibrium* model representing the market for a particular good. His proposal was as follows. The buying side of the market consisted of a large number of potential buyers 'hidden' behind the market demand function Q ('la loi de débit', as he called it) specifying, at each price p, the aggregate quantity $Q(p)$ demanded by them. As for the selling side of the market, he imagined several scenarios, according to the *number* of sellers participating in the production and exchange of the commodity. A single seller gives rise to a *monopoly* market, while a *duopoly* market corresponds to the case of two sellers. More generally, an *oligopoly* market represents a situation in which the market consists of a few sellers, say n, without assigning a precise value to n. Nonetheless, when the number n tends to infinity, we are assumed to leave the world of oligopoly and enter into a *competitive* market.

In the above representation, Cournot assigned an *asymmetric* behaviour to the economic agents operating in the market. While buyers were assumed to be *price-takers* and behave competitively, sellers were assumed on the contrary to be conscious that the market price was, at least partially, under their individual control. Probably he wanted thereby to capture the idea that, in several markets, sellers are few while buyers are many. In order to identify the partial control of the sellers over market price, he proceeded in the following way. Let $p(Q)$ denote *the inverse market demand function* for the product, namely

$$p(Q) = Q^{-1}(p);$$

$p(Q)$ represents the price p at which aggregate demand $Q(p)$ is equal to Q. In other words, if Q represents the aggregate quantity supplied by the sellers, – say $Q = \sum_{i=1}^{n} q_i$ in the case in which there are n sellers with q_i denoting the quantity supplied by seller i – the *magnitude $p(Q)$ corresponds to the equilibrium price in the market*. Then it is easy to see how a particular seller, say seller k, can exert a partial control on the equilibrium exchange price p. Since $p(Q) = p(q_k + \sum_{i=1,i\neq k}^{n} q_i)$, seller k can manipulate the price p by changing his individual supply q_k of the product. In particular, assuming that the inverse demand function $p(Q)$ is decreasing, each oligopolist k can decrease (increase) the market price by increasing (decreasing) his individual supply q_k.

Imagine that each seller k produces the commodity exchanged in the market and that he produces a quantity q_k, at a total cost $C_k(q_k)$, $k = 1, \cdots, n$. Then his profit function Π_k is written as

$$\Pi_k \left(q_k, \sum_{i=1,i\neq k}^{n} q_i \right) = p \left(q_k + \sum_{i=1,i\neq k}^{n} q_i \right) q_k - C_k(q_k). \qquad (4.1)$$

If production is realised without any coordinating device among the sellers, each producer k will individually select the quantity q_k in order to maximise his profit Π_k taking into account the control he can exert over the equilibrium market price, as described above. However, this control is only partial since it also depends on the quantities q_i, $i = 1, \cdots, n$,

$i \neq k$, supplied by the other producers i. This can be best perceived by taking the first order necessary condition for a maximum of (4.1), namely

$$\frac{\partial \Pi_k}{\partial q_k} = \frac{\partial p}{\partial q_k} q_k + p \left(q_k + \sum_{i=1, i \neq k}^{n} q_i \right) - \frac{dC}{dq_k} = 0. \qquad (4.2)$$

Denoting by $q_k(\sum_{i=1, i \neq k}^{n} q_i)$ the solution of (4.2) when it exists, we see that further conditions must necessarily be introduced in order to obtain a complete solution to the price formation mechanism which is analysed. To this end, Cournot proposed that each seller k selects the quantity q_k^* in such a way that, for all k,

$$q_k^* = q_k \left(\sum_{i=1, i \neq k}^{n} q_i^* \right).$$

In other words, the quantities $(q_1^*, ..., q_k^*, ..., q_n^*)$ constitute the joint solution of the system of equations which obtain from (4.2) when the index k runs from $k = 1$ to $k = n$: for each oligopolist k, the quantity q_k^* maximises his profit Π_k, given the quantities q_i^* selected by the other sellers i, $i = 1, \cdots, n$, $i \neq k$.

Let us sum up the main assumptions underlying the above Cournot's proposal.

1. First, Cournot considered a market for a single product (*partial equilibrium assumption*); sellers are interested only in profits, expressed in a given numéraire, while buyers are also interested in consuming the product exchanged on the market against units of numéraire. However their desired consumption at each price is not explicitly derived from preferences, but rather expressed in an aggregate manner, under the form of a decreasing demand function.

2. Behind this representation, a large number of buyers is postulated, who behave as price-takers. On the contrary, sellers behave strate-

gically because each of them perceives how the magnitude of his individual supply – their strategies are quantities – has an effect upon
the equilibrium market price (*asymmetry assumption*).

3. The price at which transactions take place makes the sum of quantities supplied by oligopolists equal to consumers' demand at that
price (*equilibrium price assumption*).

4. Finally, the quantities that the oligopolists decide to send to the
market are decided *non-cooperatively*, without any coordination device among them. In the game-theory terminology, these quantities
form a *Nash equilibrium*, in the sense that no unilateral deviation of
any firm from the supply it has selected can increase its profit: the
corresponding n-tuple of strategies is called a *Cournot equilibrium*
(*non-coordination assumption*).

To provide a simple illustration of the above, consider the following
example. Let $Q(p)$ be the market demand function for a commodity,
with

$$Q(p) = 1 - p,$$

and suppose there are n sellers i, $i = 1, \cdots, n$, of this commodity, all
sellers producing the good at zero cost. Then the profit Π_k of seller k
can be written as

$$\Pi_k \left(q_k, \sum_{i=1, i \neq k}^{n} q_i \right) = \left(1 - q_k - \sum_{i=1, i \neq k}^{n} q_i \right) \cdot q_k.$$

Given the quantities q_i, $i \neq k$, Π_k is maximal when

$$\frac{\partial \Pi_k}{\partial q_k} = 1 - 2q_k - \sum_{i=1, i \neq k}^{n} q_i = 0,$$

which gives rise to the system of equations

$$q_k = \frac{1 - \sum_{i=1, i \neq k}^{n} q_i}{2}, k = 1, ..., n. \qquad (4.3)$$

Since all the values q_k must satisfy the same expression above with respect to the aggregate value $\sum_{i=1, i \neq k}^{n} q_i$, all these values must be equal so that we obtain from (4.3)

$$q_k^* = \frac{1}{n+1}, k = 1, ..., n.$$

This example points to an interesting property which has been extensively analysed in the partial equilibrium context: *when the number of oligopolists tends to infinity, the aggregate quantity supplied in the market tends to the competitive supply.* In the above example, the competitive solution consists of a price equal to zero (due to the assumption of zero cost) and an aggregate quantity exchanged equal to 1, which are the limit price and quantity observed at the Cournot equilibrium when $n \to \infty$. We shall come back to this property later in a general equilibrium context.

4.2 A 'COURNOTIAN' EXAMPLE WITH MULTILATERAL EXCHANGE

Among the assumptions underlying Cournot's proposal, the partial equilibrium assumption (point 1 above) is not compatible with the analysis of multilateral exchange in a non-cooperative context. Accordingly, we shall initially be interested in abandoning this assumption and in extending Cournotian analysis to a system of interrelated markets. To proceed in that direction, it is useful to consider the following example of an exchange economy borrowed from Codognato and Gabszewicz (1991). It involves two goods and $n + 2$ traders. All traders have the same Cobb-Douglas utility function U defined by

$$U(x^1, x^2) = x^1 x^2,$$

while initial endowments are given by

$$\omega_i = (\frac{1}{2}, 0), i = 1, 2$$

$$= (0, \frac{1}{n}), i = 3, ..., n + 2.$$

We normalise the price of good 2 by setting it equal to one. The individual demand function $x_i(p)$, with p denoting the price of good 1, for traders $i = 3, ..., n + 2$, is easily derived from utility maximisation under the budget constraint $px^1 + x^2 = \frac{1}{n}$, namely

$$x_i(p) = (\frac{1}{2pn}, \frac{1}{2n}). \tag{4.4}$$

If agents 1 and 2 behaved competitively, taking the exchange rate p between good 1 and good 2 as given, and their similar exchange companions $i, i = 3, ..., n+2$ did the same, their individual demand for good 1 would be equal to $\frac{1}{4}$, irrespective of the value of p. Accordingly, *aggregate* demand for good 1 at price p would then be equal to $2(\frac{1}{4}) + n(\frac{1}{2pn}) = \frac{1}{2} + \frac{1}{2p}$, so that this aggregate demand would be equal to the aggregate supply of good 1, which is equal to 1 if, and only if, the price p^* is equal to one. Then the competitive allocation resulting from this price obtains as

$$x_i^* = (\frac{1}{4}, \frac{1}{4}), i = 1, 2$$

$$= (\frac{1}{2n}, \frac{1}{2n}), i = 3, ..., n + 2. \tag{4.5}$$

Assume now that the number n is large so that each agent of type 2 appears as a 'negligible' trader, in the sense that he only owns a fairly insignificant fraction $\frac{1}{n}$ of the total market endowment in good 2. In contrast, traders 1 and 2 are still keeping a significant initial share of the total market endowment in good 1. Thus it seems natural to assume that the initial owners of good 2 behave competitively, while the two owners of good 1 want to manipulate the exchange rate between the two goods. Consequently, this situation evokes, in a multilateral exchange context, the asymmetric case studied by Cournot in the partial equilibrium framework he was considering, and immediately invites the transposition of his equilibrium concept to cover the multilateral exchange example we are considering.

To this end, we notice that, as in the Cournot model, we can easily derive a market demand function for good 1 by aggregating the first component of the individual demand vectors $x_i(p)$ corresponding to the small traders i, $i = 3, ..., n + 2$, namely

$$\sum_{i=1}^{n} \frac{1}{2pn} = \frac{1}{2p} \tag{4.6}$$

(see (4.4)). However, the main difference from the Cournot approach lies in the fact that potential buyers are no longer hidden behind the market demand function since the latter is explicitly derived from their individual preferences between the two goods, as is usual in general equilibrium analysis of consumers' demand. As we shall see later, this property can also be satisfied within a general exchange framework including an arbitrary number of goods and an arbitrary initial sharing of the quantities of these goods among traders.

Now it is easy to define a Cournot equilibrium for our example. If it is advantageous to them, the duopolists $i, i = 1, 2$, can manipulate the equilibrium exchange rate p by restricting their supply of good 1 to any amount y_i which is smaller or equal to their initial endowment quantity of this good (namely, $y_i \in \left[0, \frac{1}{2}\right]$), exactly as the Cournotian oligopolists restrict their market supply – compared with the competitive supply – in order to increase the equilibrium market price expressed in units of the numéraire commodity. Yet, in this approach, the payoffs of the duopolists have to be measured in utilities. Consider duopolist $i, i = 1, 2$. If he sends a share $y_i \in \left[0, \frac{1}{2}\right]$ of his initial endowment in good 1 to the market for this good, he obtains in exchange for it a quantity py_i of good 2 when the exchange rate between goods 1 and 2 is equal to p. Consequently, using the *supply strategy* y_i, duopolist i ends up with the bundle $(\frac{1}{2} - y_i,\, py_i)$ and reaches the utility level

$$U\left(\frac{1}{2} - y_i, py_i\right) = \left(\frac{1}{2} - y_i\right)(py_i). \qquad (4.7)$$

But, as in Cournot, duopolist i has a partial control over the equilibrium market price p via his supply strategy y_i since, by (4.6) and the equilibrium price assumption (point 3 above), this price must satisfy the market clearing condition:

$$\frac{1}{2p} = y_1 + y_2,$$

or

$$p(y_1, y_2) = \frac{1}{2(y_1 + y_2)}. \qquad (4.8)$$

Substituting (4.8) into (4.7), we obtain the *payoff* V_i of oligopolist i when he uses the supply strategy y_i and his rival the strategy y_k, $k \neq i$, namely

$$V_i(y_1, y_2) = \left(\frac{1}{2} - y_i\right)\frac{y_i}{2(y_1 + y_2)}. \qquad (4.9)$$

To determine the quantity which is optimal for duopolist i to send to the market, it is then sufficient to maximise V_i, given the quantity y_k supplied by his opponent $k, k \neq i$. Solving the problem for $i = 1$, we obtain the first-order necessary condition

$$y_2 - 2y_1^2 - 4y_1 y_2 = 0. \tag{4.10}$$

Similarly, for $i = 2$, we get

$$y_1 - 2y_2^2 - 4y_1 y_2 = 0. \tag{4.11}$$

Applying the Cournot non-coordination assumption (see point 4 above), and noting that the payoffs V_i are symmetric in y_1 and y_2, we get the Cournot equilibrium (y_1°, y_2°) as the simultaneous solution to the system formed by equations (4.10) and (4.11), namely

$$y_1^\circ = y_2^\circ = \frac{1}{6}. \tag{4.12}$$

Now we are able to spell out completely the *equilibrium outcome*, namely the allocation of goods resulting from this Cournot equilibrium in the multilateral exchange context introduced in our example. Corresponding to the supply equilibrium strategies defined by (4.12), the exchange price $p(y_1^\circ, y_2^\circ)$ is obtained as

$$p^\circ = p(y_1^\circ, y_2^\circ) = \frac{3}{2} \tag{4.13}$$

(see (4.8)). Substituting this equilibrium price and the supply strategies y_i° into the bundles $(1 - y_i^\circ, p\, y_i^\circ)$ obtained from using the strategies y_i°, both oligopolists end up with the same bundle of goods

$$x_i^\circ = (\frac{1}{3}, \frac{1}{4}), i = 1, 2. \tag{4.14}$$

Similarly, substituting the equilibrium price p° into the demand function $x_i(p)$ of the competitive small traders $i, i = 3, ..., n+2$, each of these small traders obtain the commodity bundle

$$x_i^\circ = (\frac{1}{3n}, \frac{1}{2n}), i = 3, ..., n+2. \tag{4.15}$$

It is useful to conclude the presentation of this example with the following two remarks. First, let us compare the allocation corresponding to the oligopoly equilibrium (see (4.14) and (4.15)) which we have just described, with the competitive allocation (4.5). We notice that the utility obtained by each duopolist at the Cournot outcome exceeds the utility they get at the competitive allocation, while the reverse is true for the small traders. This follows from the fact that, at the Cournot equilibrium, duopolists provide the market for good 1 with a smaller quantity than their competitive supply. The effect of this supply contraction is to raise the exchange rate between good 1 and good 2, which is equal to $\frac{3}{2}$ at the Cournot equilibrium, while it is equal to 1 at the competitive equilibrium. Consequently, we notice that the same phenomenon occurs in the strategic multilateral exchange context and in the Cournotian partial equilibrium approach: *agents endowed with market power contract their output supply in order to increase the relative value of it*, compared with their supply when they behave as price-takers.

Second, let us extend our example to the case of an *oligopoly*, by replicating our exchange economy in the same manner as we did in Part 1 in order to study the asymptotic behaviour of the core. Define the economy E_m as the mth replica of the economy considered above, say E_1, namely, the economy E_m includes $m(n+2)$ agents, with all agents sharing the same utility function $U(x^1, x^2) = x^1 x^2$. Among them, $2m$ agents (the oligopolists) have as initial endowment

$$\omega_{1j} = \omega_{2j} = (\frac{1}{2}, 0), j = 1, ..., m,$$

while the nm agents of type 2 have an initial endowment ω_{ij} defined by

$$\omega_{ij} = (0, \frac{1}{n}), j = 1, ..., m; i = 3, ..., n+2.$$

First, it is easy to check that the competitive equilibrium in the economy E_m is given by the allocation

$$x_{ij}^*(m) = (\frac{1}{4}, \frac{1}{4}), i = 1, 2; \; j = 1, \cdots, m;$$
$$= (\frac{1}{2n}, \frac{1}{2n}), i = 3, ..., n+2; \; j = 1, \cdots, m, \qquad (4.16)$$

and the competitive price $p^* = 1$ (again we normalise the price of commodity 2 to be equal to one). To identify the Cournot equilibrium in the economy E_m, we suppose that the $2m$ agents replicating the duopolists of the economy E_1 behave strategically while the nm agents who replicate the competitive sector of E_1 take the price p as given. We denote by y_{ij} the supply strategy of oligopolist $ij, i = 1, 2; j = 1, \cdots, m$. First we notice that the aggregate demand function of the competitive sector is now equal to $mn(x_i(p)) = (\frac{m}{2p}, \frac{m}{2})$. Furthermore, duopolist ij obtains, in exchange for y_{ij}, a quantity py_{ij} of good 2 when the exchange rate between the two goods is equal to p. Consequently, using the supply strategy y_{ij} gives him the bundle $(\frac{1}{2} - y_{ij}, py_{ij})$, so that he obtains the utility level

$$U(\frac{1}{2} - y_{ij}, py_{ij}) = (\frac{1}{2} - y_{ij})(py_{ij}). \qquad (4.17)$$

By the equilibrium price assumption (point 3 above), the corresponding exchange rate p must satisfy the market clearing condition

$$\frac{m}{2p} = \sum_{k=1}^{m} y_{1k} + \sum_{k=1}^{m} y_{2k},$$

or

$$p = \frac{m}{2(\sum_{k=1}^{m} y_{1k} + \sum_{k=1}^{m} y_{2k})}. \qquad (4.18)$$

Substituting (4.18) into (4.16), oligopolist ij obtains the bundle

$$\left(\frac{1}{2} - y_{ij}, \frac{my_{ij}}{2(\sum_{k=1}^{m} y_{1k} + \sum_{k=1}^{m} y_{2k})}\right), \tag{4.19}$$

and the resulting utility level is given by

$$
V_{ij}(y_{11},...,y_{1j}, ..., y_{1m}; y_{21}, ...y_{2m})
$$
$$
= \left(\frac{1}{2} - y_{ij}\right)\left(\frac{my_{ij}}{2(\sum_{k=1}^{m} y_{1k} + \sum_{k=1}^{m} y_{2k})}\right), i = 1, 2; j = 1, ..., m.
$$

Using the first-order necessary conditions, the Cournot equilibrium in the economy E_m obtains as the solution to the system

$$\frac{\partial V_{ij}}{\partial y_{ij}} = 0, i = 1, 2; j = 1, ..., m.$$

Since all the payoffs V_{ij} are symmetric in the occurence of y_{ij}, we can solve the above system by letting $y_{ij} = y, i = 1, 2; j = 1, ..., m$, and we get

$$y_{ij}^{\circ}(m) = \frac{2m - 1}{2(4m - 1)}. \tag{4.20}$$

The resulting equilibrium price $p^{\circ}(m)$ in E_m is then obtained as

$$p^{\circ}(m) = \frac{4m - 1}{2(2m - 1)}. \tag{4.21}$$

Substituting (4.20) and (4.21) into (4.16), each oligopolist ends up in E_m with the bundle of goods

$$x_{ij}^{\circ}(m) = (\frac{m}{4m - 1}, \frac{1}{4}), i = 1, 2; j = 1, \cdots, m. \tag{4.22}$$

Similarly, substituting (4.21) into the demand function of each small trader, each of them obtains in E_m the bundle

$$x_{ij}^\circ(m) = \left(\frac{2m-1}{n(4m-1)}, \frac{1}{2n}\right), i = 1, 2; j = 1, \cdots, m. \tag{4.23}$$

Expressions (4.22) and (4.23) spell out the allocation of goods in E_m resulting from the Cournot equilibrium supply strategies (4.20), while the corresponding price of good 1 is given by (4.21). If we consider now the *sequence* that these allocations form in the corresponding sequence of replica economies $\{E_m\}$, we observe that

$$\lim_{m\to\infty} \{x_{ij}^\circ(m)\} = \lim_{m\to\infty} \left\{\left(\frac{m}{4m-1}, \frac{1}{4}\right)\right\} = \left(\frac{1}{4}, \frac{1}{4}\right) = x_i^*, i = 1, 2,$$

(see (4.16)). Similarly, considering the sequence of equilibrium prices $\{p^\circ(m)\}$ in the economies E_m, we see that

$$\lim_{m\to\infty} \{p^\circ(m)\} = 1 = p^*.$$

Thus we conclude that, at least in our example, as in the one considered above in the partial equilibrium approach, the aggregate quantity supplied by the oligopolists tends to the competitive supply when the number of oligopolists tends to increase without limit, causing the resulting prices and allocations to converge to the competitive equilibrium of the economy E_1.

The treatment of the above example reveals firstly that there is no conceptual difficulty in casting the classical Cournot model into a general equilibrium framework. Even though this example encompasses only two goods, it satisfies the major property required from general equilibrium analysis: the model is closed and its solution does not depend on (often implicit) considerations of the type 'all other things being equal', which make partial analysis so vulnerable. Furthermore, the example also shows that the most popular property of the Cournot solution – its convergence to the competitive equilibrium when the number of oligopolists increases without limit – may also appear as an expected outcome in a general equilibrium framework. As we shall see in the next section, the use of this framework also allows us to dispense with the awkward asymmetry assumption (point 2 above) which was introduced by Cournot in partial equilibrium in order to represent the asymmetry between the number of buyers and the number of sellers.

4.3 AN EXTENSION OF THE EXAMPLE TO THE CASE OF SYMMETRIC STRATEGIC BEHAVIOUR

The asymmetry assumption (point 3 in Section 4.1) introduced by Cournot in his partial equilibrium model was justified, at least partially, because in several markets the number of sellers is rather small, compared with the number of potential buyers. Nonetheless, some product markets have few agents both on the buying side *and* the selling side. This is the case, for instance, for intermediate goods which are produced by a few firms, and utilised by the producers of a small number of final goods. These are situations of *bilateral oligopolies*, the extreme case of which consists of a market structure corresponding to a *bilateral monopoly*, with one firm on each side of the market. In such structures, there is no reason why strategic consciousness should be assumed only for those economic agents belonging to one particular side of the market: *all* agents should *a priori* be treated symmetrically and assumed to adopt a strategic behaviour. This is particularly true in the framework of multilateral exchange, in which goods are exchanged for goods: by its very nature, exchange implies that all agents are simultaneously buyers on some markets and sellers on others. As the following extension of the above example shows, there is no difficulty in dispensing with the asymmetry assumption when the exchange model is adopted.

Consider again an alternative version of the exchange economy defined above, which now assumes that there are $r + n$ oligopolists, $r \geq$

$2, n \geq 2$, with a number r among them owning $\frac{1}{r}$ units of commodity 1 and a number n owning $\frac{1}{n}$ units of commodity 2. As in the example above, we assume that all agents have the same utility function $U(x^1, x^2) = x^1 x^2$. Initial endowments are thus defined by

$$\omega_i = (\frac{1}{r}, 0), i = 1, ..., r$$
$$= (0, \frac{1}{n}), i = r + 1, ..., r + n.$$

The unique competitive allocation of this economy is easily derived as

$$x_i^* = (\frac{1}{2r}, \frac{1}{2r}), i = 1, ..., r$$
$$= (\frac{1}{2n}, \frac{1}{2n}), i = r + 1, ..., r + n$$

with the corresponding equilibrium price $p^* = 1$ for good 1 (we set the price of good 2 to be equal to one). Notice that, when $r = 2$, we obtain the particular duopolistic exchange economy considered in our initial example. Abandoning the asymmetry assumption used in the initial example (point 3 in Section 4.1), *we assume now that all agents are oligopolists and behave strategically*, that is, all agents of type 1 as well as type 2. In other words, agents of type 2 are also allowed to take advantage of the fact that each of them can manipulate the exchange rate between good 1 and good 2 by contracting his supply in good 2 by any amount $z_i, i \in \{r + 1, ..., r + n\}$, which is smaller or equal to his initial endowment of this good (namely, $z_i \in [0, \frac{1}{n}]$). In that case, he obtains in exchange for z_i a quantity of good 1 equal to $\frac{z_i}{p}$, and ends up accordingly with the bundle of goods

$$\left(\frac{z_i}{p}, \frac{1}{n} - z_i \right), \qquad (4.24)$$

with a corresponding utility level

$$U\left(\frac{z_i}{p}, \frac{1}{n} - z_i\right) = \frac{z_i}{p} \cdot \left(\frac{1}{n} - z_i\right). \tag{4.25}$$

As for an oligopolist i, $i = 1, ..., r$, owning commodity 1, who selects the supply strategy $y_i, y_i \in \left[0, \frac{1}{r}\right]$, he gets the bundle

$$\left(\frac{1}{r} - y_i, py_i\right) \tag{4.26}$$

and the corresponding utility level

$$U\left(\frac{1}{r} - y_i, py_i\right) = \left(\frac{1}{r} - y_i\right)py_i. \tag{4.27}$$

Consequently, given a $(r + n)$-tuple of supply strategies $(y_1, ..., y_r;$ $z_{r+1,...}, z_{r+n})$ corresponding to the $r + n$ oligopolists, the equilibrium price assumption (point 2 in Section 4.1) implies that the exchange rate p must satisfy the market clearing condition

$$\frac{1}{p} \sum_{k=r+1}^{r+n} z_k = \sum_{k=1}^{r} y_k$$

or

$$p = \frac{\sum_{k=r+1}^{r+n} z_k}{\sum_{k=1}^{r} y_k}. \tag{4.28}$$

We observe that the exchange rate (4.28) depends on the supply strategies of *all* agents, contrary to the exchange rate obtained in our first example (see (4.8)), which depended only on the strategies of the duopolists. Substituting (4.28) into (4.25) and (4.27), we obtain the payoffs, at the vector of strategies $(y_1, ..., y_r; z_{r+1,...}, z_{r+n})$, for each of the market participants, namely

$$V_i(y_1, ..., y_r; z_{r+1}, ..., z_{r+n}) = \left(\frac{1}{r} - y_i\right) \frac{\sum_{k=r+1}^{r+n} z_k}{\sum_{k=1}^{r} y_k} y_i \qquad (4.29)$$

for the oligopolists owning initially commodity 1 ($i \in \{1, ..., r\}$), and

$$V_i(y_1, ..., y_r; z_{r+1}, ..., z_{r+n}) = z_i \frac{\sum_{k=1}^{r} y_k}{\sum_{k=r+1}^{r+n} z_k} \left(\frac{1}{n} - z_i\right) \qquad (4.30)$$

for the oligopolists owning initially commodity 2 ($i \in \{r + 1, ..., r + n\}$). To determine the quantity of good 1 which is optimal for oligopolist $i \in \{1, ..., r\}$ to send to the market, it is sufficient to maximise (4.29) with respect to y_i. Similarly, the quantity of good 2 which is optimal for oligopolist $i \in \{r + 1, ..., r + n\}$ is obtained from maximising (4.30) with respect to z_i. Now we apply the Cournotian non-coordination assumption (point 4 in Section 4.1) and use the fact that payoffs are symmetric among the agents of type 1 as well as those of type 2, respectively. Simple calculations, applied to the first-order necessary conditions resulting from the above maximisation problems, reveal that, at the oligopoly equilibrium, we have

$$y_i^{\circ} = \frac{r - 1}{r(2r - 1)}, i = 1, ..., r \qquad (4.31)$$

and

$$z_i^{\circ} = \frac{(n - 1)}{n(2n - 1)}, i = r + 1, ..., r + n. \qquad (4.32)$$

Using (4.28), (4.31) and (4.32), the exchange rate p° between the two goods is given at equilibrium by

$$p^{\circ} = \frac{(n - 1)(2r - 1)}{(2n - 1)(r - 1)}. \qquad (4.33)$$

First we observe that, when we fix r to remain equal to 2 and let the number $n \to \infty$, the price obtained in (4.33) converges to the value $p^\circ = \frac{3}{2}$ identified in our first duopoly example (see (4.13)), where it was assumed that only the agents of type 1 behaved strategically while the agents of type 2 were supposed to behave as price-takers. This convergence reflects the following property. In spite *of the fact that type-2 agents are now assumed to behave strategically as well, they progressively lose their market power because the ownership of good 2 is spread over a larger and larger number of them in proportion as n increases, while the ownership of commodity 1 still remains concentrated between the two agents of type 1, since r remains fixed at the value $r = 2$.* It follows that each oligopolist of type 2 becomes 'negligible' when n becomes large: we are thus getting closer and closer to the asymmetric case analysed in our first duopolistic example. Accordingly, we can conclude that the assumption of behavioural asymmetry introduced by Cournot and formalised in this example, correctly approximates a situation in which *all* agents behaved strategically, but with one side of the bilateral market embodying a much larger number of oligopolists than the other. This should be contrasted with the result obtained when *both* the numbers r and n tend to infinity. In that case, we notice that the equilibrium price p° defined by (4.33) converges to 1, which is the competitive price, while the oligopolistic supplies y_i° and z_i° both tend to the competitive supply, which is equal to $\frac{1}{2}$ (see (4.31) and (4.32)): when the number of oligopolists *on each side* of the bilateral market is simultaneously increased, the oligopoly equilibrium now converges to the competitive equilibrium. This property of course portrays, for the *symmetric case*, the phenomenon which was already observed twice above under the Cournot asymmetric assumption. We shall now propose a general definition of oligopoly equilibrium introduced in Gabszewicz and Michel (1997) and using concepts directly borrowed from non-cooperative game theory.

4.4 A FORMAL DEFINITION OF OLIGOPOLY EQUILIBRIUM

Non-cooperative game theory constitutes the natural framework in which the Cournotian theory of markets should be formulated. The basic concepts which constitute this framework are the *players*, the *strategies* and the *payoffs*, which define together a *normal-form game*. The set of *players* $\{1, ..., i, ..., n\}$ is given *a priori*, as well as the set S_i of *strategies* available to player $i, i = 1, .., n$. The *payoff* of the game to player i is a real-valued function V_i defined on the cartesian product $\Pi_{i=1}^{n} S_i$. Intuitively, the function $V_i\left(s_1, ..., s_i, ..., s_n\right)$ expresses the payoff accruing to player i when he uses the strategy s_i, s_i in S_i, and players k use strategies $s_k, s_k \in S_k, k \neq i$. To denote this payoff we shall often use the notation $V_i(s_i, s_{-i})$, where s_{-i} denotes the $(n-1)$-vector of strategies used by players $k, k \neq i$. Given a normal-form game, a *non-cooperative equilibrium* of this game is an n-tuple $(s_1^\circ, .., s_i^\circ, .., s_n^\circ)$ of strategies such that, for all $i, = 1, .., n$, and all $s_i \in S_i$,

$$V_i(s_i, s_{-i}^\circ) \leq V_i(s_i^\circ, s_{-i}^\circ).$$

A non-cooperative equilibrium constitutes the natural strategic outcome of a game when players do not use any coordination device to select their strategies. Each player then individually selects a strategy which is a 'best response' to the vector of strategies selected by the other players, as measured by the value of the corresponding payoff. At a non-cooperative equilibrium, no player has an advantageous unilateral deviation from the strategy he has selected since none of them can increase his payoff $V_i(s_i^\circ, s_{-i}^\circ)$ by deviating from s_i° to any alternative strategy $s_i \in S_i$ while the other players k stick to their equilibrium strategies $s_k^\circ, k = 1, ..., n$.

To apply the above framework and concepts to multilateral exchange, we start from our usual definition of an exchange economy, as stated in Part 1. Consider such an exchange economy with ℓ goods $h, h = 1, \cdots, \ell$, and n agents (or traders) $i, i = 1, ..., n$, with utility functions

$U_i(x)$ – satisfying the assumptions (i)–(iv) listed in Part 1, p. 15 – and initial endowments ω_i, $\omega_i \in R_+^\ell$. Since the objective of each agent in the game is to manipulate equilibrium exchange prices to his best individual advantage by selecting a particular supply y^h on each market h, $h = 1, \cdots, \ell$, we identify the set S_i of strategies open to agent i with the set of all such supply strategies which are feasible for this agent, namely

$$S_i = \left\{(y^1, \cdots, y^h, \cdots, y^\ell) : 0 \le y^h \le \omega_i^h, h = 1, \cdots, \ell\right\}$$

or, using vector notation,

$$S_i = \{y : 0 \le y \le \omega_i\} : \tag{4.34}$$

agent i can supply whatever quantity y^h in market h he wishes as long as this quantity does not exceed his initial resources ω_i^h in good h.

Now let us assume that agent i, $i = 1, .., n$, has selected a strategy y_i in S_i, and consider a price system $p = (p^1, .., p^h, .., p^\ell)$, $p \ne 0$. Given y_i, the value of resources agent i has brought to the markets is equal to the scalar product $p \cdot y_i$. With this value he can buy in exchange any bundle x such that $p \cdot x \le p \cdot y_i$. Since he has 'kept at home' the bundle $\omega_i - y_i$, he will then end up with the bundle $\omega_i - y_i + x$ for consumption after trade. Accordingly, given p and y_i, the choice of x is dictated by the solution to the program

$$\max_x U_i(\omega_i - y_i + x) \tag{4.35}$$

$$\text{s.t. } p.x \le p.y_i$$
$$x \ge 0.$$

Let $x_i(p, y_i)$ be the solution to (4.35): by monotonicity, continuity and strict quasi-concavity of U_i, this solution exists and is unique. Now let us consider a *vector* of strategies $(y_1, \cdots, y_i, \cdots, y_n), y_i \in S_i, i = 1, \cdots, n$. Let $p(y_1, \cdots, y_i, \cdots, y_n)$ be a price system which clears all markets in the exchange economy in which traders i, $i = 1, ..., n$, are endowed with initial holdings y_i, that is, $p(y_1, .., y_i, .., y_n)$ solves

$$\sum_{i=1}^{n} x_i(p, y_i) = \sum_{i=1}^{n} y_i.$$

Standard assumptions guarantee the existence of a price system $p(y_1, .., y_i, .., y_n)$ for any n-tuple of strategies $(y_1, \cdots, y_i, \cdots, y_n)$, $y_i \in S_i$; we shall assume hereafter that this price system is unique. The payoff V_i of agent i, at the vector of strategies $(y_1, .., y_i, .., y_n)$, is then obtained as

$$V_i(y_i, y_{-i}) = U_i(\omega_i - y_i + x_i(p(y_1, .., y_i, .., y_n))).$$

Notice that, in the particular case in which, for all $i, i = 1, \cdots, n$, $y_i = 0$, no trade can occur since no agent has sent a positive amount of any good to the markets for trade. Then each agent necessarily ends up with his initial endowment and consumes as in an 'autarky'. Consequently we define the corresponding payoff at the n-tuple of strategies $(0, \cdots, 0, \cdots, 0)$ by

$$V_i(0, \cdots, 0, \cdots, 0) = U_i(\omega_i).$$

Finally, we define an *oligopoly equilibrium* as an n-tuple $(y_1^\circ, \cdots, y_i^\circ, \cdots, y_n^\circ), y_i^\circ \in S_i$, such that, for all $i = 1, \cdots, n$ and for all $y_i \in S_i$,

$$V_i(y_i, y_{-i}^\circ) \le V_i(y_i^\circ, y_{-i}^\circ).$$

At an oligopoly equilibrium, each trader i selects his supply on each market h in such a way that, given the supplies chosen by the other traders, no unilateral deviation from his choice at equilibrium can increase his utility, taking into account the impact of such a deviation on the resulting equilibrium price vector.

Among the four assumptions (points 1–4 in Section 4.1) underlying the Cournot proposal, the generalisation of his equilibrium notion which has just been proposed still relies on two of them (equilibrium price assumption, non-coordination), while the two remaining ones (partial equilibrium, asymmetry) have now disappeared. It must be emphasised however that one could easily reintroduce asymmetry – as in the duopoly example considered in Section 4.2 – simply by restricting adequately the strategy sets available to some agents. For example, in this duopoly example, let us assume that the strategy sets S_i' of the duopolists i, $i = 1, 2$ are defined by

$$S_i' = \left\{ (y^1, y^2) : 0 \le y^1 \le \frac{1}{2}; y^2 = 0 \right\},$$

and by

$$S_i' = \left\{ (0, \frac{1}{n}) \right\}$$

for the 'negligible' agents $i = 3, \cdots, n + 2$. In other words, we allow the duopolists to send to the market for good 1 whatever amount they wish, so long as it does not exceed their initial endowment in this good, while we restrict the strategy set of the negligible traders solely to their *whole* initial endowment in good 2. It is easy to understand that this restriction imposed on their strategy sets forces them to adopt a competitive behaviour: they are unable to manipulate the market exchange rate by restricting their supply of good 2 since their whole endowment in this good must be sent to the market. It is easy to check that the oligopoly equilibrium of the game in which the strategy sets of the agents are S_i', coincides with the oligopoly equilibrium we have identified in Section 4.2. By contrast, the Cournot equilibrium in the example considered in Section 4.3, corresponds exactly to the general definition of oligopoly equilibrium which has just been proposed since, in this example, all agents are treated symmetrically: *all* of them are allowed to send to the market whatever amount they wish, insofar as it does not exceed their initial endowment in the corresponding good. This shows how flexible the above definition of an oligopoly equilibrium is. According to the restriction imposed on the strategy sets of the agents, several forms of oligopolistic contexts considered in partial equilibrium can be captured by this definition. The example in Section 4.2 corresponds to the context of *homogeneous oligopoly*, since all oligopolists sell the *same* commodity to the competitive sector. The example in Section 4.3 corresponds to the case of *bilateral oligopoly*. Even the context of *competitive markets* can be viewed as a particular case of the above formulation. Consider indeed a given exchange economy and the game in which the strategy set S_i of each trader reduces to the singleton $\{\omega_i\}$. Then, given a price system p, problem (4.35) now reduces necessarily to $\max_x U_i(\omega_i - \omega_i + x)$ subject to $p \cdot x \leq p \cdot \omega_i$, so that its solution $x_i(p, \omega_i)$ coincides with the Walrasian demand at p. Accordingly, the price system $p(\omega_1, \cdots, \omega_i, .., \omega_n)$, which solves

$$\sum_{i=1}^{n} x_.(p, \omega_i) = \sum_{i=1}^{n} \omega_i,$$

is a competitive price system, and the resulting allocation which assigns the vector $x_i(p(\omega_1, \cdots, \omega_i, \cdots, \omega_n))$ to agent $i, i = 1, \cdots, n$, is a competitive allocation. It follows that the n-tuple $(\omega_1, \cdots, \omega_i, \cdots, \omega_n)$ is the only oligopoly equilibrium of the game, with the competitive allocation as outcome, when the strategy set of each agent coincides with his initial endowment. This is a totally expected result since, with this restriction, no strategic freedom is offered to traders with a view to influencing the equilibrium price by manipulation of their individual supplies.

In the next chapter, we examine the problem of the existence of an oligopoly equilibrium. Unfortunately, as will become apparent soon, this problem is difficult and far from being solved. We shall try however to pave the way for those who could be tempted to tackle this open question in a more thorough way.

5. The existence problem

5.1 THE NOTION OF AUTARKIC EQUILIBRIUM

When defining the payoffs in the exchange game leading to the definition of an oligopoly equilibrium, we have explicitly considered the possibility that all traders might simultaneously use the strategy $y_i = 0$, in which case the payoff of each of them is equal to $U_i(\omega_i)$. Consider then the n-tuple of strategies $(0, .., 0, .., 0)$, and assume that one of the agents – say, agent i – deviates unilaterally from the strategy $y_i = 0$ to an alternative strategy $y_i' \in S_i$. Then at least one of the coordinates of y_i', say $y_i'^h$, is strictly larger than zero, which means that, for at least good h, trader i supplies the market with a strictly positive amount of it. However, since no other trader has sent a positive amount of any good to the market – remember that $y_k = 0$ for all $k \neq i$ – trader i does not obtain anything in exchange for this amount of good h, so that he ends up with the commodity bundle $\omega_i - y_i'$ and a utility level $U_i(\omega_i - y_i') < U_i(\omega_i)$, where the last equality follows from strict monotonicity of U_i. It follows from the above reasoning that no unilateral deviation from the strategy $y_i = 0$ can be profitable for any trader, when the others have selected the same strategy and stuck to it. This proves that the n-tuple of strategies $(0, \cdots, 0, \cdots, 0)$ is an oligopoly equilibrium. We call it the *autarkic equilibrium*.

This simple above reasoning reveals that there always exists at least one oligopoly equilibrium, namely, the autarkic one, at which no trade occurs. Let us show that there are at least two circumstances in which the autarkic equilibrium is the *only* equilibrium. The first circumstance corresponds to the case of an exchange economy with two commodities and two traders, as in the example in Section 4.3, with $r = n = 1$. Without loss of generality, let $\omega_1 = (\omega_1^1, 0)$ and $\omega_2 = (0, \omega_2^2)$, and denote by U_i the utility function of trader $i, i = 1, 2$. Then, given a pair of strategies $(y_1, y_2), y_1 \in S_1 = \left[0, \omega_1^1\right], y_2 \in S_2 = \left[0, \omega_2^2\right]$, and a price p for commodity 1 (we normalise $p^2 = 1$), the bundle obtained by trader 1 (2) is $(1 - y_1, py_1)$ $((\frac{y_2}{p}, 1 - y_2)$ for trader 2). Furthermore, since p must satisfy the equilibrium condition

$$py_1 = y_2,$$

the bundles rewrite as $(1 - y_1, y_2)$ for trader 1 and $(y_1, 1 - y_2)$ for trader 2, with corresponding payoffs

$$V_1(1 - y_1, y_2) = U_1 \left(1 - y_1, y_2\right)$$

for trader 1, and

$$V_2(y_1, 1 - y_2) = U_2 \left(y_1, 1 - y_2\right)$$

for trader 2. Since U_i is monotone in $y_i, i = 1, 2$, it is clear that V_i reaches its maximal value for $y_i = 0$, whatever the value of $y_{k,}, k \neq i$. Consequently, the vector $(0, 0)$ is an oligopoly equilibrium, and it is the only one.

The second circumstance in which the autarkic equilibrium is the only equilibrium corresponds to the case of an exchange economy in which the initial allocation of the commodities among traders is Pareto-optimal. By the very definition of Pareto-optimality, no agent can gain in utility by deviating unilaterally from his initial endowment if the initial allocation of the goods is Pareto-optimal, which makes the n-tuple of strategies $(0, \cdots, 0, \cdots, 0)$ an oligopoly equilibrium. Now suppose that there was another oligopoly equilibrium $(y_1^\circ, \cdots, y_i^\circ, \cdots, y_n^\circ)$ with at least some y_i° different from 0. Let $p(y_1^\circ, \cdots, y_i^\circ, \cdots, y_n^\circ)$ be the price system for which $\sum_{k=1}^{n} x_k(p(y_1^\circ, \cdots, y_i^\circ, \cdots, y_n^\circ)) = \sum_{k=1}^{n} y_k^\circ$, with, for all k, $x_k(p(y_1^\circ, \cdots, y_i^\circ, \cdots, y_n^\circ))$ maximising $U_k((\omega_k - y_k^\circ + x)$ subject to $p \cdot x \leq p \cdot y_k^\circ$. At the allocation of goods which assigns the bundle $(\omega_k - y_k^\circ + x_k(p(y_1^\circ, \cdots, y_i^\circ, \cdots, y_n^\circ)))$ to trader $k, k = 1, .., n$, at least one trader k reaches a utility level smaller than $U_k(\omega_k)$, for otherwise, the initial allocation of the goods would not have been Pareto-optimal. However this trader can reach this utility level by playing $y_k = 0$, so that there exists for trader k an advantageous deviation from y_k°, namely $y_k = 0$, and we obtain the desired contradiction.

We may summarise the above comments in the following way. First, there always exists an oligopoly equilibrium, the autarkic one. In two particular cases, it is the only one. Unfortunately, these two cases are not very interesting since, in the case of the two goods-two agents, the strategic context of exchange is degenerate due to the fact that the quantity of the good received by a trader must necessarily, as a consequence of the equilibrium price assumption, be equal to the quantity that his *alter ego* has decided to send to the market. As for the case of an initial allocation which is Pareto-optimal, the fact that this allocation is also the outcome of a Nash equilibrium at which no market exists, is not very interesting either: no gains from trade can in any case be realised at a Pareto-optimal allocation. In conclusion, the problem of the existence of an oligopoly equilibrium should be reformulated in the following manner: *is there always an oligopoly equilibrium which differs from the autarkic one, in any exchange economy including at least three traders and in which, given the initial allocation of the goods among these traders, there are some potential gains from trade?* Unfortunately, as shown by Cordella and Gabszewicz (1998), the answer to this question is negative.

5.2 A COUNTEREXAMPLE TO THE EXISTENCE OF AN OLIGOPOLY EQUILIBRIUM

Consider an exchange economy consisting of n traders, falling into two types, with $\frac{n}{2}$ of each type; there are two goods and we normalise the price of good 2 to be equal to one. For traders i, $i = 1, \cdots, \frac{n}{2}$, preferences and endowments are defined by

$$U_i(x^1 x^2) = \beta x^1 + x^2; \omega_i = (1, 0);$$

similarly, for traders i, $i = \frac{n}{2} + 1, \cdots, n$, we have

$$U_i(x^1 x^2) = x^1 + \beta x^2; \omega_2 = (0, 1)$$

with $0 < \beta < 1$. This exchange economy has a unique competitive equilibrium given by $p^* = (1, 1)$ and the allocation

$$x_i^* = (0, 1), i = 1, .., \frac{n}{2}$$
$$= (1, 0), i = \frac{n}{2} + 1, .., n.$$

Now consider the associated game with strategy sets defined by

$$S_i = \left\{ (y_i^1, y_i^2) : 0 \le y_i^1 \le 1; y_i^2 = 0 \right\}$$

for $i = 1, .., \frac{n}{2}$, and by

$$S_i = \left\{ (z_i^1, z_i^2) : z_i^1 = 0; 0 \le z_i^2 \le 1 \right\}$$

for $i = \frac{n}{2} + 1, .., n$. Given an n-tuple of strategies, with $(y_i^1, y_i^2) \in S_i$, $i = 1, .., \frac{n}{2}$, and $(z_i^1, z_i^2) \in S_i$, $i = \frac{n}{2} + 1, .., n$, the price of good 1 is obtained as

$$p^1 = \frac{\sum_{k=\frac{n}{2}+1}^{n} z_k^2}{\sum_{k=1}^{\frac{n}{2}} y_k^1},$$

with corresponding payoffs

$$V_i(y_i^1, y_i^2) = \beta(1 - y_i^1) + y_i^1 \frac{\sum_{k=\frac{n}{2}+1}^{n} z_k^2}{\sum_{k=1}^{n} y_k^1} \tag{5.1}$$

for $i = 1, .., \frac{n}{2}$ and

$$V_i(z_i^1, z_i^2) = z_i^2 \frac{\sum_{k=1}^{\frac{n}{2}} y_k^1}{\sum_{k=\frac{n}{2}+1}^{n} z_k^2} + \beta(1 - z_i^2) \tag{5.2}$$

for $i = \frac{n}{2} + 1, .., n$.

By the symmetry of the problem and the first-order necessary and sufficient conditions, it is easy to check that the only possible candidate for an oligopoly equilibrium, *with the exception of the autarkic one*, consists of the n-tuple of strategies where each trader sells the whole amount of the good he is initially endowed with, with the competitive allocation as outcome. Suppose that all agents $k, k = 1, .., \frac{n}{2}$, play $(y_k^1, y_k^2) = (1, 0)$ and all agents k, $k = \frac{n}{2} + 1, .., n$, play $(z_k^1, z_k^2) = (0, 1)$. Select an agent $i, i \in \{1, .., \frac{n}{2}\}$, and assume that he considers a unilateral deviation from the strategy $(1, 0)$. From (5.1), we notice that

$$\frac{\partial V_i}{\partial y_i^1} = \frac{(\sum_{k=\frac{n}{2}+1}^{n} z_k^2)(\sum_{k=1}^{\frac{n}{2}} y_k^1 - y_i^1)}{(\sum_{k=1}^{\frac{n}{2}} y_k^1)^2} - \beta \geq 0 \Leftrightarrow \beta \leq \frac{n-2}{n}, \tag{5.3}$$

with $(y_k^1, y_k^2) = (1, 0), k = 1, .., \frac{n}{2}, k \neq i$, and $(z_k^1, z_k^2) = (0, 1)$, $k = \frac{n}{2} + 1, .., n$, so that (5.3) is a necessary and sufficient condition for $(1, 0)$ to be a best reply from the viewpoint of agent $i \in \{1, .., \frac{n}{2}\}$. Using (5.2), the same condition applies for an agent $i \in \{\frac{n}{2} + 1, .., n\}$, so that (5.3) is a necessary and sufficient condition for the n-tuple of strategies where each agent sells his whole endowment to be an oligopoly equilibrium. *Therefore, the exchange game defined above has the autarkic equilibrium as a unique oligopoly equilibrium when* $\frac{n-2}{n} < \beta$. Hence, as stated above, we have identified an exchange economy including more than two traders in which there exists no oligopoly equilibrium which differs from the autarkic one, in spite of the fact that the initial allocation of the goods among these traders allows for considerable potential gains from trade.

Of course, the above example exhibits linear utility functions which do not satisfy the usual assumptions of strict quasi-concavity and strict monotonicity. Nevertheless, this example can be extended to the case in which agents have strictly quasi-concave and monotone utility functions. In the above example, rewriting the condition $\beta > \frac{n-2}{n}$ as $1 - \beta < \frac{2}{n}$, we observe that the left-hand side of this inequality measures the difference between the equilibrium price ($p = 1$) and the marginal rate of substitution between the good the agents own and the good they can obtain in the market (β), i.e. the gains from trading at any 'type-symmetric' allocation. The right-hand side measures the gains from manipulating prices at such an allocation ($\frac{2}{n} = y_i^1(\frac{\partial p}{\partial y_i^1}) = z_i^2(\frac{\partial p}{\partial z_i^2})$). With linear utility functions, the marginal rate of substitution is constant and can thus be evaluated at any type-symmetric allocation. When we try to extend the example to exchange economies with *non-linear* quasi-concave utility functions, a condition analogous to the one obtained in the above example can be identified. As before, this condition compares the marginal rate of substitution between the goods at the autarkic equilibrium with the agents' ability to manipulate prices, which is constant at any type-symmetric allocation. To confirm this, consider the following extension of the example. There are again two goods and n traders falling into two types, with $\frac{n}{2}$ of each type. But now, let $U_i(x^1, x^2)$ be utility functions representing the preferences of type-i traders, $i = 1, 2$, and assume that: (i) U_i is increasing, quasi-concave, strictly monotone, and twice differentiable; (ii) the marginal rate of substitution between goods 1 and 2 is defined everywhere in R_+^2; (iii) for any point (z^1, z^2) in R_+^2, $U_i(z^1, z^2) = U_i(z^2, z^1)$. Finally, the initial endowment of type-1 traders is given by $\omega_1 = (1, 0)$ and the initial endowment of type-2 traders by $\omega_2 = (0, 1)$. For this extension of the example, it can be proved that, *when the marginal rate of substitution between the two goods for type-1 traders exceeds* $\frac{n-2}{n}$ *at* $\omega_1 = (1,0)$, *the only oligopoly equilibrium is the autarkic one* (see Cordella and Gabszewicz 1998). This shows that the counterexample to the existence of an oligopoly equilibrium provided in this section is not pathological since it can easily be extended to fall into the category of exchange economies satisfying the usual assumptions on preferences. In fact, it is not surprising that existence does not follow easily from very general assumptions on the economy. Even in partial analysis, the existence of a Cournot equilibrium cannot be established in full generality and requires a bundle of specific assumptions. One should not be astonished that such specific assumptions have also to be accepted if one wishes to establish the existence of a Cournot equilibrium in a general equilibrium approach. In fact, this constitutes an open field for future research in this area. The only positive result concerning the existence of an oligopoly equilibrium has been established by Bonnisseau and Florig (2000) in the framework of *linear* exchange economies.

5.3 OLIGOPOLY EQUILIBRIUM AND LINEAR EXCHANGE ECONOMIES

Consider a linear exchange economy, namely, an exchange economy in which the utility function of agent i is specified as

$$U_i(x) = b_i \cdot x$$

for some given vector $b_i \in R^\ell_{++}$. An example of a linear exchange economy is provided in the preceding section, with $b_i = (\beta, 1)$ for i =1,..., $\frac{n}{2}$, and $b_i = (1, \beta)$ for $i = \frac{n}{2} + 1, ..., n$. Given an n-tuple of strategies $(y_1, ..., y_i, ...y_n)$, problem (4.35) takes in this case the particular form

$$\max_x b_i \cdot (\omega_i - y_i + x)$$

s.t. $p \cdot x \leq p \cdot y_i$ and $x \geq 0$. Then it follows from Gale (1976) that there exists a non-empty set of equilibrium price vectors such that the n-tuple of solutions $x_i(p, y_i)$ to the above problems forms a competitive equilibrium with any of these price vectors in the exchange economy having the vectors y_i as initial endowments. Even if the equilibrium price vector p does not need to be unique, the corresponding utility levels $V_i(y_i, y_{-i})$ are unique however, with

$$V_i(y_i, y_{-i}) = b_i \cdot (\omega_i - y_i) + y_i \cdot \max_{h=1,..,\ell} \left\{ \frac{b_{ih}}{p_h} \right\}$$

for any price vector p with which the vectors $x_i(p, y_i)$, $i = 1, ..., n$ define a competitive equilibrium.

We now proceed as in Part 1, and replicate the basic economy E_1, which was just described, by defining, for each integer k, the economy E_k as follows. In the economy E_k, there are nk agents divided into n groups of k identical agents. Each agent of the ith group has the same characteristics b_i, ω_i as agent i in the economy E_1. Finally, let us introduce the notion of *regular initial endowments*, as defined by Bonnisseau and Florig (2000) for the case of linear exchange economies. The initial endowments $\omega_1, ..., \omega_i, ..., \omega_n$ are *regular* when the corresponding equilibrium price vector p is unique and, if for some competitive allocation $(x_1, .., x_i, .., x_n)$ and for all $h \in \left\{ h : \frac{b_{iih}}{p_h} = \max_{k=1,..,l} \left\{ \frac{b_{ik}}{p^k} \right\} \right\}$, we have

$$x_{ih} > 0.$$

The example considered in Section 5.2 involves regular initial endowments. In fact, Bonnisseau, Florig and Jofré (1997a,b) have shown that the set of regular initial endowments is open, dense and of full Lebesgue measure in $(R_+^\ell)^n$. Bonnisseau and Florig (2000) then prove the following:

Proposition 5.1.

If the initial endowments $\omega_1, ..., \omega_i, ..., \omega_n$ are regular, then there exists an integer k_o such that, for every $k \geq k_o$, the vector of strategies $(\omega_1, ..., \omega_i, ..., \omega_n)$ is an oligopoly equilibrium of the economy E_k.

This proposition shows that, if the exchange economy is finite but sufficiently large (depending on the basic data of its definition, endowments and preferences), price-taking behaviour leads to an oligopoly equilibrium. The strength of this result follows precisely from the fact that it is based on the fundamentals of the economy, and not on some untestable assumptions, like the assumption of strict-quasi concavity of the payoff functions. Considering linear utility functions only is, without any doubt, a very strong assumption. Nevertheless, it constitutes a large class of exchange economies which can be viewed as a first approximation of standard exchange economies in which utility functions are assumed to be strictly quasi-concave. On the other hand, the assumption of regularity of endowments is very mild since almost every vector of initial endowments satisfies it. Furthermore, it may seem a little strange to prove the non-emptiness of the oligopoly equilibrium set by showing that it contains in particular the vector of strategies having as outcome a competitive allocation. This method however has its tradition: it has already been used by K. Roberts (1980) in another, but related context. On the other hand, nothing precludes other oligopoly equilibria from existing which differ from the one leading to the competitive outcome. In particular we know that this is always true for the autarkic equilibrium, which belongs to the set of oligopoly equilibria in all replicas $E_k, k = 1, 2, ...$

The above proposition is best illustrated using our example in Section 5.2. As stated above, this example satisfies the assumption of regular initial endowments. Assume that $\beta = \frac{3}{4}$, so that, when $n = 4$, $\frac{n-2}{n} = \frac{1}{2} < \beta = \frac{3}{4}$. Consequently, the only oligopoly equilibrium in the economy E_1, consisting of two agents of each type, is the autarkic equilibrium. This, however, is no longer true in the economy E_2 consisting of *four* agents of each type since then we obtain

$$\frac{n-2}{n} = \frac{3}{4} = \beta,$$

so that the necessary and sufficient condition (5.3) is now fulfilled. Consequently, in this economy, as well as in all economies $E_k, k > 2 = k_0$, the strategies $(1,0) = w_i$, for $i = 1, .., \frac{n}{2}$, and $(0,1) = w_i$, for $i = \frac{n}{2} + 1, .., n$, leading to the competitive outcome, also constitute an oligopoly equilibrium, as predicted by Proposition 5.1.

5.4 A LIMIT THEOREM

Starting with a replication procedure analogous to the one used several times above, Lahmandi-Ayed (2001) proves that, under standard assumptions, a sequence of symmetric oligopoly equilibria of a replicated exchange economy necessarily leads to a competitive equilibrium of the basic economy. This confirms the observation which was made through the various examples considered above, and already noted by Cournot in the framework of partial equilibrium. The basic economy E_1 is a pure exchange economy with ℓ goods $h, h = 1, ..., \ell$ and n agents, $i = 1, ..., n$ each represented by his initial endowment $\omega_i \in R_+^\ell$ and his utility function U_i. The usual assumptions on the functions U_i are satisfied. The replicated economy E_k contains nk agents. There are k agents of each type i, with the same utility function U_i, the same initial endowment ω_i and the same strategy space $Y_i = \{y : 0 \leq y \leq \omega_i\}$. In the economy E_k, a *symmetric nk-tuple of strategies* is an nk-tuple $(y_{11}^k, .., y_{1k}^k; ...; y_{n1}^k, .., y_{nk}^k)$ of strategies such that all agents of the same type play the same strategy, i.e $y_{ij}^k = y_{ih}^k, j \neq h$. Let $\{(y_{11}^k, .., y_{1k}^k; ...y_{n1}^k, .., y_{nk}^k)\}$ be any sequence of nk-tuple of strategies which are symmetric and form oligopoly equilibria in the successive economies E_k. Denote by y_i^k the vector $\frac{1}{k} \sum_{j=1}^k y_{ik}^k$; and let $\{[p(y_1^k, ..., y_n^k); (x_1^k, .., x_n^k)]\}$ be the corresponding sequence of outcomes giving the prices and allocations associated with these equilibria.

Proposition 5.2.

The sequence $\left\{ \left[p(y_1^k, ..., y_n^k); (x_1^k, .., x_n^k) \right] \right\}$ converges to an outcome

$[p(y_1, ..., y_n); (x_1, .., x_n)]$ which is the competitive equilibrium of the economy E_1.

Notice that this proposition ensures the convergence of the price allocations corresponding to the oligopoly equilibria of the successive economies without ensuring the convergence of the *strategies* corresponding to these oligopoly equilibria. Notice also that convergence is proved only for symmetric equilibria. In the case of asymmetric equilibria, as the economy is replicated, the dimension of the price-allocations space increases unboundedly, making it difficult to link these magnitudes to those of the basic economy. In the next chapter, we study several applications of the concept of oligopoly equilibrium, borrowed from trade theory, intertemporal economics and public economics.

6. Economic applications

6.1 COMPARATIVE ADVANTAGE AND OLIGOPOLY EQUILIBRIUM

As a preliminary economic application of the concept of oligopoly equilibrium, we study the problem of *comparative advantage* in the pure Ricardian model of international trade (Ricardo 1848,1951). The simplicity of this model, and the clarity of its conclusions, have often obscured the fact that they rest on the assumption of a *competitive* world market. In particular, the question has not been raised whether the use of market power by economic agents on the world market would alter the predictions of Ricardian theory or the extent to which this might happen. The concept of an oligopoly equilibrium introduced above allows a precise formulation of this question: what happens with the principle of comparative advantage when, contrary to the competitive assumption, economic units perceive the influence of their individual supply on the world equilibrium exchange rate of goods, and make strategic use of it? Even if we do not provide a full answer to this problem, the following example, formulated in a very Ricardian framework (two-country, two-commodity case, with a single productive factor, labour, and linear technologies), sheds some light on its complexity (this example is based on Cordella and Gabszewicz 1998).

We consider two countries $i = 1, 2$ with n agents in each country, $n \geq 2$. The whole analysis below could go through without assuming an equal number of agents in each country. However, assuming different numbers of agents in countries 1 and 2 does not add anything to our purpose, but complicates notations. Accordingly, we have preferred to stick to the assumption that $n_1 = n_2 = n$. There are two consumption goods, x^1 and x^2, produced by labour; each agent is endowed with one unit of labour, irrespective of the country. All agents $1j$, $j = 1, \cdots, n$, in country 1 have access to the same production frontier in R^2_+ defined by the locus $\{(a_{11}y_{1j}, a_{12}(1 - y_{1j})) \mid y_{1j} \in [0, 1]\}$ where y_{1j} is the quantity of labour assigned by the agent $1j$ to the production of good 1. Similarly, all agents $2j$, $j = 1, \cdots, n$, in country 2 can produce any pair of the two goods $(a_{21}y_{2j}, a_{22}(1 - y_{2j}))$, where y_{2j} denotes the quantity of labour assigned by the agent $2j$ to the production of good 1. Without loss of generality, we shall suppose that the agents in country 1 have a comparative advantage in the production of good 1,

$$\frac{a_{11}}{a_{12}} > \frac{a_{21}}{a_{22}}. \tag{6.1}$$

We suppose also that $a_{11} > 0$, $a_{12} > 0$, $a_{21} > 0$, $a_{22} > 0$. Finally we assume that the agents in each country are only interested in consuming the good when they have a comparative *disadvantage* in its production. The utility function U_{1j} of an agent $1j$ in country 1 is thus defined by

$$U_{1j}(x^1, x^2) = x^2, \qquad j = 1, \cdots, n$$

and the utility function U_{2j} of an agent $2j$ in country 2 by

$$U_{2j}(x^1, x^2) = x^1, \quad j = 1, \cdots, n.$$

Clearly these preferences generate the largest incentives to organise trade between the two countries, since the citizens of each of them prefer precisely that commodity which the citizens of the other country produce more efficiently.

Among the Ricardian competitive economies $(a_{11}, a_{12}, a_{21}, a_{22})$ compatible with (6.1), three cases have to be considered. In the first, the agents of country 1 have an absolute advantage in the production of good 1 and those in country 2 in the production of good 2. Then $a_{11} > a_{21}$ and $a_{22} > a_{12}$. Figure 6.1 depicts this situation, and the corresponding competitive equilibrium.

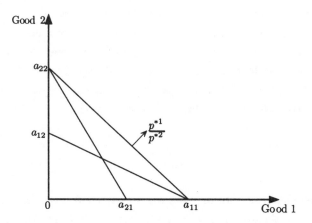

Figure 6.1

In this case, it is clear that the equilibrium world price ratio $\frac{p^{*1}}{p^{*2}}$ is given by the slope of the line $a_{22}a_{11}$ so that all agents in each country specialise completely in the production of the good in which they have an absolute advantage, i.e. $y_{1j}^* = 1, j = 1, \cdots, n$, and $y_{2j}^* = 0, j = 1, \cdots, n$, with corresponding production plans $(na_{11}, 0)$ in country 1 and $(0, na_{22})$ in country 2, where y_{ij}^* denotes the quantity of labour assigned to the production of good 1 at the competitive equilibrium. Then exchange takes place at the price ratio $\frac{p^{*1}}{p^{*2}}$, and each agent $1j$ $(2j)$ in country 1 (country 2) gets a_{22} (a_{11}) of good 2 (good 1) at equilibrium.

In the second case, each agent $2j$ in country 2 has an absolute advantage in the production of both goods, even if the agents $1j$ in country 1 still have a comparative advantage in the production of good 1. Then $a_{21} > a_{11}$ and $a_{22} > a_{12}$. This case is covered by Figure 6.2.

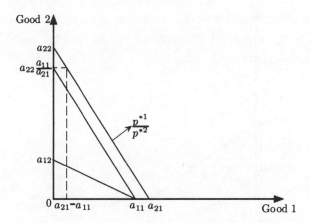

Figure 6.2

Then the terms of trade $\frac{p^{*1}}{p^{*2}}$ are given by the slope of the line $a_{22}a_{21}$. At this world exchange price, each individual $1j$ in country 1 chooses $y_{1j}^* = 1$ and again specialises completely in the production of good 1. With the resulting revenue, agent $1j$ can buy the amount $a_{22} \cdot \frac{a_{11}}{a_{21}}$ of good 2. As for the agents $2j$ in country 2, all production plans on their production frontier lead to the same revenue but, if we restrict ourselves to symmetric supplies, the choice of $y_{2j}^* = 1 - \frac{a_{11}}{a_{21}}$ by all agents $2j$ is the sole means of balancing supply and demand for good 2 at the world equilibrium price, $na_{22}(1 - y_{2j}^*) = a_{22}\frac{a_{11}}{a_{21}}n$. With the corresponding revenue, all agents $2j$ buy an amount a_{11} of good 1 and consume a_{21} of the same good so that, in aggregate, supply equals demand on both markets.

Finally, consider the case in which each agent $1j$ in country 1 has an absolute advantage in the production of both goods as depicted on Figure 6.3. Then the competitive world price is given by the slope of the line $a_{12}a_{11}$; now the agents in country 2 fully specialise in the production of good 2, so that $y_{2j}^* = 0$, $j = 1, \cdots, n$, while the agents in country 1 choose $y_{1j}^* = \frac{a_{22}}{a_{12}}$.

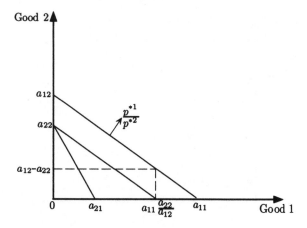

Figure 6.3

In the preceding analysis, the agents in both countries consider that the terms of trade are not under their control. They take the world price as given when they make their production decision. By contrast, and in line with the concept of oligopoly equilibrium, we shall now assume that they are aware of the influence of their individual supply on the equilibrium exchange rate of goods. Since their revenue, and thus their purchasing power as consumers, depends on this real exchange rate, they should take it into account when making their production decision. But the influence of each agent on the world price is only partial. All the other agents in both countries compete with him in the same manner on the world market. Accordingly, the equilibrium notion must reflect this complex system of rivalry among the producers of both countries. We shall be interested in a situation in which their supplies in both goods yield an oligopoly equilibrium in the game where each of them aims at influencing the world exchange rate to his own advantage. Now, as usual, let us define this game precisely. A *strategy* of an agent ij is a quantity $y_{ij}, y_{ij} \in [0, 1]$, of labour he decides to assign to the production of good 1. Notice that this quantity determines the quantity of both goods he supplies on the exchange market. Let each agent ij choose a strategy y_{ij} and consider an exchange rate $\frac{p^1}{p^2} = p^1$ on the world market. We normalise $p^2 = 1$. The revenue of an agent $1j$ in country 1 is given by

$$p^1 a_{11} y_{1j} + a_{12}(1 - y_{1j}), \qquad j = 1, \cdots, n$$

and by

$$p^1 a_{21} y_{2j} + a_{22}(1 - y_{2j}), \qquad j = 1, \cdots, n$$

for an agent $2j$ in country 2. Accordingly, at a price p^1 on the world market, agent $1j$ in country 1 maximises his utility when spending his total income on good 2, so that the corresponding utility U_{1j} is given by

$$U_{1j}(0, x^2) = p^1 a_{11} y_{1j} + a_{12}(1 - y_{1j}). \qquad (6.2)$$

Similarly an agent $2j$ maximises his utility when spending his total income on good 1 only, and getting a utility level U_{2j} given by

$$U_{2j}(x^1, 0) = a_{21} y_{2j} + \frac{a_{22}}{p^1}(1 - y_{2j}). \qquad (6.3)$$

Given a $2n$-tuple of strategies $(y_{11}, \cdots, y_{1j}, \cdots, y_{1n}; y_{21}, \cdots, y_{2j}, \cdots y_{2n})$, the resulting equilibrium world price clearing the market for good 1 must satisfy

$$a_{21} \sum_{k=1}^{n} y_{2k} + \frac{a_{22}}{p_1}\left(n - \sum_{k=1}^{n} y_{2k} \right) = a_{11} \sum_{k=1}^{n} y_{1k} + a_{21} \sum_{k=1}^{n} y_{2k},$$

where the left term of this equality represents total demand for good 1 and the right term total supply. Accordingly, we get as equilibrium price

$$p^1 \left(\sum_{k=1}^{n} y_k, \sum_{k=1}^{n} y_{2k} \right) = \frac{a_{22} \left(n - \sum_{k=1}^{n} y_{2k} \right)}{a_{11} \sum_{k=1}^{n} y_{1k}}. \qquad (6.4)$$

Substituting the equilibrium price (6.4) into (6.2) and (6.3), we express the utility level of each agent as a function of his and other agents' strategies,

$$U_{1j}(y_{1j}, y_{-ij}) = \frac{a_{22} \left(n - \sum_{k=1}^{n} y_{2k} \right)}{\sum_{k=1}^{n} y_{1k}} y_{1j} + a_{12}(1 - y_{ij}), \qquad j = 1, \cdots, n$$

$$(6.5)$$

and

$$U_{2j}(y_{2j}, y_{-ij}) = a_{21} y_{2j} + \frac{a_{11} \sum_{k=1}^{n} y_{1k}}{n - \sum_{k=1}^{n} y_{2k}} (1 - y_{2j}), \qquad j = 1, \cdots, n, \quad (6.6)$$

where y_{-ij} denotes the $(2n - 1)$-tuple of strategies of agents different from $1j$ or $2j$. Nevertheless, when $\forall j, y_{1j} = 0$ and $y_{2j} = 1$, no exchange can occur, and each agent acts in autarky. Utilities are then simply given by a_{12} in country 1 and a_{21} in country 2. This is the autarkic outcome. An *oligopoly equilibrium* is a Nash equilibrium of the game in which agent ij has $U_{ij}(y_{ij}, y_{-ij})$ as payoff. More precisely, an oligopoly equilibrium is a $2n$-tuple of strategies $\tilde{y}_{ij}$ such that, for all ij, for all $y_{ij} \in [0, 1]$,

$$U_{ij}(\tilde{y}_{ij}, \tilde{y}_{-ij}) \geq U_{ij}(y_{ij}, \tilde{y}_{-ij}).$$

At an oligopoly equilibrium, each agent ij chooses his production plan in such a way that, given the production plans chosen by the other agents and the resulting world exchange rate, no unilateral deviation from this choice can give him better market opportunities.

Of particular interest in the analysis of non-cooperative trade is the autarkic $2n$-tuple of strategies envisaged above, namely, when each country specialises in the production of the good in which it has a comparative *disadvantage*, i.e. $\tilde{y}_{1j} = 0$ and $\tilde{y}_{2j} = 1$, $\forall\, j = 1, \cdots, n$. Indeed, we show that

Proposition 6.1.
The $2n$-tuple of autarkic strategies $(0, \cdots, 0, \cdots 0; 1, \cdots, 1, \cdots, 1)$ is always an oligopoly equilibrium.

Proof First, assume on the contrary that an agent $1j$ can increase his utility level a_{12} obtained at the no-trade outcome. Then he must choose his strategy y_{1j} in the semi-open interval $]0, 1]$, in which case he obtains a utility level given by (6.5), with $y_{1k} = 0$, $\forall\, k \neq j$ and $y_{2k} = 1$ for all $k = 1, \cdots, n$, i.e.

$$U_{1j}(y_{1j}, \tilde{y}_{-ij}) = a_{12}(1 - y_{1j}) < a_{12} = U_{1j}(\tilde{y}_{1j}, \tilde{y}_{-ij}),$$

a contradiction. Similarly, if an agent $2j$ deviated from $\tilde{y}_{2j} = 1$, he would have to choose his strategy y_{2j} in the semi-open interval $[0, 1[$, in which case he obtains a utility level given by (6.6) with $y_{1k} = 0, \forall\, k = 1, \cdots, n$ and $y_{2k} = 1$, $k \neq j$, i.e.

$$U_{2j}(y_{2j}, \tilde{y}_{-ij}) = a_{21}y_{2j} < a_{21} = U_{2j}(\tilde{y}_{2j}, \tilde{y}_{-ij}),$$

a contradiction.

Proposition (6.1) states a property which is simply that the n-tuple of autarkic strategies is always an oligopoly equilibrium, a proposition which was already discovered in the framework of exchange economies (see Section 5.1). But the interest of this proposition would be considerably enhanced if we could show that, for some Ricardian economies, this n-tuple of strategies would be the *unique* oligopoly equilibrium. Then, and in spite of, possibly huge comparative advantages and strong incentives to organise advantageous exchange, the potential gains from trade would be inexorably wasted due to the non-cooperative strategic interaction among the agents. That this is the case for large classes of Ricardian economies follows from the next analysis. First, it is proved in Cordella and Gabszewicz (1998) that, excluding the autarkic equilibrium, the only remaining possibilities for an n-tuple of strategies $(y_{11}, \cdots, y_{1n}; y_{21}, \cdots, y_{2n})$ to be an oligopoly equilibrium are the following:

1. $\forall\, j = 1, \cdots, n : \tilde{y}_{1j} = 1$ and $\tilde{y}_{2j} = 0$;
2. $\forall\, j = 1, \cdots, n : \tilde{y}_{2j} \in\,]0,1[$ and $\tilde{y}_{1j} = 1$;
3. $\forall\, j = 1, \cdots, n : \tilde{y}_{2j} = 0$ and $\tilde{y}_{1j} \in\,]0,1[$.

To identify the class of Ricardian economies in which the n-tuple of autarkic strategies is the unique oligopoly equilibrium, we may thus restrict ourselves to these three candidates, and find the conditions under which all of them are simultaneously excluded. The first candidate corresponds to the situation where all agents in each country fully specialise in the production of the good in which they have a comparative advantage. When each country has an absolute advantage in the production of the good desired by the other country, as in Figure 6.1, this candidate is the competitive equilibrium. The second and third candidates represent situations in which all the agents in one country fully specialise in the production of the good in which they have a comparative advantage, while in the other country the agents choose a strategy which is interior to their strategy set. The competitive equilibrium in the case of Figure 6.2 corresponds to such a situation, with country 1 fully specialising in the production of good 1, and all agents in country 2 using the interior solution $y_{2j}^* = 1 - \frac{a_{11}}{a_{21}}$. Similarly, the competitive equilibrium in the case of Figure 6.3, $y_{1j}^* = \frac{a_{22}}{a_{12}}$, $y_{2j}^* = 0$, can be a candidate of type (3) as an oligopoly equilibrium.

In order to identify Ricardian economies for which the only oligopoly equilibrium is the n-tuple of autarkic strategies, we now study the necessary and sufficient conditions which must be satisfied by the three possibilities listed above if they are indeed to be an oligopoly equilibrium.

First consider candidate (1): $(1, \cdots, 1, \cdots, 1; 0, \cdots, 0, \cdots, 0)$. Differentiation of (6.5) with respect to y_{1j} yields

$$\frac{\partial U_{1j}}{\partial y_{1j}} = \frac{a_{22}\left(n - \sum_{k=1}^{n} y_{2k}\right)}{\left(\sum_{k=1}^{n} y_{1k}\right)^2} \left(\sum_{k=1}^{n} y_{1k} - y_{1j}\right) - a_{12}. \qquad (6.7)$$

A necessary condition for $\tilde{y}_{1j} = 1$, $\tilde{y}_{2j} = 0$ to be an oligopoly equilibrium is that

$$\frac{\partial U_{1j}}{\partial y_{1j}}\bigg|_{\substack{y_{1j}=1 \\ y_{2j}=0}} \geq 0 \iff \frac{a_{12}}{a_{22}} \leq \frac{n-1}{n}.$$

Similarly, differentiating (6.6) with respect to $y_{2j}, \tilde{y}_{1j} = 1, \tilde{y}_{2j} = 0$ can be an oligopoly equilibrium only if

$$\frac{\partial U_{2j}}{\partial y_{2j}}\bigg|_{\substack{\tilde{y}_{1j}=1 \\ \tilde{y}_{2j}=0}} = a_{21} - \frac{a_{11}\sum_{k=1}^{n} y_{1k}}{\left(n - \sum_{k=1}^{n} y_{2k}\right)^2}\left(n - \sum_{k=1}^{n} y_{2k} - 1 + y_{2j}\right) \leq 0$$

$$\iff \frac{a_{11}}{a_{21}} \geq \frac{n}{n-1}. \qquad (6.8)$$

Furthermore, it is easily checked that $\dfrac{\partial^2 U_{1j}}{\partial y_{1j}^2} < 0$ and $\dfrac{\partial^2 U_{2j}}{\partial y_{2j}^2} < 0$, so that $\frac{a_{12}}{a_{22}} \leq \frac{n-1}{n}$ and $\frac{a_{11}}{a_{21}} \geq \frac{n}{n-1}$ are also sufficient conditions for $(1, \cdots, 1; 0, \cdots, 0)$ to be an oligopoly equilibrium.

Summarising the above, we get

Lemma 6.1.

The $2n$-tuple $(1, \cdots, 1; 0, \cdots, 0)$ is an oligopoly equilibrium if, and only if,

$$\frac{a_{12}}{a_{22}} \leq \frac{n-1}{n} \quad \text{and} \quad \frac{a_{11}}{a_{21}} \geq \frac{n}{n-1}. \tag{6.9}$$

Now, consider a candidate of type (2), $\tilde{y}_{2j} \in]0,1[$ and $\tilde{y}_{1j} = 1$, $\forall \, j = 1, \cdots, n$. For it to be an oligopoly equilibrium, the necessary conditions

$$\frac{\partial U_{2j}}{\partial y_{2j}} = 0, \qquad \forall \, j = 1, \cdots, n \tag{6.10}$$

must hold for all agents of country 2 with $\tilde{y}_{1j} = 1$, while we must have

$$\frac{\partial U_{1j}}{\partial y_{1j}} \Big|_{\substack{\tilde{y}_{1j}=1 \\ \tilde{y}_{2j} \in]0,1[}} \geq 0 \tag{6.11}$$

for the agents of country 1. Using (6.8) and (6.10) with $\tilde{y}_{1j} = 1$ for all j, we obtain

$$\forall j = 1, \cdots, n, \quad \frac{a_{11}n}{\left(n - \sum\limits_{k=1}^{n} \tilde{y}_{2k}\right)^2} \left(n - 1 - \sum_{k=1}^{n} \tilde{y}_{2k} + \tilde{y}_{2j}\right) = a_{21}. \tag{6.12}$$

Since all the values $\tilde{y}_{2j}$ must satisfy the same expression in (6.12) with respect to the aggregate quantity $\sum_{k=1}^{n} \tilde{y}_{2k}$, the n quantities $\tilde{y}_{2j}$ must be equal, i.e. $\tilde{y}_{2j} \stackrel{\text{def}}{=} \tilde{y}_2$ for all $j = 1, \cdots, n$, so that

$$\sum_{k=1}^{n} \tilde{y}_{2k} = n\tilde{y}_2. \tag{6.13}$$

Substituting (6.13) into (6.12) we obtain

$$\tilde{y}_2 = 1 - \frac{n-1}{n} \frac{a_{11}}{a_{21}}. \tag{6.14}$$

A necessary condition for $\tilde{y}_{1j} = 1$, $\tilde{y}_{2j} = \tilde{y}_2$ to be an oligopoly equilibrium with $\tilde{y}_2 \in]0, 1[$ is thus

$$\frac{a_{11}}{a_{21}} < \frac{n}{n-1}.$$

On the other hand, substituting (6.14) into (6.7) with $\tilde{y}_{1j} = 1$, $\forall j = 1, \cdots, n$, we see that (6.11) holds if, and only if

$$\frac{a_{11}}{a_{21}} \geq \frac{a_{12}}{a_{22}} \frac{n^2}{(n-1)^2}.$$

Moreover, by the concavity of the payoff function, these necessary conditions are also sufficient for $(1, \cdots, 1; \tilde{y}_2, \cdots, \tilde{y}_2)$ to be an oligopoly equilibrium.

Summarising the above, we get

Lemma 6.2.
The $2n$-tuple $(1, \cdots, 1; \tilde{y}_2, \cdots, \tilde{y}_2)$, with $\tilde{y}_2 = 1 - \frac{n-1}{n} \frac{a_{11}}{a_{21}}$, is an oligopoly equilibrium if, and only if

$$\frac{n^2}{(n-1)^2} \frac{a_{12}}{a_{22}} \leq \frac{a_{11}}{a_{21}} < \frac{n}{n-1}. \tag{6.15}$$

Finally, consider a candidate of type (3), i.e. $\tilde{y}_{1j} \in]0, 1[$, $\tilde{y}_{2j} = 0$. If this is to be an oligopoly equilibrium, the necessary conditions

$$\frac{\partial U_{1j}}{\partial y_{1j}} = 0, \qquad j = 1, \cdots, n \tag{6.16}$$

must hold for all agents of country 1 with $\tilde{y}_{2j} = 0$, while we must have

$$\left.\frac{\partial U_{2j}}{\partial y_{2j}}\right|_{\substack{\tilde{y}_{1j} \in]0,1[\\ \tilde{y}_{2j}=0}} \leq 0 \tag{6.17}$$

for the agents of country 2. Using (6.7) and (6.16) with $\tilde{y}_{2j} = 0$, $\forall\, j$, we obtain

$$\frac{a_{22}n}{\left(\displaystyle\sum_{k=1}^{n} \tilde{y}_{1k}\right)^2} \left(\sum_{k=1}^{n} \tilde{y}_{1k} - \tilde{y}_{1j}\right) - a_{12} = 0, \qquad \forall\, j = 1, \cdots, n. \tag{6.18}$$

Since all the values $\tilde{y}_{1j}$ must satisfy the same expression in (6.18) with respect to the aggregate quantity $\sum_{k=1}^{n} \tilde{y}_{1k}$, the n quantities $\tilde{y}_{1j}$ must be equal, i.e. $\tilde{y}_{1j} \stackrel{\text{def}}{=} \tilde{y}_1$, for all $j = 1, \cdots, n$, so that

$$\sum_{k=1}^{n} \tilde{y}_{1j} = n\tilde{y}_1. \tag{6.19}$$

Substituting (6.19) into (6.18) we obtain

$$\tilde{y}_1 = \frac{a_{22}}{a_{12}} \frac{n-1}{n}. \tag{6.20}$$

A necessary condition for $\tilde{y}_{1j} = \tilde{y}_1, \tilde{y}_{2j} = 0$ to be an oligopoly equilibrium with $\tilde{y}_1 \in]0,1[$ is thus $\frac{a_{22}}{a_{12}} \frac{n-1}{n} < 1$, or $\frac{n-1}{n} < \frac{a_{12}}{a_{22}}$. On the other hand, substituting (6.20) into (6.8) with $\tilde{y}_{2j} = 0$, $\forall\, j = 1, \cdots, n$, we see that (6.17) holds if, and only if $\frac{a_{12}}{a_{22}} \leq \frac{a_{11}}{a_{21}} \frac{(n-1)^2}{n^2}$. As before these conditions are also sufficient for $(\tilde{y}_1, \cdots, \tilde{y}_1; 0, \cdots, 0)$ to be an oligopoly equilibrium.

Summarising the above, we get:

Lemma 6.3.

The $2n$-tuple $(\tilde{y}_1, \cdots, \tilde{y}_1; 0, \cdots, 0)$, **with** $\tilde{y}_1 = \frac{a_{22}}{a_{12}} \frac{n-1}{n}$ **is an oligopoly equilibrium if, and only if,**

$$\frac{n-1}{n} < \frac{a_{12}}{a_{22}} \leq \frac{a_{11}}{a_{21}} \frac{(n-1)^2}{n^2}. \tag{6.21}$$

We notice immediately, from the necessary conditions (6.9), (6.15) and (6.21), that $(1, \cdots, 1; 0, \cdots, 0)$ is an oligopoly equilibrium only if neither $(\tilde{y}_1, \cdots, \tilde{y}_1; 0, \cdots 0)$, nor $(1, \cdots, 1; \tilde{y}_2, \cdots, \tilde{y}_2)$ are oligopoly equilibria: $(\tilde{y}_1, \cdots, \tilde{y}_1; 0, \cdots, 0)$ is excluded because the left inequality of (6.9) is not compatible with the left inequality of (6.21); similarly $(1, \cdots, 1; \tilde{y}_2, \cdots, \tilde{y}_2)$ is excluded because the right inequality of (6.9) is not compatible with the right inequality of (6.15). On the other hand, it is readily seen from the same necessary conditions (6.15) and (6.21) that $(\tilde{y}_1, \cdots, \tilde{y}_1; 0, \cdots, 0)$ and $(1, \cdots, 1; \tilde{y}_2, \cdots, \tilde{y}_2)$ cannot be oligopoly equilibria simultaneously. Moreover, it turns out from (6.9) that $(1, \cdots, 1; 0, \cdots, 0)$ can be an oligopoly equilibrium only if $a_{11} \geq a_{21} \frac{n}{n-1}$ and $a_{22} > a_{12} \frac{n}{n-1}$, which implies that $a_{11} > a_{21}$ and $a_{22} > a_{12}$. In other words, $(1, \cdots, 1; 0, \cdots, 0)$ can be an oligopoly equilibrium only if country 1 has an absolute advantage in the production of good 1, and country 2 in the production of good 2.

Now we are able to identify several classes of Ricardian economies for which the only oligopoly equilibrium is the autarkic one. We have, indeed:

Proposition 6.2.

For any fixed n, **and any values for** $\frac{a_{11}}{a_{21}}$ **and** $\frac{a_{12}}{a_{22}}$ **satisfying**

$$\frac{n-1}{n} < \frac{a_{12}}{a_{22}} < \frac{a_{11}}{a_{21}} < \frac{n}{n-1}, \tag{6.22}$$

the corresponding Ricardian economy has the n-tuple of autarkic strategies as a unique oligopoly equilibrium.

Proof   First, both the inequalities in (6.22) contradict the fact that $(1, \cdots, 1; 0, \cdots, 0)$ is an oligopoly equilibrium (Lemma 6.1). Now, assume that $(1, \cdots, 1; \tilde{y}_2, \cdots, \tilde{y}_2)$ is an oligopoly equilibrium. Then, by Lemma 6.2, the left inequality of (6.15) must hold

$$\frac{a_{12}}{a_{22}} \frac{n^2}{(n-1)^2} \leq \frac{a_{11}}{a_{21}},$$

which, with the right inequality of (6.22), implies that

$$\frac{a_{12}}{a_{22}} \frac{n^2}{(n-1)^2} < \frac{n}{n-1},$$

which, in turn, implies that

$$\frac{a_{12}}{a_{22}} < \frac{n-1}{n},$$

an inequality which contradicts the left inequality of (6.22). Consequently, $(1, \cdots, 1; \tilde{y}_2, \cdots, \tilde{y}_2)$ is not an oligopoly equilibrium. Finally assume that $(\tilde{y}_1, \cdots, \tilde{y}_1; 0, \cdots, 0)$ is an oligopoly equilibrium. Then, by Lemma 6.3, the right inequality of (6.21) must hold,

$$\frac{a_{12}}{a_{22}} \leq \frac{a_{11}}{a_{21}} \frac{(n-1)^2}{n^2},$$

which, with the left inequality of (6.22), implies that

$$\frac{n-1}{n} < \frac{a_{11}}{a_{21}} \cdot \frac{(n-1)^2}{n^2},$$

an inequality which contradicts the right inequality of (6.22). This completes the proof of Proposition 6.2.

To illustrate the above proposition, it is worthwhile to consider the following example of a Ricardian economy, corresponding to the case of Figure 6.1, namely

$$a_{11} = a_{22} = 3; a_{21} = a_{12} = 2; n = 2.$$

By Proposition 6.2, the autarkic equilibrium is the only oligopoly equilibrium, and $\tilde{y}_{1j} = 0$, $\tilde{y}_{2j} = 1$, so that the world production of the two goods is (4,4). At the competitive equilibrium, we have $y_{1j}^* = 1$, $y_{2j}^* = 0$, so that the world output is (6,6). Strategic behaviour causes a reduction of world production by one third. Surprisingly enough, Proposition 6.2 identifies many situations in which the comparative advantages are not exploited in the international exchange of goods. As shown by Propositions 6.3 and 6.4, this class can even be widened to several other situations.

Proposition 6.3.
For any fixed n, and to any value of $\frac{a_{11}}{a_{21}}$ in the interval $]\frac{n-1}{n}, \frac{n}{n-1}[$, there corresponds a non-degenerate interval of values for $\frac{a_{12}}{a_{22}}$ such that the Ricardian economy $(a_{11}, a_{12}, a_{21}, a_{22})$ has the n-tuple of autarkic strategies as a unique oligopoly equilibrium.

Proof Let n, a_{11} and a_{21} be given and satisfying

$$\frac{n-1}{n} < \frac{a_{11}}{a_{21}} < \frac{n}{n-1}. \qquad (6.23)$$

Choose any triplet $(a_{12}, a_{22}, \varepsilon)$ such that

$$\frac{a_{12}}{a_{22}} = \frac{n-1}{n}(1-\varepsilon), \qquad\qquad (6.24)$$

with $0 < \varepsilon < 1 - \frac{n-1}{n}\frac{a_{11}}{a_{21}}$, so that, by (6.24), $\frac{a_{12}}{a_{22}} < \frac{n-1}{n}$ and (6.1) is verified. There is a non-degenerate interval of values for $\frac{a_{12}}{a_{22}}$ which can be chosen in that way since, from the right inequality in (6.23), we obtain $\frac{a_{11}}{a_{21}} < \frac{n}{n-1} \Rightarrow 1 - \frac{n-1}{n}\frac{a_{11}}{a_{21}} > 0$. First, it follows from the right inequality of (6.23) and Lemma 6.1 that $(1, \cdots, 1; 0, \cdots, 0)$ is not an oligopoly equilibrium. Second, it follows from the fact that $\frac{a_{12}}{a_{22}} < \frac{n-1}{n}$ and Lemma 6.3 that $(\tilde{y}_1, \cdots, \tilde{y}_1; 0, \cdots, 0)$ with $\tilde{y}_1$ defined by (6.20) is not an oligopoly equilibrium either. Consequently, the only remaining possibility is the $2n$-tuple $(1, \cdots, 1; \tilde{y}_2; \cdots, \tilde{y}_2)$, with $\tilde{y}_2$ defined by (6.14). But, by Lemma 6.2, this $2n$-tuple would not be an oligopoly equilibrium if the left inequality of (6.15) were violated, namely if

$$\frac{a_{11}}{a_{21}} < \frac{n^2}{(n-1)^2}\frac{a_{12}}{a_{22}},$$

or, by (6.24) if

$$\frac{a_{11}}{a_{21}} < \frac{n}{(n-1)}(1-\varepsilon),$$

an inequality which must hold, since ε has been chosen in the interval $]0, 1 - \frac{n-1}{n}\frac{a_{11}}{a_{21}}[$.

Proposition 6.4.

For any fixed n, and to any value $\frac{a_{12}}{a_{22}}$ in the interval $]\frac{n-1}{n}, \frac{n}{n-1}[$, there corresponds a non-degenerate interval of values for $\frac{a_{11}}{a_{21}}$ such that the Ricardian economy $(a_{11}, a_{12}, a_{21}, a_{22})$ has the n-tuple of autarkic strategies as unique oligopoly equilibrium.

Proof Let n, a_{12} and a_{22} be given, and satisfying

$$\frac{n-1}{n} < \frac{a_{12}}{a_{22}} < \frac{n}{n-1}. \tag{6.25}$$

Choose any triplet $(a_{11}, a_{21}, \varepsilon)$ such that

$$\frac{a_{11}}{a_{21}} = \frac{n}{n-1}(1+\varepsilon), \tag{6.26}$$

with $0 < \varepsilon < \frac{a_{12}}{a_{22}} \frac{n}{n-1} - 1$, so that, by (6.26), $\frac{a_{11}}{a_{21}} > \frac{n}{n-1}$ and (6.1) is verified. There is a non-degenerate interval of values for $\frac{a_{11}}{a_{21}}$ which can be chosen in that way since, from (6.25), we obtain $\frac{a_{12}}{a_{22}} > \frac{n-1}{n} \Leftrightarrow \frac{a_{12}}{a_{22}} \frac{n}{n-1} - 1 > 0$. First, it follows from the left inequality of (6.25) and Lemma 6.4 that $(1, \cdots, 1; 0, \cdots, 0)$ is not an oligopoly equilibrium. Second, it follows from the fact that $\frac{a_{11}}{a_{21}} > \frac{n}{n-1}$ and Lemma 6.5 that $(1, \cdots, 1; \tilde{y}_2, \cdots, \tilde{y}_2)$ with $\tilde{y}_2$ defined by (6.14) is not an oligopoly equilibrium either. Consequently, the only remaining possibility is the $2n$-tuple $(\tilde{y}_1, \cdots, \tilde{y}_1; 0, \cdots, 0)$, with $\tilde{y}_1$ defined by (6.20). But, by Lemma 6.3, this $2n$-tuple would not be an oligopoly equilibrum if the right inequality of (6.21) were violated, namely if

$$\frac{a_{11}}{a_{21}} < \frac{a_{12}}{a_{22}} \cdot \frac{n^2}{(n-1)^2},$$

or, by (6.26), if

$$(1+\varepsilon) < \frac{a_{12}}{a_{22}} \frac{n}{(n-1)},$$

an inequality which must hold since ε has been chosen in this interval $]0, \frac{a_{12}}{a_{22}} \frac{n}{n-1} - 1[$. Consequently, $(\tilde{y}_1, \cdots, \tilde{y}_1; 0, \cdots, 0)$ is not an oligopoly equilibrium, so that the only remaining outcome is the n-tuple of autarkic strategies.

Propositions 6.2, 6.3 and 6.4 show that a non-cooperative behaviour of the economic agents on the international market can have devastating effects on the efficiency of trade when there is 'competition among the few'. In spite of the existence of possibly huge comparative advantages, each country may prefer to remain in autarky, wasting the advantageous opportunities opened by the possibility of free trade. We notice also that the sets of Ricardian economies where this waste is observed, exist, however large the number n of agents in each country. Nevertheless, as revealed by the following propositions, these sets tend to vanish when n tends to infinity.

Proposition 6.5.

In the case where the agents in country 1 have an absolute advantage in the production of good 1, and those in country 2 in the production of good 2, there exists a number $\bar{n}$ such that, if the number of agents in both countries exceeds $\bar{n}$, the set of oligopoly equilibria consists exactly of the autarkic equilibrium and the competitive equilibrium.

Proof When the agents in country 1 (2) have an absolute advantage in the production of good 1 (2), we find that $a_{11} > a_{21}$ and $a_{22} > a_{12}$. Accordingly, it must be that $\frac{a_{11}}{a_{21}} > 1 > \frac{a_{12}}{a_{22}}$. Consequently, there exists $\bar{n}$ such that, $\forall n \geq \bar{n}$, the inequalities $\frac{a_{11}}{a_{21}} \geq \frac{n}{n-1} > \frac{n-1}{n} \geq \frac{a_{12}}{a_{22}}$ must hold. By Lemma 6.4, this implies that the $2n$-tuple $(1, \cdots, 1; 0, \cdots, 0)$ – which is the competitive equilibrium when $a_{11} > a_{21}$ and $a_{22} > a_{12}$ – is an oligopoly equilibrium for all $n \geq \bar{n}$.

Proposition 6.6.

In the case where the agents in country 2 have an absolute advantage in the production of both goods, there exists a number $\bar{n}$ such that, if the number of agents in both countries exceeds $\bar{n}$, the set of oligopoly equilibria consists exactly of the autarkic equilibrium and the oligopoly equilibrium $(1, \cdots, 1; \tilde{y}_2, \cdots, \tilde{y}_2)$. Furthermore, when $n \to \infty$, $(1, \cdots, 1; \tilde{y}_2, \cdots, \tilde{y}_2)$ converges to the

competitive equilibrium

$$\left(1, \cdots, 1; 1 - \frac{a_{11}}{a_{21}}, \cdots, 1 - \frac{a_{11}}{a_{21}}\right).$$

Proof In the case where the agents in country 2 have an absolute advantage in the production of both goods, we find that $a_{21} > a_{11}$ and $a_{22} > a_{12}$, so that, with (6.1), the inequalities

$$1 > \frac{a_{11}}{a_{21}} > \frac{a_{12}}{a_{22}}$$

must necessarily hold. Consequently, there exists $\bar{n}$ such that $\forall n \geq \bar{n}$, so the inequality

$$\frac{a_{11}}{a_{21}} \geq \frac{a_{12}}{a_{22}} \frac{n^2}{(n-1)^2}$$

must hold. It follows directly from Lemma 6.5 that $(1, \cdots, 1; \tilde{y}_2, \cdots, \tilde{y}_2)$ is an oligopoly equilibrium. Since $\tilde{y}_2 = 1 - \frac{n-1}{n} \frac{a_{11}}{a_{21}}$ (see (6.14)), $\lim_{n \to \infty} \tilde{y}_2 = 1 - \frac{a_{11}}{a_{21}}$, which corresponds to the competitive supply in country 2.

To test the robustness of our example with respect to the somewhat extreme preferences of the agents, postulated above, Cordella and Gabszewicz (1998) have considered a variation of it in which agents have strictly monotone preferences in both goods. More precisely, they assume that the utility of the agents in country 1 (country 2) are given by $U_{1j}(x^1, x^2) = \varepsilon \ln x_1 + x_2$ ($U_{2j}(x_1, x_2) = x_1 + \varepsilon \ln x_2$), with $\varepsilon > 0$ small. As for the technological coefficients and the number of agents, we choose, as in the example provided above, $a_{11} = a_{22} = 3$; $a_{21} = a_{12} = 2$; $n = 2$. For ε small, the preferences of the agents in this example are close to the extreme preferences considered in the above analysis. Furthermore, when $0 < \varepsilon < \frac{3}{5}$, it can be checked that, in the world market, there exists a unique oligopoly equilibrium, which is interior, and given by

$\tilde{y}_{1j} = \frac{5\varepsilon}{3}$, $\tilde{y}_{2j} = 1 - \tilde{y}_{1j}$, $j = 1, 2$. Accordingly, when ε tends to zero, the unique oligopoly equilibrium on the world market tends to the autarkic equilibrium. Thus we conclude that our findings, in the extreme case in which agents are only interested in one good ($\varepsilon = 0$), are robust to a slight perturbation of preferences implying strict monotonicity in both goods.

'Of the four possible [Ricardian competitive] equilibria in which at least one country specialises in production, the principle of comparative costs rules out only one: the inefficient case where both countries specialize according to comparative *disadvantage*' (Jones and Neary 1984, p. 11). As seen above, this inefficient case is the *only* one to be realised in a wide class of Ricardian economies when the world market is oligopolistic. No doubt, in many situations, the loss to be incurred by interacting agents exploiting their market power can be considerable, compared with the gains which would accrue from cooperation. Nevertheless, it really comes as a surprise that non-cooperation in production and trade can be so harmful, since it fully destroys advantageous exchange. It is only when sufficient competitive forces are restored, i.e., when the number of agents involved in trade increases, that this system of perfectly free commerce starts to operate again.

6.2 INTERTEMPORAL OLIGOPOLY EQUILIBRIUM

In this section we present another application of the concept of oligopoly equilibrium, which is proposed by Cordella and Datta (2002), who provide a dynamic version of the model, embodying two types of agents and two goods. As in our first application, agents control their consumption, but also a technological production process which allows them to use the consumption good owned at time t as an input to produce future output. More precisely, the authors assume that each type of agent controls the production of one good, and the type is identified with the corresponding good. There exists at each period a spot market in which agents can trade the two goods between them, while no trade is allowed across periods. Input invested in period t generates output at period $t + 1$. At each period, the agents consume a part of their current output, sell a part of it on the spot market, and use the rest as input in order to produce output which will be made available in the next period. Accordingly, there are two channels through which each agent can influence the current and future relative prices. First they can restrict their present output supply on the exchange spot market by increasing their current consumption in order to increase the relative price for the good they control: this is the usual channel described in the models we have considered above. Furthermore, they can also consume a larger share of the good they are endowed with in order to improve their future terms of trade, by restricting the amount they invest for future production. As we shall see, *this new opportunity may have dramatic effects on the convergence of oligopoly equilibrium outcomes to competitive allocations.*

In the following, the superscript i stands for an agent of type 1 and the superscript j for an agent of type 2. There are n agents of each type $(i, j = 1, ..., n)$. The notation z_{1t}^i (z_{2t}^j) designates the stock of good 1 (good 2) held by the i-th agent (j-th agent) in period t. In period $t = 0$, the stock is the initial endowment, specialised in good 1 for agents of type i, and in good 2 for agents of type j. In the following periods, the stock corresponds to the output resulting from investment in the preceding period. A part, y_{1t}^i (y_{2t}^j), of the stock is used for consumption and the rest, $z_{1t}^i - y_{1t}^i$ $(z_{2t}^j - y_{2t}^j)$, is used as input, in period t, by agents i and j respectively. The production generated by these investments in period $t + 1$ is assumed to be given by the production functions

$$z_{1(t+1)}^i = (z_{1t}^i - y_{1t}^i)^\alpha \qquad (6.27)$$

$$z_{2(t+1)}^j = (z_{2t}^j - y_{2t}^j)^\alpha \qquad (6.28)$$

with $\alpha \leq 1$. The initial endowments z_{10}^i and z_{20}^j are assumed to be equal and strictly larger than 0. The i-th agent consumes a fraction of y_{1t}^i and trades the rest for an amount of good 2 for his own consumption in period t. If (c_{1t}^i, c_{2t}^i) $((c_{1t}^j, c_{2t}^j))$ represents the vector of consumption at period t of agent i (agent j), his (instantaneous) utility is assumed to be given by

$$u(c_{1t}^i, c_{2t}^i) = \ln c_{1t}^i + \ln c_{2t}^i \qquad (u(c_{1t}^j, c_{2t}^j) = \ln c_{1t}^j + \ln c_{2t}^j).$$

Finally, his intertemporal utility for consumption sequences $\{(c_{1t}^i, c_{2t}^i)\}$ is represented by the discounted sum of instantaneous utilities

$$\sum_{t=0}^{\infty} \partial^t (\ln c_{1t}^i + \ln c_{2t}^i),$$

where $\partial < 1$ is the discount factor. The budget constraint in period t for agent i (j) can be written as

$$p_{1t}c_{1t}^j + p_{2t}c_{2t}^i = p_{1t}y_{1t}^i \qquad (p_{1t}c_{1t}^j + p_{2t}c_{2t}^i = p_{1t}y_{2t}^j),$$

with p_{1t} and p_{2t} representing the spot prices for good 1 and 2 respectively, in period t. Given a sequence of such prices, agent i's intertemporal optimisation problem can be written as

$$\max_{\{c_{1t}^i, c_{2t}^i, y_{1t}^i\}} \sum_{t=0}^{\infty} \partial^t (\ln c_{1t}^i + \ln c_{2t}^i), \qquad (6.29)$$

subject to :

$$p_{1t}c_{1t}^i + p_{2t}c_{2t}^i = p_{1t}y_{1t}^i$$
$$0 \leq y_{1t}^i \leq z_{1t}^i = (z_{1(t-1)}^i - y_{1(t-1)}^i)^\alpha$$
$$c_{1t}^i > 0; c_{2t}^i > 0,$$

and similarly for agent j, with the appropriate changes in the indices of the variables. Assuming the equality of aggregate supply and demand on each spot market at period t, and taking into account the fact that type-1 agents supply good 1 and type-2 agents supply good 2, this gives us, as market clearing price ratio,

$$p_t = \frac{p_{2t}}{p_{1t}} = \frac{\sum_{i=1}^{n}(y_{1t}^i - c_{1t}^j)}{\sum_{j=1}^{n}(y_{2t}^j - c_{2t}^j)}. \tag{6.30}$$

At an intertemporal competitive equilibrium each agent solves the above problem taking the prices as given, and prices clear the markets at each period. Formally, an *intertemporal competitive equilibrium* is a $(2 \times 2n)$-tuple of sequences $\{(y_{1t}^{*i}, c_{1t}^{*i})\}_{t=0}^{\infty}, \{(y_{2t}^{*j}, c_{2t}^{*j})\}_{t=0}^{\infty}$ of decisions for the $2n$ agents, $i, j = 1, ..., n$, and a sequence $\{p_t^*\}_{t=0}^{\infty}$ of relative prices such that (i)$\{(y_{1t}^{*i}, c_{1t}^{*i})\}_{t=0}^{\infty}$ maximises $U\left(\left\{c_{1t}^i, \frac{1}{p_t^*}(y_{1t}^i - c_{1t}^j)\right\}\right)$, subject to the technological constraint (6.27) for $i = 1, ..., n$; (ii) $\left\{(y_{2t}^{*j}, c_{2t}^{*j})\right\}_{t=0}^{\infty}$ maximises $U\left(\left\{(p_t^*((y_{2t}^j - c_{2t}^j), c_{2t}^j)\right\}\right)$ subject to the technological constraint (6.28) for $j = 1, ..., n$; and (iii) the price ratio p_t^* clears the spot market in period t, $t = 1, 2, ...$

Using the analogy between the optimisation problems (6.29) and (6.30) at given prices and the unique solution of a one-sector optimal growth model, the authors show that the unique intertemporal competitive equilibrium is given by the values

$$y_{1t}^{*i} = (1 - \partial \alpha) z_{1t}^i \tag{6.31}$$

$$c_{1t}^{*i} = \frac{(1 - \partial \alpha) z_{1t}^i}{2} \tag{6.32}$$

$$c_{2t}^{*i} = \frac{(1 - \partial \alpha) z_{1t}^i}{2 p_t^*}, \tag{6.33}$$

$$y_{2t}^{*j} = (1 - \partial\alpha)z_{2t}^{j} \qquad (6.34)$$

$$c_{1t}^{*j} = \frac{(1 - \partial\alpha)p_t^* z_{2t}^{j}}{2} \qquad (6.35)$$

$$c_{2t}^{*j} = \frac{(1 - \partial\alpha)z_{2t}^{j}}{2}. \qquad (6.36)$$

As for the equilibrium relative price p_t^*, it is given, for all periods t, by

$$p_t^* = \frac{(1 - \partial\alpha)z_{1t}}{(1 - \partial\alpha)z_{2t}},$$

an expression in which we have omitted the indices i and j since the agents inside each type are identical. Furthermore, since we have assumed that $z_{10}^i = z_{10}^j$, we have $p_t^* = 1$ for all t.

We now extend the definition of an oligopoly equilibrium to cover the problem of intertemporal strategic interaction. A *strategy* for a type-1 agent i is a sequence $\{y_{1t}^i, c_{1t}^i\}_{t=0}^{\infty}$ such that $0 \leq c_{1t}^i \leq y_{1t}^i \leq z_{1t}^i = (z_{1(t-1)}^i - y_{1(t-1)}^i)^\alpha$ for $t \geq 1$ and $0 \leq c_{10}^i \leq y_{10}^i \leq z_{10}^i$. A strategy for a type-2 agent is defined analogously with the appropriate change of indices. The payoffs for type-1 and type-2 agents are defined, respectively, by

$$V_i(\{y_{1t}^i, c_{1t}^i\}_{t=0}^{\infty}, (\{y_{1t}^k, c_{1t}^k\}_{t=0}^{\infty})_{k=1;k\neq i}^{n}; (\{y_{2t}^i, c_{1t}^i\}_{t=0}^{\infty})_{j=1}^{n})$$
$$= \sum_{t=0}^{\infty} \partial^t \left[\ln c_{1t}^i + \ln\left\{\frac{p_{1t}}{p_{2t}}(y_{1t}^i - c_{1t}^i)\right\} \right]$$

$$V_j(\{y_{2t}^j, c_{2t}^j\}_{t=0}^{\infty}; (\{y_{1t}^i, c_{1t}^i\}_{t=0}^{\infty})_{i=1}^{n}, (\{y_{2t}^l, c_{2t}^l\}_{t=0}^{\infty})_{l=1;l\neq j}^{n})$$
$$= \sum_{t=0}^{\infty} \partial^t \left[\ln c_{2t}^j + \ln\left\{\frac{p_{1t}}{p_{2t}}(y_{2t}^j - c_{2t}^j)\right\} \right]$$

where $i, j = 1, ..., n; k = 1, ..., n$; $k \neq i, l = 1, ..., n; l \neq j$. These payoffs depend on the price ratios $p_t = \frac{p_{2t}}{p_{1t}}$ due to the fact that agent i's consumption of good 2 at period t is given by $\frac{(y_{1t}^i - c_{1t}^i)}{p_t}$ and agent j's consumption of good 1 at date t by $p_t(y_{2t}^j - c_{2t}^j)$ from their respective budget constraints. Since agents behave strategically, they take into account the influence of their individual decisions on the market clearing price ratio at each point. Consequently, in the above payoffs, the price ratio $\frac{p_{2t}}{p_{1t}}$ must satisfy

$$p_t = \frac{p_{2t}}{p_{1t}} = \frac{\sum_{i=1}^n (y_{1t}^i - c_{1t}^j)}{\sum_{j=1}^n (y_{2t}^j - c_{2t}^j)},$$

as given by (6.30). *An intertemporal oligopoly equilibrium* is a Nash equilibrium of the above game.

Focusing on the space of type-symmetric and stationary strategies (namely, strategies for which consumption and investment decisions at date t only depend on the current output stock), Cordella and Datta (2002) have proved the following:

Proposition 6.7.
The $(2 \times 2n)$-tuple of strategies $\left\{ (y_{1t}^{i^\circ}, c_{1t}^{i^\circ}), (y_{2t}^{i^\circ}, c_{2t}^{i^\circ}) \right\}_{t=0}^\infty$, $i, j = 1, ..., n$

$$y_{1t}^{i^\circ} = \frac{(2n-1)(1 - \partial\alpha)z_{1t}}{(2n-1)(1 - \partial\alpha) + n\partial\alpha}$$

$$c_{1t}^{i^\circ} = \frac{ny_{1t}^{i^\circ}}{(2n-1)}$$

and

$$y_{2t}^{i^\circ} = \frac{(2n-1)(1 - \partial\alpha)z_{2t}}{(2n-1)(1 - \partial\alpha) + n\partial\alpha}$$

$$c_{1t}^{i^\circ} = \frac{ny_{2t}^{i^\circ}}{(2n-1)}$$

is an intertemporal oligopoly equilibrium.

Comparing the proportions of consumption $(\frac{c_{1t}^{i^o}}{y_{1t}^{i^o}}, \frac{c_{2t}^{i^o}}{y_{2t}^{i^o}})$ of own good at the intertemporal oligopoly equilibrium just identified, with the proportions $(\frac{c_{1t}^{i*}}{y_{1t}^{i*}}, \frac{c_{2t}^{i*}}{y_{2t}^{i*}})$ obtained at the competitive equilibrium (see (6.31)-(6.36) above), we find that *the proportion of own good consumed in each period at the intertemporal oligopoly equilibrium exceeds the proportion consumed at the intertemporal competitive equilibrium. However, as the number of strategic agents increases, the oligopoly proportion decreases and, when the number of strategic agents tends to infinity, it converges to the competitive equilibrium proportion.* This result is in conformity with our findings in static oligopoly equilibrium theory: agents consume more of their own good in order to restrict their market supply and accordingly obtain better terms of trade. Also, increased competition removes this manipulating effect. But there is another dynamic distortion in this model, due to the influence that agents can exert on future prices via their *investment* decisions. To analyse this effect, we must compare the proportions $(\frac{z_{1t}-y_{1t}}{z_{1t}}, \frac{z_{2t}-y_{2t}}{z_{2t}})$ of stock to be invested in each period to allow for future consumption. Using Proposition 6.7, (6.31) and (6.34), we observe that *the proportion of stock invested in each period is lower at the intertemporal oligopoly equilibrium than at the competitive equilibrium. Moreover, this proportion decreases when the number of agents increases.* The first part of this statement again reflects the fact that agents have an incentive to invest less in each period to benefit from better terms of trade in the next period. The second part of the statement is explained by the fact that investment decisions of agents of the same type are strategic complements: if agent i invests less, commodity 1 becomes more scarce in the future (its price increases), and the marginal rate of substitution between future and present consumption decreases in absolute terms for all agents of type 1. They are better off consuming more in the current period and investing a smaller proportion of their stock. The ratio of aggregate consumption to investment is equal to

$$\frac{y_{1t}^*}{(z_{1t}^* - y_{1t}^*)} = \frac{1 - \partial\alpha}{\partial\alpha}$$

at the intertemporal competitive equilibrium, while the corresponding ratio is given by

$$\frac{\overset{\circ}{y}_{1t}}{(\overset{\circ}{z}_{1t} - \overset{\circ}{y}_{1t})} = \frac{1 - \partial \alpha}{\partial \alpha}(1 + \frac{n-1}{n})$$

at the intertemporal oligopoly equilibrium. These equations reveal how the difference between intertemporal oligopoly and competitive equilibria aggregate consumption to investment increases monotonically with n. It follows from the above that, contrary to the usual statement about convergence of oligopoly equilibria, *the consumption and investment allocations corresponding to intertemporal oligopoly equilibria do not converge, with the number of agents, to the corresponding allocations in the intertemporal competitive equilibrium.*

Cordella and Datta (2002) summarise the above analysis as follows.

In order to better understand the implication of strategic behavior on efficiency, we recall that there are two sources of strategic interaction in this model: the consumption, or trading decisions, and the investment decisions. The consumption decisions are intra- or within-period trading decisions while the investment decisions capture the inter- or across-period effect through their influence on future output and, hence, on future consumption and investment decisions. The within-period effect of strategic behavior is a static effect and is well understood: strategic agents consume more of the good they are endowed with in order to have better terms of trade. But, as the number of agents increases, each agent's market power diminishes and, when n becomes very large, the strategic and competitive agents consume the same proportion of the two goods, in each time period. That is, at the limit, the static distortions vanish. The across-period investment effect is essentially dynamic and the associated distortionary effects are relatively less understood. The allocative distortions associated with the strategic investment behavior, or the dynamic distortions, increase with the number of agents. When the economy is replicated, each agent finds it profitable to invest less in each time period because if he does so all the other agents of his own type would also find it profitable to underinvest. Thus, in our model, the investment decisions are strategic complements while the consumption or trading decisions are strategic substitutes. The strategic incentives for overconsumption (as a proportion of own stock) decrease and the strategic incentives for underinvestment (as a proportion of own stock) increase with the number of strategic agents.

6.3 OLIGOPOLY EQUILIBRIUM AND TAXATION

Because it provides the simplest version of market interactions, the exchange model constitutes a natural starting point for exploring specific issues in general equilibrium theory. In this section, we investigate the effectiveness and welfare implications of fiscal policies in a context of multilateral exchange, when traders behave strategically.

One of the objectives pursued when taxing economic agents is to collect resources for redistributive purposes. With imperfect competition, taxation can also serve the purpose of correcting distortions generated by the market mechanism. The present approach deals simultaneously with these two facets of fiscal policies, in an exchange economy in which some agents – the 'inside agents' – participate in exchange while the remaining ones – the 'outside agents' – are excluded from trade, simply because they do not own any initial resources: this constitutes a stylised formulation of more elaborate redistributive schemes. In the present context, the redistributive purpose of taxation consists accordingly in transferring to the outside agents initial resources levied on inside agents, in order to guarantee them some minimal survival resources. The first question we raise is whether these transfers can reach a Pareto-optimal overall allocation, providing preassigned utility levels to outside agents, and taking into account the fact that inside agents play strategically when exchanging goods among themselves. Here the second facet of fiscal policy enters into the picture. Indeed, strategic behaviour generally affects trade in a way which destroys Pareto-efficiency, complicating thereby the possibility of reaching a Pareto-optimal outcome via transfers. Nevertheless, Gabszewicz and Grazzini (2001) have shown that there exist lump-sum taxes and transfers reaching a Pareto-optimal overall allocation of goods among inside and outside agents, which simultaneously constitutes a Nash equilibrium outcome in the strategic market game played by the inside agents. This result is reminiscent of the second welfare theorem, but this time applies to strategic trade.

The significance of this result should, however, be tempered due to the well-known drawbacks of lump-sum taxes: the informational requirements needed to make them effective, and non-anonymity, since they can be required to be personalized on the basis of the characteristics of each agent. It is thus natural to examine whether it would be possible for alternative methods of taxation to be effective in reaching a Pareto-optimal outcome while avoiding the drawbacks we have just referred to. Leaving aside the informational problem of identifying these characteristics, we examine whether non-anonymity can be somewhat relaxed by imposing taxes affecting each good in the same proportion, as is particularly the case for commodity taxation, which bears on transactions, and if taxes on initial endowments had the same tax rate per good for all agents (endowment taxation). Using a simple example, we show that such fiscal policies are not sufficient tools to reach an overall Pareto-optimal allocation: trade distortions due to imperfect competition cannot be wiped out via such methods. Finally, we propose an alternative method combining anonymous endowment taxation and transfers among inside agents, proportional to the amount sent for exchange, and test it on the particular example of Section 5.2. We show that this method is effective both in resorbing trade distortions due to strategic behaviour, and in providing an overall allocation among inside and outside agents which is Pareto-optimal.

6.3.1. Strategic Market Games and Pareto-optimality

Consider an exchange economy involving $n+m$ agents i, $i = 1, ..., n+m$, and ℓ goods h, $h = 1, ..., \ell$. The initial ownership of these goods is fully concentrated in the hands of the first n agents, ω_i, $\omega_i \in R^\ell_+$, $\omega_i \neq 0$, denoting the *initial endowment* of agent i, $i = 1, ..., n$. By assumption, we set $\omega_i = 0$, for agents i, $i = n + 1, ..., n + m$: only agents i, $i = 1, ..., n$, named hereafter the *inside agents*, participate in the exchange and are accordingly the *players* in the market game. Agents i, $i = n+1, ..., n+m$, are excluded from trade and we call them the *outside agents*. We denote by U_i, $i = 1, ..., n + m$, the *utility function* of agent i, representing his preference relation among the commodity bundles x, $x \in R^\ell_+$. Standard assumptions on U_i – continuity, strict monotonicity and strict quasi-concavity – are made from the outset.

In the following we are interested in identifying tax and transfer schemes through which outside agents i, $i = n + 1, ..., n + m$, obtain a share of the resources initially owned by inside agents who participate directly in the exchange process described in the strategic market game above. The redistributive purpose pursued with such schemes consists in providing agents, who are initially deprived of any resource, with some amount of the various commodities, thereby allowing them to survive, in spite of the fact that they are unable to participate directly in trade. Formally, we assume that these survival levels are represented by utility levels – say $\overline{U}_i$ – for the outside agents i, $i = n + 1, .., n + m$. These utility levels accordingly constrain the set of transfers and corresponding taxes which can be used in order to meet these preassigned levels. In this spirit, we define utility levels $\overline{U}_i$, $i = n + 1, .., n + m$, as *feasible* if there exists lump-sum taxes t_i, $t_i \in R^\ell_+$, $i = 1, \cdots, n$, and transfers s_i, $s_i \in R^\ell_+$, $i = n + 1, .., n + m$, such that

1. $t_i \leq \omega_i$, $i = 1, ..., n$;
2. $\sum_{i=n+1}^{n+m} s_i = \sum_{i=1}^{n} t_i$;
3. $U_i(s_i) \geq \overline{U}_i$, $i = n + 1, ..., n + m$.

Given taxes t_i, a *post-tax allocation* among inside agents is an n-tuple of commodity bundles $(x_1, ..., x_i, ..., x_n)$ such that

$$\sum_{i=1}^{n} x_i = \sum_{i=1}^{n} (\omega_i - t_i).$$

Now we are in a position to state the following:

Proposition 6.8.

Given any preassigned feasible utility levels $\overline{U}_i$ for outside agents i, $i = n + 1, ..., n + m$, there exist lump-sum taxes t_i on inside agents' endowments ω_i, $i = 1, ..., n$, and transfers s_i from inside agents to outside agents such that (i) the overall allocation of goods $(\omega_1 - t_1, ..., \omega_n - t_n; s_{n+1}, ..., s_{n+m})$ among inside and outside agents is Pareto-optimal, and outside agents obtain, at that overall- allocation, commodity bundles providing utility levels $\overline{U}_i$, $i = n + 1, ..., n + m$; (ii) the post-tax allocation $(\omega_1 - t_1, ..., \omega_n - t_n)$ among inside agents is the unique oligopoly equilibrium of the strategic market game in which the strategy sets of inside agents are defined by $S_i = \{y_i \mid 0 \leq y_i \leq \omega_i - t_i\}$.

Proof   In the exchange economy with $(n + m)$ agents made of inside agents $i = 1, ..., n$ and outside agents $i = n + 1, ..., n + m$, an $(n + m)$-tuple of commodity bundles $(x_1^*, ..., x_n^*; x_{n+1}^*, ..., x_{n+m}^*)$ is Pareto-optimal if it solves the problem $\max_{x_1, ..., x_{n+m}} \sum_{i=1}^{n+m} U_i(x_i)$ s.t.

$$1. \quad \sum_{i=1}^{n+m} x_i = \sum_{i=1}^{n} \omega_i$$
$$2. \quad x_i \geq 0, \qquad i = 1, ..., n + m. \tag{6.37}$$

Furthermore, since the preassigned utility levels $\overline{U}_i$, $i = n + 1, ..., n + m$, are feasible for lump-sum taxes t_i and transfers s_i, the $(n + m)$-tuple of commodity bundles $(x_1^*, ..., x_n^*; x_{n+1}^*, ..., x_{n+m}^*)$ can be chosen eventually in order to solve the problem $\max_{x_1, ..., x_{n+m}} \sum_{i=1}^{n} U_i(x_i)$ s.t.

$$1. \quad \sum_{i=n+1}^{n+m} s_i = \sum_{i=1}^{n} t_i$$
$$2. \quad x_i = \omega_i - t_i \geq 0; \quad i = 1, ..., n;$$

3. $x_i = s_i \geq 0;$ $i = n+1, ..., n+m;$

4. $U_i(x_i) = U_i(s_i) \geq \overline{U}_i,$ $i = n+1, ..., n+m.$ (6.38)

Since the function $\sum_{i=1}^{n} U_i(x_i)$ is continuous as a sum of continuous functions, and the set of vectors satisfying (1), (2), (3) and (4) is non-empty and compact, there exists an $(n+m)$-tuple of commodity bundles $(x_1^*, , ..., x_n^*; x_{n+1}^*, ..., x_{n+m}^*) = (\omega_1 - t_1^*, ..., \omega_n - t_n^*; s_{n+1}^*, ..., s_{n+m}^*)$, which is a solution to problem (6.38).

Now consider the exchange economy consisting of the n inside traders with initial endowments $\omega_i - t_i^*$, $i = 1, ..., n$. The allocation $(\omega_1 - t_1^*, ..., \omega_n - t_n^*)$ of the resources $\sum_{i=1}^{n}(\omega_i - t_i^*)$ among inside agents is also Pareto-optimal in the subeconomy consisting of these inside agents. If some agent $i \in \{1, ..., n\}$ uses a strategy y_i which differs from the null vector, he reaches a utility level $V_i(y_i, y_{-i})$, with $y_{-i} = (0, ..., 0)$, smaller or equal to $V_i(0, ..., 0)$, in the subeconomy consisting of n inside agents. Accordingly, no unilateral deviation from the allocation $(\omega_1 - t_1^*, ..., \omega_n - t_n^*)$ can increase the utility of an inside agent, so that $(\omega_1 - t_1^*, ..., \omega_n - t_n^*)$ is an oligopoly equilibrium in the strategic market game in which the set of strategies S_i of agent i is given by $S_i = \{y_i \mid 0 \leq y_i \leq \omega_i - t_i^*\}$, $i = 1, ..., n$.

Finally, the uniqueness of equilibrium follows from the fact that any alternative strategic equilibrium would generate an allocation which is Pareto-dominated by the allocation $(\omega_1 - t_1^*, ..., \omega_n - t_n^*)$. Accordingly, at least one inside agent can deviate from the strategy he has selected at this alternative oligopoly equilibrium by playing the strategy 0, and obtain a higher payoff, a contradiction.

Proposition 6.8 is simply a restatement of the second welfare theorem formulated for our particular setting with some agents excluded from trade and the remaining ones behaving strategically while, in the usual formulation of this theorem, the Pareto-optimal allocation is viewed as sustained by competitive prices. The proof of this proposition takes advantage of the fact that a Pareto-optimal allocation of an exchange economy always appears as the outcome of a Nash equilibrium in the associated market game. The usual criticisms against lump-sum taxes and transfers needed to sustain a particular Pareto-optimal allocation as a competitive outcome, applies as well in our attempt to sustain such an allocation as an oligopoly equilibrium. In particular, these taxes and transfers need to be personalized since they vary across agents depending on the quantity of resources required to achieve the particular Pareto-optimal allocation. Thus, it is natural to wonder whether it is possible to design taxes which are not linked to individual characteristics, but rather to the commodities themselves, as in the case of commodity taxation. Such taxes appear as more *anonymous*, to the extent that they are imposed on all consumers in the same manner for the same good. In an exchange economy, one can think of two types of taxes satisfying this anonymity criterion. The first one consists in imposing a tax t^h on good h, to be collected on transactions concerning good h: this is *commodity taxation*. The second one consists in imposing a tax t^h on the hth-component of ω_i, independently of i, before transactions take place: this is *endowment taxation*. Now, we examine whether using these tax instruments could be sufficient to perform the job which we have just seen to be feasible with personalized lump-sum taxes and transfers.

6.3.2. Commodity Taxation

In this section, we construct a particular example of an exchange economy reminiscent of the example considered in Section 4.3 and show that commodity taxation is not a sufficient instrument in order to realize a Pareto-optimal allocation when inside agents behave strategically. Consider an exchange economy with two goods, 1 and 2, and consisting of $n + 1$ agents, namely n inside agents and one outside agent. The inside agents fall into two *types*, with $\frac{n}{2}$ agents of each type. All agents i, $i = 1, ..., n + 1$, have the same utility function U, which is defined by

$$U(x^1, x^2) = x^1 x^2. \tag{6.39}$$

Initial endowments are defined by

$$\omega_i = (1,0), \qquad i = 1, ..., \frac{n}{2} \qquad\qquad (6.40)$$

$$\omega_i = (0,1), \qquad i = \frac{n}{2} + 1, ..., n \qquad\qquad (6.41)$$

$$\omega_i = (0,0), \qquad i = n + 1. \qquad\qquad (6.42)$$

To the exchange economy consisting of the n inside agents, we may associate a strategic market game as follows. For all agents, the *strategy set* S_i consists of the $[0,1]$-interval. For an agent $i \in \{1, ..., \frac{n}{2}\}$, we denote by q_i a strategy in $[0,1]$: as usual, q_i is to be interpreted as the quantity of good 1 that agent i sends to the market for trade. Similarly, b_i, $b_i \in [0,1]$, denotes a strategy of agent i, $i \in \{\frac{n}{2} + 1, ..., n\}$.

As shown in Gabszewicz and Michel (1997) where this example is introduced, all traders of the same type must adopt the same strategy at equilibrium and, apart from the autarkic one, the *vector of strategies* (q^*, b^*) *defined by*

$$(q^*, b^*) = \left(\frac{n-2}{2(n-1)}, \frac{n-2}{2(n-1)} \right) \qquad\qquad (6.43)$$

is the only oligopoly equilibrium of this exchange game.

Now suppose that commodity taxes t^h, $h = 1, 2$, are levied on transactions in order to provide the outside agent $n + 1$ with some amount of the two goods and realise thereby a feasible utility level $\overline{U}$ for him. More specifically, suppose that, *when exchange takes place*, a per unit tax t^1, $0 < t^1 < 1$, is levied on the supply of good 1 and a per unit tax t^2, $0 < t^2 < 1$, is levied on the supply of good 2, giving rise to a total tax product equal to $t^1 \sum_{k=1}^{\frac{n}{2}} q_k$ units of good 1, and $t^2 \sum_{k=\frac{n}{2}+1}^{n} b_k$ units of good 2. Furthermore, suppose that, *after trade has occurred* at an n-tuple of strategies $(q_1, ..., q_{\frac{n}{2}}; b_{\frac{n}{2}+1}, ..., b_n)$, the total product of the tax $t^1 \sum_{k=1}^{\frac{n}{2}} q_k$ in good 1 and $t^2 \sum_{k=\frac{n}{2}+1}^{n} b_k$ in good 2 is transferred to the outside agent $n + 1$. Consequently, this commodity tax and transfer scheme generates a new exchange game as follows. Given a commodity tax t^1, $0 < t^1 < 1$, and a commodity tax t^2, $0 < t^2 < 1$, the strategy set of inside agents i, $i = 1, ..., n$, is the interval $[0,1]$. Furthermore, the initial endowments are still $\omega_i = (1,0)$, $i \in \left\{1, ..., \frac{n}{2}\right\}$ and $\omega_i = (0,1)$, $i \in \left\{\frac{n}{2} + 1, ..., n\right\}$. However, the price $p(q_1, ..., q_{\frac{n}{2}}; b_{\frac{n}{2}+1}, ..., b_n)$ is now obtained as

$$p(q_1, ..., q_{\frac{n}{2}}; b_{\frac{n}{2}+1}, ..., b_n) = \frac{(1 - t^2) \sum_{k=\frac{n}{2}+1}^{n} b_k}{(1 - t^1) \sum_{k=1}^{\frac{n}{2}} q_k},$$

and the resulting post-tax allocation of goods in the new game is given by

$$x_i = \left(1 - q_i, \frac{(1 - t^2) \sum_{k=\frac{n}{2}+1}^{n} b_k}{(1 - t^1) \sum_{k=1}^{\frac{n}{2}} q_k} q_i (1 - t^1)\right), \quad i = 1, ..., \frac{n}{2} \quad (6.44)$$

$$x_i = \left(\frac{(1 - t^1) \sum_{k=1}^{\frac{n}{2}} q_k}{(1 - t^2) \sum_{k=\frac{n}{2}+1}^{n} b_k} b_i (1 - t^2), 1 - b_i\right). \quad i = \frac{n}{2} + 1, ..., n \quad (6.45)$$

It gives rise to utility levels

$$V_i(q, b) = (1 - q_i) \left(\frac{(1 - t^2) \sum_{k=\frac{n}{2}+1}^{n} b_k}{\sum_{k=1}^{\frac{n}{2}} q_k} q_i\right), \quad i = 1, ..., \frac{n}{2} \quad (6.46)$$

and

$$V_i(q, b) = \left(\frac{(1 - t^1) \sum_{k=1}^{\frac{n}{2}} q_k}{\sum_{k=\frac{n}{2}+1}^{n} b_k} b_i\right) (1 - b_i), \quad i = \frac{n}{2} + 1, ..., n. \quad (6.47)$$

In the following proposition, we show that the commodity taxes and transfers scheme defined above does not permit a Pareto-optimal overall allocation, with the outside agent obtaining the preassigned utility level $\overline{U}$ at the outcome of the new market game which has just been defined.

Proposition 6.9.

Given any utility level $\overline{U}$ for the outside agent $n + 1$, there are no commodity taxes t^h, $h = 1, 2$ such that, when the product of these taxes is transferred to agent $n+1$, (i) the overall allocation resulting from this transfer and from the oligopoly equilibrium of the new exchange game is Pareto-optimal and (ii) the utility of the outside agent after transfer is at least equal to $\overline{U}$.

Proof Suppose, contrary to Proposition 6.9, that there are commodity taxes t^h, $h = 1, 2$, for which requirements (i) and (ii) are met. First, we show that, even with these taxes t^h, $h = 1, 2$, the vector of strategies (q^*, b^*) of the exchange game, as obtained in (6.32), remains the unique interior Nash equilibrium of the new exchange game. The first order conditions which must be satisfied at an interior equilibrium are

$$\frac{\partial V_i}{\partial q_i} = (1 - q_i) \left(\frac{\sum_{k=\frac{n}{2}+1}^{n} b_k \left(\sum_{k=1}^{\frac{n}{2}} q_k - q_i \right)}{\left(\sum_{k=1}^{\frac{n}{2}} q_k \right)^2} \right)$$

$$- \frac{\sum_{k=\frac{n}{2}+1}^{n} b_k}{\sum_{k=1}^{\frac{n}{2}} q_k} q_i = 0, \quad i = 1, ..., \frac{n}{2}$$

$$\frac{\partial V_i}{\partial b_i} = (1 - b_i) \left(\frac{\sum_{k=1}^{\frac{n}{2}} q_k \left(\sum_{k=\frac{n}{2}+1}^{n} b_k - b_i \right)}{\left(\sum_{k=\frac{n}{2}+1}^{n} b_k \right)^2} \right)$$

$$- \frac{\sum_{k=1}^{\frac{n}{2}} q_k}{\sum_{k=\frac{n}{2}+1}^{n} b_k} b_i = 0, \quad i = \frac{n}{2} + 1, ..., n.$$

Using the fact that all traders of the same type must adopt the same strategy at equilibrium (for a formal proof, see Gabszewicz and Grazzini 1999, Appendix, p.493) we may denote by q (b) the supply of inside agents $i \in \left\{ 1, ..., \frac{n}{2} \right\}$ ($i \in \left\{ \frac{n}{2} + 1, ..., n \right\}$) on the market. Using this property, the first order conditions which must be satisfied at an interior oligopoly equilibrium can be rewritten as

$$\frac{(n-2)(1-q)}{nq} - 1 = 0, \quad i = 1, ..., \frac{n}{2} \tag{6.48}$$

$$\frac{(n-2)(1-b)}{nb} - 1 = 0, \quad i = \frac{n}{2} + 1, ..., n, \tag{6.49}$$

so that the interior equilibrium is given by $(q^*, b^*) = \left(\frac{n-2}{2(n-1)}, \frac{n-2}{2(n-1)}\right)$ (simple calculations show that this vector of strategies is the unique interior equilibrium). Furthermore, notice that, at the oligopoly equilibrium, we have

$$p(q^*, b^*) = \frac{1 - t^2}{1 - t^1}. \tag{6.50}$$

Substituting the equilibrium values q^* and b^* into the payoffs V_i (see (6.48) and (6.49)), we obtain

$$V_i(q^*, b^*) = \frac{n(n-2)(1-t^2)}{4(n-1)^2}, \quad i = 1, ..., \frac{n}{2} \tag{6.51}$$

and

$$V_i(q^*, b^*) = \frac{n(n-2)(1-t^1)}{4(n-1)^2}, \quad i = \frac{n}{2} + 1, ..., n. \tag{6.52}$$

Any Pareto-optimal allocation, which would follow from commodity taxes t^1 and t^2 and provide agent $n+1$ with utility level $\overline{U}$, must solve the problem

$$\max_{t^1, t^2} \sum_{i=1}^{n} V_i(q^*, b^*) \quad s.t.$$

$$U(\frac{n}{2}t^1 q^*, \frac{n}{2}t^2 b^*) = \overline{U},$$

or

$$\max_{t^1,t^2} \frac{n}{2} \cdot \frac{n(n-2)(1-t^2)}{4(n-1)^2} + \frac{n}{2} \cdot \frac{n(n-2)(1-t^1)}{4(n-1)^2} \qquad s.t.$$

$$\left(t^1 \frac{n}{2} \frac{(n-2)}{2(n-1)}\right)\left(t^2 \frac{n}{2} \frac{(n-2)}{2(n-1)}\right) = \overline{U}. \qquad (6.53)$$

Simple calculations show that the unique solution to this problem is $t^1 = t^2 = t^* = \frac{4(n-1)\sqrt{\overline{U}}}{n(n-2)}$. Substituting the value t^* into (6.44) and (6.45) reveals that the marginal rate of substitution between good 1 and good 2 is equal to $1 - \frac{2(1+2\sqrt{\overline{U}})}{n} + \frac{4\sqrt{\overline{U}}}{n^2}$ for the inside agents i, $i = 1, ..., \frac{n}{2}$, to $1/\left(1 - \frac{2(1+2\sqrt{\overline{U}})}{n} + \frac{4\sqrt{\overline{U}}}{n^2}\right)$ for the inside agents i, $i = \frac{n}{2}+1, ..., n$, and to 1 for the outside agent $n+1$. Consequently, these marginal rates of substitution vary across agents, so that the resulting overall allocation cannot be Pareto-optimal, a contradiction to our initial assumption.

Having reached this negative outcome, we then examine whether endowment taxation can realize the objective which was unsuccessfully pursued with commodity taxation.

6.3.3. Endowment Taxation

Consider now the following tax and transfer scheme. Firstly, *before exchange takes place*, taxes are introduced which consist in collecting, for each good, and each inside agent, a share t^h, $h = 1, 2$, of the amount of commodity h he owns initially: we call this tax scheme *endowment taxation*. Secondly, *after trade has occurred*, the product of these taxes is redistributed in favor of the outside agent, who gets accordingly $\frac{n}{2}t^h$ of good $h = 1, 2$.

More specifically, consider again the same example of exchange economy as considered in Section 6.3.2. The endowment tax and transfer scheme we have just considered generates a new market game as follows. Since, after taxation, traders are deprived of a share of their initial endowment, they start the game with strategy sets S_i equal to the interval $[0, 1 - t^1]$ for agents $i = 1, ..., \frac{n}{2}$, and to the interval $[0, 1 - t^2]$ for $i = \frac{n}{2} + 1, ..., n$. Given any n-tuple of strategies $(q_1, ..., q_{\frac{n}{2}}; b_{\frac{n}{2}+1}, ..., b_n)$ the resulting price is

$$p(q_1, ..., q_{\frac{n}{2}}; b_{\frac{n}{2}+1}, ..., b_n) = \frac{\sum_{k=\frac{n}{2}+1}^{n} b_k}{\sum_{k=1}^{\frac{n}{2}} q_k},$$

giving rise to the post-tax allocation of goods

$$x_i = \left(1 - t^1 - q_i, \frac{\sum_{k=\frac{n}{2}+1}^{n} b_k}{\sum_{k=1}^{\frac{n}{2}} q_k} q_i \right), \qquad i = 1, ..., \frac{n}{2} \qquad (6.54)$$

$$x_i = \left(\frac{\sum_{k=1}^{\frac{n}{2}} q_k}{\sum_{k=\frac{n}{2}+1}^{n} b_k} b_i, 1 - t^2 - b_i \right), \qquad i = \frac{n}{2} + 1, ..., n. \quad (6.55)$$

These outcomes generate utility levels

$$V_i(q, b) = (1 - t^1 - q_i) \left(\frac{\sum_{k=\frac{n}{2}+1}^{n} b_k}{\sum_{k=1}^{\frac{n}{2}} q_k} q_i \right), \qquad i = 1, ..., \frac{n}{2} \qquad (6.56)$$

and

$$V_i(q, b) = \left(\frac{\sum_{k=1}^{\frac{n}{2}} q_k}{\sum_{k=\frac{n}{2}+1}^{n} b_k} b_i \right) (1 - t^2 - b_i), \qquad i = \frac{n}{2} + 1, ..., n. \quad (6.57)$$

In the following proposition, we show that the endowment tax and transfer scheme we consider above also does not allow a Pareto-optimal overall allocation, with the outside agent obtaining the preassigned utility level $\overline{U}$, at the outcome of the new market game which was just defined.

Proposition 6.10.
Given any utility level $\overline{U}$ for the outside agent $n + 1$, there are no endowment taxes t^h, $h = 1, 2$ such that, when the product of

these taxes is transferred to agent $n+1$, **(i) the overall allocation resulting from this transfer and from the oligopoly equilibrium of the new game is Pareto-optimal and (ii) the utility of the outside agent after transfer is at least equal to $\overline{U}$.**

Proof Suppose, contrary to Proposition 6.10, that there are endowment taxes t^h, $h = 1, 2$, for which requirements (i) and (ii) are met. First, we show that (q^*, b^*) defined by

$$(q^*, b^*) = \left(\frac{(1 - t^1)(n - 2)}{2(n - 1)}, \frac{(1 - t^2)(n - 2)}{2(n - 1)} \right), \qquad (6.58)$$

is the unique interior oligopoly equilibrium of the new exchange game. Using the fact that all traders of the same type must adopt the same strategy at equilibrium, we may denote by q (b) the supply of inside agents $i \in \left\{ 1, ..., \frac{n}{2} \right\}$ $(i \in \left\{ \frac{n}{2} + 1, ..., n \right\})$ on the market. The first order conditions which must be satisfied at an interior equilibrium can then be written as

$$\frac{(1 - t^1 - q)(n - 2)}{nq} - 1 = 0, \qquad i = 1, ..., \frac{n}{2} \qquad (6.59)$$

$$\frac{(1 - t^2 - b)(n - 2)}{nb} - 1 = 0, \qquad i = \frac{n}{2} + 1, ..., n. \qquad (6.60)$$

Simple calculations show that the vector of strategies (q^*, b^*) in (6.58) is the unique interior equilibrium. Furthermore, notice that, at the oligopoly equilibrium, we have

$$p(q^*, b^*) = \frac{1 - t^2}{1 - t^1}. \qquad (6.61)$$

Substituting the equilibrium values q^* and b^* into the payoffs V_i (see (6.56) and (6.57), we obtain

$$V_i(q^*, b^*) = \frac{n(n-2)(1-t^1)(1-t^2)}{4(n-1)^2}, \qquad i = 1, ..., n. \qquad (6.62)$$

Any Pareto-optimal allocation which would follow from endowment taxes t^1 and t^2 and provide agent $n+1$ with utility level $\overline{U}$ must solve the problem

$$\max_{t^1, t^2} \sum_{i=1}^{n} V_i(q^*, b^*) \qquad s.t.$$

$$U(\frac{n}{2}t^1, \frac{n}{2}t^2) = \overline{U},$$

or

$$\max_{t^1, t^2} n \cdot \frac{n(n-2)(1-t^1)(1-t^2)}{4(n-1)^2} \qquad s.t.$$

$$(6.63)$$

$$\left(\frac{n}{2}t^1\right)\left(\frac{n}{2}t^2\right) = \overline{U}.$$

Simple calculations show that the unique solution to this problem is $t^1 = t^2 = t^* = \frac{2\sqrt{\overline{u}}}{n}$. Substituting the optimal value t^* into (6.54) and (6.55) reveals that the marginal rate of substitution between good 1 and good 2 is equal to $\frac{n-2}{n}$ for the inside agents i, $i = 1, ..., \frac{n}{2}$, to $\frac{n}{n-2}$ for the inside agents i, $i = \frac{n}{2} + 1, ..., n$, and to 1 for the outside agent $n+1$. Consequently, these marginal rates of substitution vary across agents, so that the resulting overall allocation cannot be Pareto-optimal, a contradiction.

The negative results in Propositions 6.9 and 6.10 both follow from the same cause: the tax schemes proposed are not powerful enough to wipe out the distortions introduced by the strategic behaviour of inside agents. Optimal taxes corresponding to these schemes can only reach second best because they are unable to manipulate the game sufficiently in order to neutralize the market power of inside agents.

We now propose a tax and transfer scheme relying again on endowment taxation, but combined with a more elaborate system of transfers: these will not only go from the inside agents to the outside one, but also take place among the inside agents themselves. As will be shown, when applied to our example, this method will prove to be a powerful instrument both as a counter-distortionary measure and as an efficient redistributive tool.

6.3.4. Endowment Taxation and Incentive Transfers

In this section, we start by defining a tax and transfer scheme which is specific to the exchange economy considered in Sections 6.3.2 and 6.3.3. The aim of this tax and transfer scheme is not only to ensure a preassigned utility level to the outside agent, but also to resorb the distortion resulting from the strategic behaviour of inside agents. First, *before exchange takes place*, suppose that endowment taxes are levied, as above, on the goods owned initially by inside agents. Furthermore, *after trade has occurred*, a share of the product of these taxes is redistributed among inside agents, while the remaining part is transferred to the outside one. More specifically, the share received by inside agents is redistributed among them *in a manner assigning to them a quantity of the good they did not own initially, which is proportional to the amount of the good they owned initially and supplied for exchange.* In other words, the transfer received by each inside agent, in units of the good which is not initially owned, increases as he raises the amount of the initially owned good he sends to the market. Furthermore, the transfer received by the outside agent must assign a commodity bundle providing him the utility level $\overline{U}$.

Clearly, the imposition of this tax and transfer scheme allows a manipulation of the market game defined above. On the one hand, the strategy set of inside agents is no longer the unit interval $[0, 1]$, but an interval strictly included in it. On the other hand, transfers among inside agents of the share of the tax product they receive reshape their payoffs in the game since these transfers have now to be added to the outcomes already obtained from strategic exchange. In the following, we show that there exists a tax and transfer scheme which manipulates the game in such a way that the allocation corresponding to the interior oligopoly equilibrium of this game is a competitive allocation in the subeconomy consisting of the inside agents. Furthermore, the transfer obtained by the agent $n+1$ generates a utility level $\overline{U}$, and the overall allocation is Pareto-optimal.

In the following, we suppose that $\overline{U} < \frac{n^2}{4}$, which is equivalent to assuming that the utility level $\overline{U}$ is feasible. Let a tax t^h, $t^h = t = \tau + \frac{2\sqrt{\overline{U}}}{n}$, be levied on both goods $h = 1, 2$. Furthermore, assume that, after trade has occurred at an n-tuple of strategies $(q_1, ..., q_{\frac{n}{2}}; b_{\frac{n}{2}+1}, ..., b_n)$, a share $\frac{\tau}{\frac{1}{2}-\tau-\frac{\sqrt{\overline{U}}}{n}}, 0 < \tau < \frac{1}{4} - \frac{\sqrt{\overline{U}}}{2n}$, of the total tax product in good 1 (good 2) is transferred to each agent $i \in \{\frac{n}{2}+1, ..., n\}$ $(i \in \{1, ..., \frac{n}{2}\})$, while the remaining share of the tax product in each good $(\sqrt{\overline{U}})$ is redistributed to the outside agent. This tax and transfers scheme generates a new market game as follows. The strategy set of all agents is the interval $[0, 1-t]$. The post-tax allocation of the game at a vector of strategies $(q_1, ..., q_{\frac{n}{2}}; b_{\frac{n}{2}+1}, ..., b_n)$ is now obtained as

$$x_i = \left(1 - \tau - \frac{2\sqrt{\overline{U}}}{n} - q_i, \frac{\sum_{k=\frac{n}{2}+1}^{n} b_k}{\sum_{k=1}^{\frac{n}{2}} q_k} q_i + \frac{\tau}{\frac{1}{2} - \tau - \frac{\sqrt{\overline{U}}}{n}} q_i\right),$$

$$i = 1, ..., \frac{n}{2} \qquad (6.64)$$

$$x_i = \left(\frac{\sum_{k=1}^{\frac{n}{2}} q_k}{\sum_{k=\frac{n}{2}+1}^{n} b_k} b_i + \frac{\tau}{\frac{1}{2} - \tau - \frac{\sqrt{\overline{U}}}{n}} b_i, 1 - \tau - \frac{2\sqrt{\overline{U}}}{n} - b_i\right),$$

$$i = \frac{n}{2} + 1, ..., n \qquad (6.65)$$

giving rise to utility levels

$$V_i(q, b) = \left(1 - \tau - \frac{2\sqrt{\overline{U}}}{n} - q_i\right) \left(\frac{\sum_{k=\frac{n}{2}+1}^{n} b_k}{\sum_{k=1}^{\frac{n}{2}} q_k} q_i + \frac{\tau}{\frac{1}{2} - \tau - \frac{\sqrt{\overline{U}}}{n}} q_i\right),$$

$$i = 1, ..., \frac{n}{2} \qquad (6.66)$$

and

$$V_i(q, b) = \left(\frac{\sum_{k=1}^{\frac{n}{2}} q_k}{\sum_{k=\frac{n}{2}+1}^{n} b_k} b_i + \frac{\tau}{\frac{1}{2} - \tau - \frac{\sqrt{\overline{U}}}{n}} b_i\right) \left(1 - \tau - \frac{2\sqrt{\overline{U}}}{n} - b_i\right),$$

$$i = \frac{n}{2} + 1, ..., n. \qquad (6.67)$$

Proposition 6.11.
Given a feasible preassigned utility level $\overline{U}$ for the outside agent $n + 1$, there exists endowment taxes t^h, $h = 1, 2$, and incentive transfers of a share of the resulting tax product among inside agents such that, (i) when the remaining share of this product is transferred to the outside agent, the overall allocation resulting from this transfer and from the oligopoly equilibrium of the resulting exchange game is Pareto-optimal and (ii) the utility of the outside agent at the commodity bundle obtained from the transfer is equal to $\overline{U}$.

Proof First, remove from the initial endowment of the inside agent i, an amount equal to $\frac{2\sqrt{\overline{U}}}{n}$ from the good he owns initially, and transfer it to the outside agent. Then the latter gets the bundle $(\sqrt{\overline{U}}, \sqrt{\overline{U}})$ and obtains accordingly a utility level equal to $\overline{U}$. Furthermore, impose also, on each inside agent i's endowment a levy τ on the good he owns initially, with

$$\tau = \frac{n - 2\sqrt{\overline{U}}}{n(n+2)}. \qquad (6.68)$$

Using the fact that all inside agents of the same type must adopt the same strategy at equilibrium, we denote by q (b) the strategy inside agents $i \in \{1, ..., \frac{n}{2}\}$ $(i \in \{\frac{n}{2}+1, ..., n\})$ use at such an equilibrium. Using this property, the first order conditions which must be satisfied at an interior oligopoly equilibrium can be written as

$$\left(1-\tau-\frac{2\sqrt{\overline{U}}}{n}-q\right)\left(\frac{n-2}{n}\frac{b}{q}+\frac{\tau}{\frac{1}{2}-\tau-\frac{\sqrt{\overline{U}}}{n}}\right)-\left(b+\frac{\tau}{\frac{1}{2}-\tau-\frac{\sqrt{\overline{U}}}{n}}q\right)=0,$$

$$\left(1-\tau-\frac{2\sqrt{\overline{U}}}{n}-b\right)\left(\frac{n-2}{n}\frac{q}{b}+\frac{\tau}{\frac{1}{2}-\tau-\frac{\sqrt{\overline{U}}}{n}}\right)-\left(q+\frac{\tau}{\frac{1}{2}-\tau-\frac{\sqrt{\overline{U}}}{n}}b\right)=0,$$

with τ as defined in (6.68). The only solution of the above system is given by (q^*, b^*) with

$$q^* = b^* = \frac{n-2\sqrt{\overline{U}}}{2(n+2)},$$

which is accordingly the unique oligopoly equilibrium of the resulting game. Furthermore, it is easily checked that the transfers among inside agents are feasible at equilibrium. Substituting these values into (6.64) and (6.65), we obtain

$$x_i^* = \left(\frac{1}{2}-\frac{\sqrt{\overline{U}}}{n}, \frac{1}{2}-\frac{\sqrt{\overline{U}}}{n}\right), \qquad i = 1, ..., n.$$

Accordingly, the common marginal rate of substitution between the two goods, at the post-tax allocation, is equal to one for all inside agents, which is also the value of the marginal rate of substitution of the outside agent $n+1$ at the commodity bundle $(\sqrt{\overline{U}}, \sqrt{\overline{U}})$ he gets from the transfer. We conclude that the overall allocation is Pareto-optimal.

7. Oligopoly equilibrium with a productive sector

In the economic applications considered in Sections 6.1 and 6.2, the agents were assumed not only to participate in the exchange activity, but also to take decisions as producers. In the Ricardian model of Section 6.1, the agents are assumed to have access to a linear production set resulting from the allocation of the unit of labour they own between the production of the two goods available for consumption. In the intertemporal model proposed in Section 6.2, consumers decide not only about their present consumption, but also about the amount to be invested for consumption in the next period. Nevertheless, in both cases, these production decisions were not taken by these agents as being the members of a particular firm, viewed as an economic entity distinct from the agents themselves. As in the popular 'Robinson Crusoe' paradigm, a 'firm' is identified in these models as a single agent exerting both the activities of consumption and production, whose final objective consists in maximising, through production and exchange, the utility he can obtain using these economic activities.

Yet, in reality, as well as in its transcription into the traditional general equilibrium model 'à *la* Arrow-Debreu', firms constitute economic agents which are not only distinct from consumers, but which are also guided by a different decision criterion, *profit-maximisation at given prices*. A firm is now viewed as a technology (its production set) transforming inputs into outputs and generating thereby profits to be shared among those consumers who have preassigned shares in the economic value of this transformation activity, as measured by these profits. It is a major virtue of the competitive model that nothing is lost by the consumers through the decentralisation process underlying the above mechanism: profit maximisation by firms at given prices guarantees income maximisation for the owners of the firm, allowing them to reach the highest possible utility through trade. It is a natural question to wonder whether a theory inspired from this traditional model could be designed in order to accomodate strategic behaviour for economic agents, including firms, involved in the production and exchange process. We propose hereafter a model, based on Gabszewicz and Vial (1972), which is a possible alternative in order to complete this program.

7.1 COURNOT-WALRAS EQUILIBRIA

We consider a productive economy with m firms, j, $j = 1, ..., m$, and n consumers, i, $i = 1, ..., n$. Consumers provide firms with labour and other types of non-consumable resources. In exchange they receive a fixed (given) share of the various consumption goods produced by the firms. Let us assume that there are ℓ such consumption goods and let θ_{ij} be the *share* of the i-th consumer in the production vector of the j-th firm, $i = 1, ..., n$; $j = 1, ..., m$; of course, for all j, $\sum_{i=1}^{n} \theta_{ij} = 1$. We denote by U_i the utility function representing the preferences of consumer i among the commodity bundles x in R_+^ℓ, which is assumed to satisfy the usual assumptions introduced in Part 1. The production possibilities for the j-th firm are defined by a compact convex subset G_j of R_+^ℓ: namely, *the production set* of firm j. After each firm has chosen a production plan y_j in its production set G_j, the resulting outputs are distributed to consumers in accordance with their preassigned shares; accordingly, consumer i obtains the bundle $\sum_{j=1}^{m} \theta_{ij} y_j$. An exchange economy is then generated, in which consumer i is initially endowed with the vector $\omega_i + \sum_{j=1}^{m} \theta_{ij} y_j$, with ω_i representing his initial holdings existing independently from the production activity of the firms; the vector $\omega_i + \sum_{j=1}^{m} \theta_{ij} y_j$ is the *intermediate endowment* of consumer i. An *allocation* is an n-tuple $(x_1, .., x_i, .., x_n)$ such that

$\sum_{i=1}^{n} x_i = \sum_{j=1}^{m} y_j + \sum_{i=1}^{n} \omega_i$. Given a price system p and production plans $(y_1, ..., y_j, ..., y_m)$, $y_j \in G_j$, a *competitive equilibrium relative to* $(y_1, ..., y_j, ..., y_m)$ is a pair $(p; (x_1, .., x_i, .., x_n))$ consisting of a price system p and an equilibrium allocation $(x_1, .., x_i, .., x_n)$ such that, for all $i = 1, ..., n$, the commodity bundle x_i maximises U_i under the constraint $p \cdot x \leq p \cdot \omega_i + p \cdot \sum_{j=1}^{m} \theta_{ij} y_j$. Assuming that, for any m-tuple of production plans $(y_1, ..., y_j, ..., y_m)$, there exists a unique competitive equilibrium relative to $(y_1, ..., y_j, ..., y_m)$, we denote by $p(y_1, ..., y_j, ..., y_m)$ the corresponding price system. Given some normalisation rule, the relation

$$(y_1, ..., y_j, ..., y_m) \rightarrow p(y_1, ..., y_j, ..., y_m)$$

appears as a function defined on $\Pi_{j=1}^{m} G_j$ with values in R_+^ℓ; we call it a *price function*. The behaviour of the firms still remains to be formally defined. This is done by considering them as the *players* of a non-cooperative m-person game with *strategy sets* G_j. Given an m-tuple of strategies $(y_1, ..., y_j, ..., y_m)$ and a price function $p(y_1, ..., y_j, ..., y_m)$, the *profits* of firm j are defined by

$$p(y_1, ..., y_j, ..., y_m) \cdot y_j = p(y_j, y_{-j}) \cdot y_j$$

and constitute its *payoffs* in the game. An m-tuple of strategies $(y_1^\circ, ..., y_j^\circ, ..., y_m^\circ)$ is an *equilibrium point* for p if for all j, $j = 1, ..., m$, and all $y_j \in G_j$,

$$p(y_j, y_{-j}^\circ) \cdot y_j \leq p(y_j^\circ, y_{-j}^\circ) \cdot y_j^\circ.$$

A *Cournot-Walras equilibrium* is a triplet $(p; (x_1^\circ, .., x_i^\circ, ..., x_n^\circ); (y_1^\circ, ..., y_j^\circ, ..., y_m^\circ))$, consisting of a price function p, an equilibrium allocation $(x_1^\circ, ..., x_i^\circ, ..., x_n^\circ)$ and an m-tuple $(y_1^\circ, ..., y_j^\circ, ..., y_m^\circ)$ of strategies such that (i) the pair $(p(y_1^\circ, ..., y_j^\circ, ..., y_m^\circ), (x_1^\circ, ..., x_i^\circ, ..., x_n^\circ))$ is a competitive equilibrium relative to $(y_1^\circ, ..., y_j^\circ, ..., y_m^\circ)$ and (ii) $(y_1^\circ, ..., y_j^\circ, ..., y_m^\circ)$ is an equilibrium point for p. A *global competitive equilibrium* is a triplet $(p, (x_1^*, ..., x_i^*, ..., x_n^*), (y_1^*, ..., y_j^*, ..., y_m^*))$ consisting of a price function p, an equilibrium allocation and an m-tuple of strategies such that $(p(y_1^*, ..., y_j^*, ..., y_m^*), (x_1^*, .., x_i^*, ..x_n^*))$ is a competitive equilibrium relative to $(y_1^*, ..., y_j^*, ..., y_m^*)$ and $p(y_1^*, ..., y_j^*, ..., y_m^*) \cdot y$ achieves its maximum on G_j at y_j^*, $j = 1, ..., m$.

The institutional organisation of the above economy can be described informally as follows. Consumers provide firms with labour and other non-consumable resources, like primary factors. With these resources, firm j can realise any commodity bundle in G_j, which is then distributed among the owners of firm j in accordance with their shares of ownership θ_{ij}. At the end of the production process each consumer is thus endowed with the sum of his shares in the various firms, plus the amount of each commodity he already owns independently from the production activity (ω_i). Exchange markets are then organised, where consumers behave competitively and aim at improving their consumption through trade. Equilibrium prices obtained in these exchange markets then serve as signals for each firm j in order to adjust its production plan in its production set G_j in the direction of the highest profit, *taking into account the strategies $y_k \in G_k$ selected by the other firms k, $k \neq j$*. As far as exchange equilibrium prices vary with a change in the relative supplies of the commodities, each firm has partial control over their value *via* the choice it makes of its production plan. An equilibrium point is simply a Nash equilibrium of the resulting game, in which firms are players, production sets are strategy sets, and profits are payoffs. A Cournot-Walras equilibrium consists of this equilibrium point, and of the resulting competitive equilibrium obtained on the exchange markets. The solution which is adopted in this model thus consists in assuming that *firms*, and not consumers, behave as the players of a non-cooperative game; namely, that their equilibrium supplies form a Nash equilibrium, the profit-payoffs being defined in terms of the corresponding price system obtained on the exchange markets. As for the consumers on the exchange side of the economy, they simply behave in a competitive way. A global competitive equilibrium corresponds to the usual notion of a competitive equilibrium in an economy with a productive sector: consumers maximise utility at given prices and firms maximise profits, also taking prices as given.

The notion of Cournot-Walras equilibrium differs from the concept of oligopoly equilibrium studied in the preceding chapters in several ways. First, it reintroduces the asymmetry of behaviour which was favoured by Cournot: since consumers are numerous, it is reasonable to assume that they behave competitively. On the contrary, firms are few, and price-taking behaviour is no longer justified, so that they behave strategically. The analog of this asymmetric behaviour in the exchange model corresponds to the example analysed above in Section 4.2. Second, consumers delegate to firms the power of selecting production plans in their production set in accordance with the profit criterion, with profits defined in terms of some normalisation rule transforming relative prices into absolute prices. This delegation procedure, which did not exist in the models underlying the concept of oligopoly equilibrium, mimics the usual Arrow-Debreu model, in which firms are viewed as collectively owned by subsets of consumers sharing profits among them. Also as in this model and contrary to the exchange model, firms' payoffs are now identified with *profits*; but, contrary to the Arrow-Debreu model, firms perceive the influence they can exert on relative prices and, accordingly, the impact of their strategies on profits transit *via* two channels: directly through the quantities they decide to produce, and indirectly through the interplay between these quantities and relative prices.

7.2 AN EXAMPLE

In order to illustrate the above concept of Cournot-Walras equilibrium, we consider a two-commodity economy with two firms and two consumers. The production sets of firms 1 and 2 are, respectively,

$$G_1 = \left\{ y_1 = (y_1^1, y_1^2) : 0 \le y_1^1 \le 2, 0 \le y_1^2 \le 8, 2y_1^1 + y_1^2 \le 10 \right\}$$

and

$$G_2 = \left\{ y_2 = (y_2^1, y_2^2) : 0 \le y_2^1 \le 8, 0 \le y_2^2 \le 2, 2y_2^1 + y_2^2 \le 10 \right\}.$$

The utility functions of consumers 1 and 2 are, respectively, $U_1(x^1, x^2) = (x^1)^{1/4}(x^2)^{3/4}$ and $U_2(x^1, x^2) = (x^1)^{3/4}(x^2)^{1/4}$, whereas their intermediate endowments are, respectively, (y_1^1, y_1^2) and (y_2^1, y_2^2). The price system p of the competitive equilibrium relative to (y_1, y_2) is constrained by the following set of equations:

$$p^1 x_1^1 + p^2 x_1^2 = p^1 y_1^1 + p^2 y_1^2$$
$$p^1 x_2^1 + p^2 x_2^2 = p^1 y_2^1 + p^2 y_2^2$$
$$3p^1 x_1^1 - p^2 x_1^2 = 0$$
$$p^1 x_2^1 - 3p^2 x_2^2 = 0$$
$$x_1^1 + x_1^2 = y_1^1 + y_1^2$$
$$x_2^1 + x_2^2 = y_2^1 + y_2^2,$$

to which we add the arbitrary normalisation rule

$$p^1 \cdot (y_1^1 + y_2^1) + p^2 \cdot (y_1^2 + y_2^2) = 1.$$

Routine calculations yield the following price function:

$$p^1(y_1, y_2) = \frac{1}{D}(y_1^2 + 3y_2^2),$$
$$p^2(y^1, y^2) = \frac{1}{D}(3y_1^1 + y_2^1)$$

with

$$D = (y_1^2 + 3y_2^2)(y_1^1 + y_2^1) + (3y_1^1 + y_2^1)(y_1^2 + y_2^2).$$

We prove that the triplet $(p(y_1^\circ, y_2^\circ); x_1^\circ, x_2^\circ; y_1^\circ, y_2^\circ)$ with $x_1^\circ = x_2^\circ = (2, 6)$ and $y_1^\circ = y_2^\circ = (6, 2)$ is a Cournot-Walras equilibrium. First, it is easy to check that $p(y_1^\circ, y_2^\circ) = p^\circ = (1/16, 1/16)$ and that $(p^\circ; x_1^\circ, x_2^\circ)$ is a competitive equilibrium relative to (y_1°, y_2°). Consider the profit function of firm 1 when firm 2's production plan is y_2°:

$$f_1(y_1, y_2^\circ) = p(y_1, y_2^\circ) \cdot y_1$$
$$= \frac{2y_1^1 y_1^2 + 3y_1^1 + 3y_1^2}{2y_1^1 y_1^2 + 6y_1^1 + 6y_1^2 + 24}.$$

The isoprofit curves $f_1(y_1, y_2^\circ) = k$ with $0 < k < 1$, defined on the non-negative orthant are branches of hyperbolas which are convex. Moreover, $f_1(y_1, y_2^\circ)$ is strictly increasing along the ray $y_1^1 = y_1^2$. Hence $f_1(y_1, y_2^\circ)$ is strictly quasi-concave and achieves its maximum on the convex set G_1 at a unique point. The Kuhn-Tucker conditions are

$$\frac{\partial f_1}{\partial y_1^1} - \lambda_1 - 2\lambda_3 \leq 0, \frac{\partial f_1}{\partial y_1^2} - \lambda_2 - 2\lambda_3 \leq 0,$$
$$y_1^1 \left(\frac{\partial f_1}{\partial y_1^1} - \lambda_1 - 2\lambda_3 \right) = 0, y_1^2 \left(\frac{\partial f_1}{\partial y_1^2} - \lambda_2 - \lambda_3 \right) = 0.$$

At $y_1 = y_1^\circ$ these conditions are satisfied with $\frac{\partial f_1}{\partial y_1^1} = 3\alpha, \frac{\partial f_1}{\partial y_1^2} = \alpha, \lambda_1 = \lambda_3 = \alpha, \lambda_2 = 0$ and $\alpha = 29/384$. It is easily checked that, for this problem the Kuhn-Tucker conditions are also sufficient to guarantee that $f_1(y_1, y_2^\circ)$ attains its maximum at y_1°. Similarly the profit function of firm 2, $f_2(y_1^\circ, y_2) = p(y_1^\circ, y_2) \cdot y_2$ attains its maximum value on G_2 at $y_2 = y_2^\circ$. Hence $(p(y_1^\circ, y_2^\circ); x_1^\circ, x_2^\circ; y_1^\circ, y_2^\circ)$ is a Cournot-Walras equilibrium. A direct inspection shows that it is not a global competitive equilibrium. In this economy the global competitive equilibrium is unique and corresponds to the triplet $(p^*; x_1^*, x_2^*; y_1^*, y_2^*)$ with $p^* = (1/18, 1/18)$, $x_1^* = (11/4, 33/4)$, $x_2^* = (33/4, 11/4)$, $y_1^* = (1, 8)$ and $y_2^* = (8, 1)$. Furthermore, one can check that the global competitive equilibrium is not a Cournot-Walras equilibrium.

7.3 THE PROFIT CRITERION AND THE ROLE OF PRICE NORMALISATION

We have already pointed out that the concept of Cournot-Walras equilibrium requires a normalisation rule to be specified in which absolute prices defining the price function are expressed. It turns out that different price normalisations entail profit functions for the firms which are in general not related to each other by monotone transformations. It follows that maximisation of profits in different normalisations amounts to firms pursuing different objectives and, accordingly, giving rise to different Cournot-Walras equilibria (an example is provided in Gabszewicz and Vial 1972). Also Dierker and Grodal (1986) have shown that the existence of a Cournot-Walras equilibrium depends on the choice of the normalisation rule. Worse than that: Grodal (1984) and Bohm (1994) have revealed that nearly every feasible allocation becomes a Cournot-Walras equilibrium with respect to some price normalisation rule.

Grodal (1984) has also shown that production plans, even if they belong to the interior of the production sets of the firms, can be strategies corresponding to a Cournot-Walras equilibrium. All these difficulties do not arise in the competitive framework since profits are then invariant with respect to the particular normalisation rule which is used to express absolute prices. A consequence of this invariance is that profit maximising firms also maximise the welfare of their shareholders since they maximise their individual wealth and thereby the utility they can derive at the given price system. A similar link between the firms' objective and shareholders' welfare fails to exist at a Cournot-Walras equilibrium: nothing can prevent unilateral deviation from an equilibrium strategy from increasing the utilities of all shareholders of a particular firm. This would arise, for instance, if the choice of an alternative strategy resulted in slightly lower wealth than at equilibrium, but in a much lower price of some particular commodity which is greatly desired by the owners of the firm. As summarised in Kreps (1990, p.727): 'The notion that shareholders want managers of their firms to maximise profits is a

long-standing component of the folklore of capitalism. But it is incorrect
folklore, if the firm has market power and if its shareholders participate,
even indirectly, in the markets that are affected by the operations of the
firm.'

Of course the difficulty relating to price normalisation does not appear in the framework of pure exchange economies since, in this context,
economic agents maximise their individual utilities, and not their profits. Similarly, if the characteristics of the shareholders of a firm could
be aggregated into a social preference ordering, that ordering could be
substituted for the profit criterion in order to define the objective of
the firm. However the possibility of aggregating shareholders' characteristics can be considered only under extremely restrictive conditions,
so that the problem of defining a meaningful decision criterion for the
firms when they retain market power remains to be solved. Dierker and
Grodal (1998) have faced this problem, which they have formulated as
follows: 'Assume that the objective function of a firm is to maximise
profits using a specific normalisation rule. For instance, suppose that
prices are normalised such that the value of a certain commodity bundle x always equals 1. Can a profit maximum then be characterised in
terms of *relative* prices only, without recourse to the specific normalisation rule ?.'

In order to investigate the problem in a simple setting, they consider
an economy with two commodities and a monopolistic firm. Good 0,
refered to as the 'numéraire', serves as input to produce good 1 by the
monopolist under a constant returns-to-scale technology: one unit of
good 1 requires c units of the numéraire. Consumers are denoted by
$i = 1, .., n$. It is also assumed that they are endowed only with a positive
amount of good 0, so that $\omega_i = (\omega_i^0, 0)$, $i = 1, ..., n$. Consumer i owns a
share θi in the firm, $\sum_{i=1}^{n} \theta_i = 1$; we denote by A the set of consumers
i for which $\theta i > 0$. Finally we shall assume that the shareholders of the
firm do not consume its product. A strategy P of the firm is the decision
to offer one unit of the product in exchange for P units of the numéraire.
Since shareholders do not consume its product, it is natural to assume
that the monopolist maximises profits by taking good 0 as numéraire.

For some strategy P, these profits are written as

$$\Pi(P) = (P - c) \sum_{i \notin A} x_i((1, P); \omega_i^0)$$

with $x_i((1, P); \omega_i^0), i \notin A$, denoting consumer i's demand for good 1.

Now consider prices $\alpha(P)(1, P)$ instead of $(1, P)$. Since individual demand functions are homogeneous of degree 0, nominal profits expressed in prices $\alpha(P)(1, P)$ are $\alpha(P)\Pi(P)$. We notice that the total amount of the numéraire good which can be bought out of these profits is the same as before $(\Pi(P))$ since one unit of this good is now priced $\alpha(P)$. Now let us show that the objective of the firm, which is here to maximise its shareholders' consumption of the numéraire good, can be expressed as well in terms of the price vector $\alpha(P)(1, P)$. To illllustrate, assume that we abandon the price normalisation rule in which we assume that the numéraire good has price 1 and that we normalise prices such that they add up to 1. Then the price of the numéraire good is now equal to $\frac{1}{1+P}$ and the price of good 1 to $\frac{P}{1+P}$, so that $\alpha(P) = \frac{1}{1+P}$. Profits in this normalisation now become

$$\Pi_\Delta(P) = \left(\frac{P}{1+P} - \frac{c}{1+P}\right) \sum_{i \notin A} x_i \left(\frac{1}{1+P}, \frac{P}{1+P}; \frac{1}{1+P}\omega_i^0\right)$$

or

$$\Pi_\Delta(P) = \frac{1}{1+P}\Pi(P).$$

Define by $\Pi^\circ = \Pi^\circ(P^\circ)$ the maximal profit corresponding to the optimal strategy P° of the monopolist if the normalisation is made by assuming a price equal to 1 for the numéraire good, and let Z° denote the amount of this good shareholders obtain from profits, namely $Z^\circ = \Pi^\circ$. Since, as noted above, the amount of the numéraire which can be bought from profits remains the same when the alternative normalisation rule (prices adding up to 1) is used, the strategy P° still allows shareholders to buy exactly Z° units of the numéraire when this alternative normalisation rule is used. Since profits are maximal at P° we have also

$$(\Pi(P) - Z^\circ) \leq 0,$$

for all P, with equality for $P = P^\circ$. Hence $\Pi(P) - \Pi^\circ$ reaches its maximum at P°. Accordingly maximising $\Pi(P) - \Pi^\circ$ or $\Pi(P)$ is an equivalent operation. Now assume that we normalise prices so that they add up to 1. Then the above expression becomes

$$\Pi_\Delta(P) - \frac{1}{1+P}Z^\circ = \frac{1}{1+P}(\Pi(P) - Z^\circ) \leq 0,$$

for all P, with equality for $P = P^\circ$. Hence the objective of the firm is also maximised with the same strategy P° under this alternative normalisation rule. Thus we conclude that the objective of the firm can also be expressed equivalently in terms of the price vector $\alpha(P)(1, P)$. The above argument can be generalised using an arbitrary normalisation rule $\alpha(P)$ as follows, when the firm has as objective to allow its shareholders to buy as many units of a given consumption bundle $x \geq 0$ out of its profits. If $\lambda^\circ x$ corresponds to an optimal strategy in the sense that $\lambda^\circ x$ is feasible and shareholders' net trade can never exceed $\lambda^\circ x$, then the firm's objective can be written using good 0 as numéraire, i.e

$$\Pi(P) - (1, P)(\lambda^\circ x).$$

In the normalisation $\alpha(P)$ leading to prices $\alpha(P)(1, P)$, this objective rewrites as

$$\alpha(P)\Pi(P) - \alpha(P)(1, P)(\lambda^\circ x) = \alpha(P)\left[\Pi(P) - (1, P)(\lambda^\circ x)\right] \leq 0.$$

Consequently, the objective of the monopolist can be expressed using any arbitrary normalisation rule α. Of course, the price to be paid in order to write profit maximisation in a way which is independent of price normalisation is that the value of shareholders' aggregate net trade enters explicitly into the formulation of the objective. Dierker and Grodal show that this does not require the firm to anticipate shareholders' optimal net trade; only the bundle x needs to be known to the firm.

Notice however that the optimal value Π° must be explicitly taken into account for the following reason. Consider any differentiable function $f(P)$ such that $\frac{d}{dP} f(P^\circ) = 0$ and let τ be a transformation with nonvanishing derivative. In our interpretation $f(P)$ and $\tau(P)f(P)$ stand for the same objective of the firm. Hence both functions should satisfy the first order condition for optimisation at identical points, i.e., at P° in our example. Obviously $\frac{d}{dP}(\tau(P)f(P)) = f(P)\frac{d}{dP}\tau(P) + \tau(P)\frac{d}{dP}f(P)$ vanishes at P° if and only if f does. This is achieved by putting $f(P) = \Pi(P) - \Pi^\circ$ (Dierker and Grodal 1998, p.158).

Dierker and Grodal generalise the above analysis by defining the objective of the monopolist without making *a priori* assumptions on the demand behaviour of the shareholders. To do so they start by considering a situation in which, given two different strategies P_1 and P_2, the corresponding aggregate budget sets $B(P_i)$ of the shareholders are strictly included into each other, say $B(P_1) \subset B(P_2)$. Consider any commodity bundle x, $x \geq 0$. Clearly the number of units of x which the shareholders can afford under the strategy P_2 is strictly larger than under the strategy P_1. Whatever bundle is used by the firm to evaluate the real wealth of the shareholders, they are always wealthier at P_1 than at P_2. The authors assume that a real wealth maximising monopolist who has to choose between P_1 and P_2 will choose P_2. When the aggregate budget set corresponding to different strategies cannot be ordered by inclusion, they say that shareholders' real wealth at a strategy P_1 can be increased by the strategy P_2, or $P_2 \succ P_1$, if the aggregate demand of the shareholders when using the strategy P_1 belongs to their aggregate budget set corresponding to the use of the strategy P_2. Finally the authors define a *real wealth maximising strategy* P° if there is no other feasible strategy P such that $P \succ P^\circ$. A firm maximises the real wealth of its shareholders if it is impossible for the firm to change its strategy in such a way that the resulting aggregate budget set of its shareholders contains a commodity bundle which is strictly larger than their present aggregate demand. Imposing a monotonicity assumption on aggregate demand, they show that the relation $\succ$ is asymmetric, which implies that the set of real wealth maximising strategies is non-empty. Furthermore, they study how the concept extends from monopoly exerted on a single good to oligopolistic Cournot competition with an arbitrary number of goods and oligopolists. They prove that if the payoff functions of the oligopolists are continuously differentiable and concave (with respect to the numéraire normalisation), shareholders' real wealth maximisation can be fully characterised by the first order optimality conditions.

In conclusion, Dierker and Grodal have proposed a method of overcoming the problem of normalisation by assuming that firms maximise the real wealth of their shareholders based on the value of shareholders' aggregate demand. As suggested by the authors, other bundles could have been used instead, like a weighted average of shareholders' demands with ownership shares as weights, or the demand of a median shareholder, or some other bundle related to the interest of the shareholders. In any case, it is clear that the introduction of a productive sector into the analysis of imperfect competition compounds the difficulties we have already met with the exchange model, because it adds to the complexity of strategic behavior the difficult group decision problem generated by the existence of multi-owner firms.

8.   Conclusion

The last chapter of Part 2 has probably thrown some light on the difficulties encountered when extending to general equilibrium the partial equilibrium approach which has been used to formulate the problems posed by imperfect competition. Nevertheless, any economic theorist who is aware of the importance of the interdependence of markets cannot be content for ever with the partial equilibrium route. Modern economies are characterised by tentacular firms operating simultaneously on several product markets, both at home and abroad; they have huge staffs of managers who devote their efforts to developing elaborate strategies whose interactions can hardly be analysed without taking into account the full complexity of the economic system. Unfortunately, this general equilibrium complexity, already apparent when competition is assumed, is now compounded with the complexity of strategic interplay. Does it mean that theorists should abandon their efforts to understand how interrelated markets operate in situations of imperfect competition? We do not think so, and this book is an attempt to show that some possibilities exist for disentangling somewhat the main components of the problem. We have done it by following traditional economic theory as closely as possible. Not only have we adopted the simplest model proposed by our predecessors for allowing the study of interrelated markets, but we have also used the most traditional concepts proposed by them for analysing imperfect competition: the core and the Cournot equilibrium. Perhaps it was not a good idea to anchor so much the general equilibrium analysis of market imperfections to this traditional approach; it may be that general equilibrium would require another type of model when imperfect competition is studied. At least we have the excuse that no alternative proposal has been formulated so far.

Of course we have only scratched the surface of what looks like a promising territory requiring further and deeper research. This research could start out from the two major drawbacks of our approach: the absence of a productive sector and the lack of analysis of the link existing between market power and increasing returns to scale. Yet these two aspects are interrelated. Chapter 7 has clearly illustrated that the usual representation of a profit-maximising firm as a convex technology owned by consumers is ill-adapted to the context of imperfect competition. In this representation, the market power of firms finds its origin in the demand conditions they face: rivalry arises because a few firms sell their products to the same pool of consumers, and struggle to obtain the largest share of it. This demand component is certainly an important element in oligopolistic rivalry. But it is not explained *why* there are few firms. This is probably because another major source of market power, which is not in the usual representation of the economy, comes from the *supply* side, namely, from the technological conditions under which firms operate. Suppose the firm size which minimises average production cost is large relative to the size of the market. A price-taking equilibrium could not have many firms, each operating at an inefficiently small scale, because such firms would have a profit incentive to increase output. Hence the market can only accomodate a few firms of efficient size. But with only a few firms, one cannot justify the assumption that firms treat prices as given, since firms must realise that their size permits them to influence prices to their own advantage. Most likely, the technological conditions determine both the number of firms which survive at equilibrium and the kind of market arrangement which results, given the aggregate demand existing in the interrelated markets for the products. An integrated view of the technological conditions, which is not restricted to convex technologies, is needed before proceeding further into the introduction of a productive sector into the model of an imperfectly competitive world. But this is beyond the purpose of the present research.

Bibliography

Amir, R., S. Sahi, M. Shubik and S. Yaho (1990), 'A strategic market game with complete markets', *Journal of Economic Theory*, 51, 126–143.

Aumann, R.J. (1964), 'Markets with a continuum of traders', *Econometrica*, 32, 39–50.

Aumann, R.J. (1973), 'Disadvantageous monopolies', *Journal of Economic Theory*, 6, 1–11.

Benassy, J.P. (1988), 'The objective demand curve in general equilibrium with price makers', *Economic Journal* (suppl.), 98, 37–49.

Bewley, T. (1973), 'Edgeworth's conjecture', *Econometrica*, 41, 425–454.

Bohm, V. (1994), 'The foundations of the theory of monopolistic competition revisited', *Journal of Economic Theory*, 63, 208–218.

Bonnisseau, J.M. and M. Florig (2000), 'Oligopoly equilibria in large, but finite, linear exchange economies', *Cahiers CERNSEM, Université de Paris I*.

Bonnisseau, J.M., M. Florig and A. Jofré (1997a), 'Continuity and uniqueness of equilibria for linear exchange economies', *Cahiers CERNSEM, Université de Paris I*.

Bonnisseau, J.M., M. Florig and A. Jofré (1997b), 'Differentiability of equilibria for linear exchange economies', *Cahiers CERNSEM, Université de Paris I*.

Champsaur, P. and G. Laroque (1976), 'A note on the core of an economy with atoms or syndicates', *Journal of Economic Theory*, 13, 458–471.

Codognato, G. and J. Gabszewicz (1991), 'Equilibres de Cournot-Walras dans une économie d'échange', *Revue Economique*, 6, 1013–1026.

Cordella, T. and M. Datta (2002), 'Intertemporal Cournot and Walras equilibria: an illustration, *International Economic Review*, 43(1), 1–17.

Cordella, T. and J. Gabszewicz (1997), 'Comparative advantage under oligopoly', *Journal of International Economics*, 43, 333–346.

Cordella, T. and J. Gabszewicz (1998), '"Nice" trivial equilibria in strategic market games', *Games and Economic Behavior*, 22, 162–169.

Cournot, A.A. (1838), *Recherches sur les Principes Mathématiques de la Théorie des Richesses*, Paris. Translation: Bacon, A. (1897) *Researches into the Mathematical Principles of the Theory of Wealth*, Macmillan, New York.

d'Aspremont, C., R. Dos Santos Ferreira, and L.-A. Gérard Varet (1997), 'General equilibrium concepts under imperfect competition', *Journal of Economic Theory*, 73(1), 199–230.

Debreu, G. (1959), *Theory of Value*, John Wiley, New York.

Debreu, G. and H. Scarf (1963), 'A limit theorem on the core of an economy', *International Economic Review*, 4, 235–246.

Dierker, E. and B. Grodal (1998), 'Modelling policy issues in a world of imperfect competition', *Scandinavian Journal of Economics*, 100, 153–179.

Dierker, E. and B. Grodal (1999), 'The price normalisation problem in imperfect competition and the objective of the firm', *Economic Theory*, 14, 257–284.

Dierker, H. and B. Grodal (1986), 'Non-existence of Cournot-Walras equilibrium in a general equilibrium model with two oligopolists' in Hildenbrand, W. and A. Mas-Colell (eds), *Contributions to Mathematical Economics in Honor of Gérard Debreu*, North-Holland, Amsterdam, 167–185.

Drèze, J., J. Gabszewicz and S. Gepts (1969), 'On cores and competitive equilibria', in *La Décision, Agrégation et Dynamique des Ordres de Préférences*, Colloques Internationaux, CNRS, Paris, 91–114.

Drèze, J., J. Gabszewicz, D. Schmeidler and K. Vind (1972), 'Cores and prices in an exchange economy with an atomless sector', *Econometrica*, 40, 1091–1108.

Dubey, P. and M. Shubik (1978), 'The noncooperative equilibria of a closed trading economy with market supply and bidding strategies', *Journal of Economic Theory*, 17, 1–20.

Edgeworth, F.Y. (1881), *Mathematical Psychics*, Paul Kegan, London.

Gabszewicz, J. (1975), 'Coalitional fairness of allocations in pure exchange economies', *Econometrica*, 43, 661–668.

Gabszewicz, J. (1977), 'Asymmetric duopoly and the core', *Journal of Economic Theory*, 14, 172–179.

Gabszewicz, J. and J. H. Drèze (1971), 'Syndicates of traders in an exchange economy', in H.W. Kuhn and G. Szegö (eds), *Differential Games and Related Topics*, North-Holland, Amsterdam.

Gabszewicz, J. and L. Grazzini (1999), 'Taxing market power', *Journal of Public Economic Theory*, 1(4), 475–497.

Gabszewicz, J. and L. Grazzini (2001), 'Strategic multilateral exchange and taxes, in G. Debreu, W. Neuefeind and W. Trockel (eds), *Economics Essays: A Festschrift for Werner Hildenbrand*, Springer, Berlin.

Gabszewicz, J. and T. Hansen (1972). 'Collusion of factor owners and distribution of social output', *Journal of Economic Theory*, 4(1), 1–18.

Gabszewicz, J. and J.-F. Mertens (1971), 'An equivalence theorem for the core of an exchange economy whose atoms are not "too" big', *Econometrica*, 39, 713–721.

Gabszewicz, J. and P. Michel (1997), 'Oligopoly equilibrium in exchange economies', in B.C. Eaton and R.G. Harris (eds), *Trade, Technology and Economics: Essays in Honor of Richard G. Lipsey*, Edward Elgar, Cheltenham, 217–240.

Gabszewicz, J. and B. Shitovitz (1992). 'The core in imperfectly competitive economies', in R. Aumann and S. Hart (eds), *Handbook of Game Theory and Economic Applications*, North-Holland, Amsterdam, 460–483.

Gabszewicz, J. and J.P. Vial (1972), 'Oligopoly "à la Cournot" in general equilibrium analysis', *Journal of Economic Theory*, 4, 381–400.

Gale, D. (1976), 'The linear exchange model', *Journal of Mathematical Economics*, 3, 205–209.

Gary-Bobo, R.J. (1989), 'Cournot-Walras and locally consistent equilibria', *Journal of Economic Theory*, 89, 10–32.

Greenberg, J. and B. Shitovitz (1977), 'Advantageous monopolies', *Journal of Economic Theory*, 16, 394–402.

Grodal, B. (1984), 'Profit maximising behavior in general equilibrium models with imperfect competition, *Økonomiske Essays*, 28, 79–90, København Akademisk Forlag.

Grodal, B. (1996), 'Profit-maximization and imperfect competition', in B. Allen (ed.), *Economics in a Changing World*, vol. 2, Macmillan, London, 3–22.

Guesnerie, R. (1977), 'Monopoly, syndicate and Shapley-value: about some conjectures', *Journal of Economic Theory*, 15, 235–251.

Hart, O. (1985), 'Imperfect competition in general equilibrium: an overview of recent work', in K.J. Arrow and S. Honkapohja (eds), *Frontiers of Economics*, Basil Blackwell, Oxford, 150–169.

Hart, S. (1974), 'The formation of cartels in large markets', *Journal of Economic Theory*, 7, 453–466.

Hildenbrand, W. (1974), *Core and Equilibria of a Large Economy*, Princeton University Press, Princeton (New Jersey).

Hildenbrand, W. and A. Kirman (1988), *Equilibrium Analysis*, North-Holland, Amsterdam.

Jones, R. and J.P. Neary (1984), 'The positive theory of international trade', in R. Jones and P. Kenen (eds), *Handbook of International Economics*, North-Holland, Amsterdam, 162–184.

Kreps, D. (1990), *A Course in Microeconomic Theory*, Harvester Wheatsheaf, Hemel Hempstead.

Laffont, J.J. and G. Laroque (1976), 'Existence d'un équilibre général de concurrence imparfaite: une introduction', *Econometrica*, 44(2), 283–304.

Lahmandi-Ayed, R. (2001), 'Oligopoly equilibria in exchange economies: a limit theorem', *Economic Theory*, 17, 665–674.

Marschak, T. and R. Selten (1974), *General Equilibrium with Price-Making Firms*, Lecture Notes in Economics and Mathematical Systems 91, Springer, Berlin.

Mas-Colell, A. (1989), 'An equivalence theorem for a bargaining set', *Journal of Mathematical Economics*, 18, 129–139.

Mas-Colell, A., Whinston, M.D. and J.R. Green (1995), *Microeconomic Theory*, Oxford University, New York.

Nash, J. (1950), 'Equilibrium points in *n*-person games', *Proceedings of the National Academy of Sciences*, 36, 48–49.

Negishi, T. (1961), 'Monopolistic competition and general equilibrium', *Review of Economic Studies*, 28, 196–201.

Ricardo, D. (1848,1951), *On the Principles of Political Economy and Taxation*, Vol. I of P. Sraffa (ed.), The Works and Correspondance of David Ricardo, Cambridge University Press, Cambridge.

Richter, H. (1963), 'Verallgemeinerung eines in der Statistik benödigten Satzes der Masstheorie', *Math Annalen*, 150, 85–90.

Roberts, K. (1980), 'The limit points of monopolistic competition', *Journal of Economic Theory* (Symposium issue), 22, 256–279.

Shapley, L. (1961), 'Values of large games, III: A corporation with two large stockholders', *R-M 2650*, Rand Corporation, Santa Monica, California.

Shapley, L. (1977), 'Non-cooperative general exchange', in S.A. Lin (ed.), *Theory and Measurement of Economic Externalities*, Academic Press, New York, 155–175.

Shapley, L. and M. Shubik (1977), 'Trade using one commodity as a means of payment', *Journal of Political Economy*, 85, 937–978.

Shitovitz, B. (1973), 'Oligopoly in markets with a continuum of traders', *Econometrica*, 41, 467–505.

Shitovitz, B. (1982), 'On exploitation in a class of differentiable mixed markets', *Economics Letters*, 9, 301–304.

Shitovitz, B. (1987), 'Notes on the bargaining set and the core of mixed markets', mimeo.

Shubik, M. (1959), 'Edgeworth market games', in A.W. Tucker and R.D. Luce (eds), *Contributions to the Theory of Games IV*, Princeton University Press, Princeton (New Jersey).

Triffin, R. (1940), *Monopolistic Competition and General Equilibrium Theory*, Harvard University Press, Cambridge (Massachusetts).

von Neumann, J. and O. Morgenstern (1944), *Theory of Games and Economic Behavior*, Princeton University Press, Princeton (New Jersey).

Index

aggregate consumption to investment
  ratio 172–3
aggregate excess supply 19
allocations 17, 80, 103–4
  collective choice 42
  definition 17
Amir, R. 6
anonymity, in taxation 179
Arrow-Debreu model 196
asymmetric behaviour 111, 128, 196
asymmetry assumption 124
  and the partial equilibrium model
    124
asymmetry of behaviour 111, 196
asymptotic approach 9, 10
  to imperfect competition, based on
    collusion 34–68
  to imperfect markets 39–55
  to perfect competition 28–38
    competitive allocations contained
      in the core 28–35
atomless approach 9
atomless coalitions 80
atomless economies, approach to
  perfect competition using 69–78
atoms ('significant traders') 2
Aumann, R.J. 2, 9, 68, 69, 70, 97,
  107
Aumann's equivalence theory 2
autarkic equilibrium 11, 135–7,
  139–40, 141
autarkic strategies 153–9
autarky 131

bargaining set 5, 106–7
behaviour, asymmetry of 111, 196

behavioural asymmetry assumption
  128
Benassy, J.P. 8
Bertrand price competition 93
Bewley, T. 31
bilateral markets 128
bilateral monopolies 124
bilateral oligopolies 124, 133
Bohm, V. 199
Bonniseau, J.M. 141, 142
budgetary exploitation theorem
  and mixed markets 78–89
  proof 86–9
budgetary exploitation, versus utility
  exploitation 96–100

Champsaur, P. 100, 104
coalitions 26, 53, 58, 77, 79–80, 101–2
Cobb-Douglas production function
  65
Cobb-Douglas utility function 115–16
Codognato, G. 115
collective allocation mechanism 10
collective bargaining 26
collusion
  and asymptotic behaviour of the core
    35–68
  of factor owners 66–7
commodity taxation 175, 179–84
comparative advantage 154, 164
  and oligopoly equilibrium 146–66
comparative advantage principle 11
comparative costs principle 166
comparative disadvantage 153, 166
competitive allocations 9, 19–23, 29,
  39, 71, 167

213